Kabbalah, Magic, and Science

KABBALAH, MAGIC, AND SCIENCE

The Cultural Universe of a
Sixteenth-Century Jewish Physician

David B. Ruderman

HARVARD UNIVERSITY PRESS

Cambridge, Massachusetts
London, England
1988

10 9 8 7 6 5 4 3 2 1

Publication of this book has been aided by a grant
from the Frederick W. Hilles Publication Fund
of Yale University.

This book is printed on acid-free paper, and its binding materials
have been chosen for strength and durability.

Library of Congress Cataloging-in-Publication Data

Ruderman, David B.
    Kabbalah, magic, and science: the cultural universe of a sixteenth-
century Jewish physician / David B. Ruderman.
        p.   cm.
    Bibliography: p.
    Includes index.
    ISBN 0-674-49660-4 (alk. paper)
    1. Jagel, Abraham ben Hananiah dei Galicchi, 16th/17th cent.
    2. Scholars. Jewish—Italy—Biography. 3. Physicians, Jewish—Italy—
    Biography. 4. Judaism and science. 5. Magic, Jewish. 6. Cabala—His-
    tory. I. Title.
BM755.J273R83   1988
181'.06—dc19   87-35271
[B]   CIP

For Phyllis

Acknowledgments

IT IS MY PLEASURE to thank those individuals and institutions who were helpful to me in writing this book. I benefited immensely from the valuable insights and sound criticisms of a number of colleagues and friends who read all or parts of the manuscript. They include Steven Fraade, Ivan Marcus, David Altshuler, George Lindbeck, Jon Butler, Kenneth Stow, Michael Heyd, Benjamin Ravid, and Reuven Bonfil. Above all, Moshe Idel generously offered me his time, his extraordinary knowledge, and his constant encouragement.

I began this study many years ago in the wonderful setting of the National Library of the History of Medicine, in Washington, D.C. Additional research followed at the libraries of Yale University and at the National and University Library of the Hebrew University in Jerusalem, especially its Institute for Microfilms of Hebrew Manuscripts and the Harry Friedenwald Collection in the History of Jewish Medicine. The Bodleian Library at Oxford and the Hebrew Union College–Jewish Institute of Religion Library kindly permitted me to quote extensively from manuscripts of Abraham Yagel in their possession. I completed the first stages of this work during a leave financed by Yale University, and the last stages in the pleasant surroundings of the Institute for Advanced Study at the Hebrew University in Jerusalem. I extend sincere gratitude to all of these institutions for their support.

A preliminary version of Chapter 4 was presented at a conference at the Center for Jewish Studies at Harvard University in March 1982 and was subsequently published as "Unicorns, Great Beasts, and the Marvelous Variety of Things in Nature in the Thought of Abraham b. Hananiah Yagel," in *Jewish Thought in the Seventeenth Century*, edited by Isidore Twersky and Bernard Septimus (Cambridge, Mass.: Harvard University Press, 1987), pp. 343–364. The second part of Chapter 5 is based on an earlier article, "Three Contemporary Perceptions of a Polish Wunderkind," which appeared in *Association for Jewish Studies Review*, 4 (1979), 143–163. An early version of Chapter 6 is to appear as "The Receptivity of Jewish

Thought to the New Astronomy of the Seventeenth Century: The Case of Abraham b. Hananiah Yagel," in the Umberto Cassuto memorial volume, recently published in Jerusalem. Chapter 7 was originally delivered as a paper at the conference Jewish Societies in Transformation in the Sixteenth and Seventeenth Centuries, at the Van Leer Institute, Jerusalem, January 1986. An earlier version of Chapter 8 was first presented at the annual meeting of the Association for Jewish Studies in December 1985 and subsequently published as "On Divine Justice, Metempsychosis, and Purgatory: Ruminations of a Sixteenth Century Italian Jew" in *Jewish History*, 1 (1986), 9–30. I thank the editor and publisher of each of these publications for permission to reprint portions of these essays.

It was my good fortune to work with Margaretta Fulton and Ann Hawthorne of Harvard University Press. I owe them special thanks for the care with which they oversaw the transformation of this work into a book.

My wife, Phyllis, and my children, Noah and Tali, have borne with patience my preoccupation with a sixteenth-century Jewish physician. They not only allow me such eccentric indulgences; they provide my life with much meaning and satisfaction.

Orange, Connecticut
Tu Be'Shevat, 5748

Contents

Kabbalah, Magic, and Science

Introduction

THIS BOOK pursues a theme familiar to historians of early modern Europe, but from a relatively unexplored perspective. It considers the relationships between religion, magic, and science, as they were understood in the late sixteenth and early seventeenth centuries, from the unique vantage point of Jewish cultural history.[1] In examining closely the intellectual and social world of Abraham ben Hananiah Yagel (1553–c.1623), a Jewish physician, kabbalist, magician, and naturalist, it attempts to incorporate the experience of a Jew into the larger setting of European culture in this era and at the same time to evaluate it in the context of contemporary Jewish civilization. Accordingly, the following chapters view a specific Jewish experience both in its own cultural terms and in its dialogue and negotiation with the larger non-Jewish world with which it came in contact.[2]

Two distinct questions emerge concerning Yagel's interest in nature: Did his religious beliefs inhibit or encourage his scientific pursuits? And how were his passionate theosophic and occult concerns integrated with his scientific ones? Both general issues have long engaged the attention of historians of early modern Christian Europe, who have approached them from sharply differing perspectives and with often contradictory conclusions.

Earlier historians of science assumed that the scientific revolution of the seventeenth century was generally hostile to Christian theology and constituted a simple triumph of reason over unreason. They stressed the progressive and cumulative nature of scientific knowledge, its antitheological orientation, and its experimental and secular approach to the study of nature.[3] Challenging this position, a revisionist interpretation claimed that Christian theology encouraged scientific innovation by emphasizing the regularity and orderliness of natural processes, on the one hand, and the contingency and passivity of matter on the other; Christian faith may even have caused the scientific revolution of the seventeenth century or, at the very least, was a necessary precondition for its emergence.[4] In recent years, both extremist positions have given way to a view that neither conflict nor harmony adequately describes the complex interaction between Christianity and early modern science. Instead of positing a causal or preconditional relationship between the two, contemporary scholars prefer to speak of a rapport between certain aspects of Christianity—especially Protestantism—and the new science,[5] or to suggest certain meaningful connections between theological and scientific discourse that became most evident by the seventeenth century.[6]

The second question, regarding the supposed congruence between "occult" and "modern scientific" mentalities, is of more recent origin. Just as earlier historians had once considered the new science to be opposed to Christian theology, so too did they view its relation to magic and mystical theosophy.[7] Some twenty years ago, this regnant "Whig" or triumphalist understanding of the origins of modern science was challenged by a number of scholars, especially the late Frances Yates.[8] They showed that Neoplatonism, Hermeticism, alchemy, astrology, and magic were important subjects for a number of key figures of early modern science and directly related to their scientific pursuits. They thus stressed the Renaissance Hermetic tradition as an immediate antecedent to the emergence of the new science. As in the case of the question of Christianity's relationship to science, the extreme positions of both sides have inevitably somewhat converged; the current interpretation no longer either ignores the occultist background of modern science or reduces science to a mere variant of either magic or religion. The continuing debate about the validity of the so-called Yates thesis has focused on the changing criteria of rationality and scientific method through the sixteenth and seventeenth centuries while recognizing the inherent difficulty of imposing fundamental unhistorical categories ("occult" and "scientific") on the complex historical data of that era.[9]

These two basic questions also elicit a third: How are the two issues—the apparent link between religion and science, and between the occult and science—fundamentally related? Historians have usually treated these two issues separately. Most discussions of the connection between Christianity and science center either on the fourteenth or on the seventeenth century, with relatively little attention to the intervening period of the fifteenth and sixteenth centuries and with little reference to the extraordinary scholarly fascination with the occult in that period. To a certain extent, this predicament is a function of the more general problem of the continuity or discontinuity between medieval and modern science, of ascertaining the actual link between fourteenth-century scientific accomplishments with those of the seventeenth, and of defining the nature of Renaissance science.[10] The question might be stated as follows: Did the Renaissance Hermetic traditions promote or retard the rapport between Christianity and the study of nature from the end of the fourteenth century until the late seventeenth century?

This study of Abraham Yagel's thought offers a unique opportunity to consider the first two issues—the relationship between religion and science and between the occult and science—from the perspective of a Jewish thinker who had not only a keen interest in contemporary natural philosophy and medicine but also an abiding commitment to Jewish mystical and magical traditions. It also allows us to consider the third question, one especially relevant to this Jewish thinker. For Yagel, as we shall see, found substantial justification and encouragement for his pursuit of the study of nature in Judaism's long involvement with the occult. From his perspective, the religious obligation of Jews to comprehend the natural world was merely a contemporary manifestation and extension of the special bond between the religious and the occult that had existed in Judaism since its inception.

There is as yet no modern work of scholarship on the meeting of Jewish thought and early modern science. This book represents a small part of such a larger undertaking now in progress.[11] It offers a comparative view of the interplay of the religious and magical with the scientific proclivities of the age, using the specific texts and context of an individual embedded in the Jewish tradition.

Yet a case study of Yagel represents more than merely a Jewish illustration of tendencies already visible in the Christian world. The richness of Yagel's scientific ruminations raises the fundamental questions whether there was a specifically Jewish pattern of response to the study of nature in the late sixteenth century and in what ways that response was similar to or different from that of contemporary Christians. Yagel read widely in the scientific and medical literature of his day, and he creatively wedded this knowledge to his own religious tradition. His originality lay not in his mastery of new scientific sources and methods but in his ability to fuse Judaism with the study of natural philosophy. As a religious thinker, he sought to reshape Jewish culture by underscoring the religious value of comprehending the natural world, by reformulating kabbalistic tradition in the language of scientific discourse so as to promote it as the highest form of human knowledge, and by pushing Jewish religious sensibilities to their limits in advocating the legitimate role of the magical arts as the ultimate expression of human creativity in Judaism. His bold new agenda for Jewish culture also sought to elevate the place of the Jewish people in European civilization. In a period of increasing anti-Jewish agitation and cultural isolation, Yagel strove to merge Judaism with European science by highlighting the centrality of the former within the latter. For Yagel, Jews since Solomon's time had always demonstrated a keen interest in naturalistic learning; they had always excelled in the occult and medical arts; and their unique kabbalistic heritage allowed them to penetrate the mysteries of the universe in a manner unattainable by the best of the natural philosophers. They were thus well suited to assume a significant role in a culture that increasingly valued such virtues. And Yagel found confirmation of the continuing validity of "the wisdom of Israel" in the fact that some Christian scholars were attracted to the study of Judaism, especially its occultist and esoteric roots.

Ultimately, Yagel's scientific vision of Judaism had limited influence on either Jewish or Christian intellectual life. Nevertheless, he was neither isolated nor unappreciated in his own lifetime. He established close and lasting contacts with some of the most important Jewish cultural figures of his day, especially the kabbalists Menahem Azariah da Fano and Mordecai Dato. Moreover, the particular fusion of medicine, science, and Judaism that he advocated was valued by a significant number of Jewish intellectuals, especially physicians, to an even greater degree than in previous generations. Accordingly, a study of Yagel's particular adaptation of sixteenth-century science to Judaism constitutes a good starting point for assessing the wider pattern of dialogue between Judaism and modern science that unfolded in subsequent centuries.

Two critical features of Yagel's integration of religion and magic with his scientific concerns warrant emphasis from the outset. Whether these features denote a unique Jewish—as opposed to a Christian—response to the study of nature in this period remains a subject for future research. Nevertheless, they invite comparison with Christian attitudes to science and perhaps suggest, at the very least, a difference of degree or of emphasis, if not of total dissimilitude between the two groups.

We already have alluded to the first, that Yagel's attraction to nature, medicine, astrology, chiromancy, demonology, and magic was fostered by the extraordinary resources of the Jewish tradition itself. Thus he appears to have had little need to rediscover and co-opt an ancient pagan past abounding with mystical insight and magical potency; he could readily locate within Jewish esoteric traditions of both ancient and medieval provenance an embarrassingly rich collection of theosophical interpretations and occult formulas. Moreover, he was fortified and encouraged by the openness and tolerance of rabbinic Judaism toward magical and theurgic activity. The ancient rabbis were magical wonder-workers; they in turn had promoted the heroic image of Solomon as the archmagician.[12] Similarly, the vocation of healing and the divine office of the physician constituted a hallowed Jewish tradition throughout antiquity and the Middle Ages. The plethora of biblical and rabbinic medical and biological wisdom testified to the fecundity of Jewish medical activity.[13] Mathematics, astrology, and astronomy were also well-established areas of Jewish endeavor.[14] Medieval Jewish literature in all these fields, especially that written in the Islamic world, provided a veritable gold mine of information and inspiration. In short, Jewish traditions of naturalistic learning authorized and encouraged Yagel's magical and scientific interests to an extraordinary degree. No doubt the prevailing passion of European learning strongly encouraged Yagel's interest in these esoteric pursuits. Nevertheless, sufficient precedents were available to him in the immense corpus of Jewish literary tradition; he only needed to locate them and to ascribe to them a more central epistemological status than before. For Yagel, the potential tension of harmonizing unorthodox practices with religious doctrine was significantly mitigated because such practices had been previously sanctioned, even sanctified, by his religious tradition.

In the second place, Yagel repeatedly linked his pursuit of the study of nature with a theme that is prominent throughout his writing: the interconnectedness of all learning.[15] He was fond of reminding his reader that even the most insignificant object in nature is pregnant with profound meaning when related to its higher source within the divine scheme of creation. Sharing the passion of many sixteenth-century Christian naturalists, Yagel enthusiastically searched for signs in nature to correlate them with other signs, so as to classify, to integrate, and thus to reaffirm the essential divine unity. But Yagel's obsession with correlating signs also appears to have been related to his status as a highly educated member of the Jewish community. His intellectual task, as he might have defined

it, was to integrate Jewish knowledge with the sources of other traditions and other disciplines. By harmonizing Jewish learning with
non-Jewish learning, whether based on observation of the physical
world or based on books, no matter how alien and dissimilar it
might appear, he would narrow the cultural distance separating Judaism from Western civilization.

Crossing the threshold of the modern era, Jews such as Yagel
needed more than ever to demonstrate that the ideas and cultural
signatures of their own tradition resembled those in the larger world
of nature and in European culture as a whole. The insights of the
Jewish tradition, especially esoteric ones, were in no way inferior to
those of other cultural legacies, including Christianity; on the contrary, they were often superior. Jews long before had loudly proclaimed the superiority of their own unadulterated traditions; but
especially in Yagel's era, such boastful claims might now fall on attentive ears. The more the Jew could assemble his own signs, pub-
licize them, and reveal their relatedness with other signs, the more
acceptable he imagined Judaism might be rendered in a larger intellectual and more cosmopolitan community. Perhaps underlying Yagel's passion for integrating and correlating all kinds of ideas and
sources from books and from the natural world was this psychological need to gain cultural respect and social acceptance for himself
and for his entire beleaguered community.

The following chapters attempt to substantiate these hypotheses
by exploring various facets of Yagel's kabbalistic, medical-magical,
and scientific pursuits. They consider the attitudes, methods, and
sources Yagel shared with some of his Christian contemporaries but
also underscore Yagel's individuality as shaped and informed by his
Jewish identity. The book opens with a broad survey of Yagel's life,
highlighting the economic and political vicissitudes of Jewish life in
late sixteenth- and early seventeenth-century Counter-Reformation
Italy. The next six chapters treat in depth Yagel's medical and naturalistic interests and involvements, including his theory and practice of medicine and his attitude toward demonology, unusual fauna,
prodigies of nature, astronomical discoveries, and the various forms
of magic. Chapters 8 and 9 consider the larger cultural context of
Yagel's thinking on nature. Yagel's particular interest in metempsychosis and his attempt to establish its veracity by appealing to ancient philosophy, contemporary science, and Christian theology
well illustrate his characteristic obsession to correlate disparate
sources of knowledge. The final chapter discusses Yagel's attitude

toward ancient theology and his understanding of kabbalah and the place of Judaism within Western civilization.

One final, methodological word is in order. At least initially, I shall deliberately avoid pinpointing the precise meaning Yagel assigned to kabbalah, magic, and especially science. Yagel's "scientific" interests emerged before the scientific revolution of the late seventeenth century; they exhibit a peculiar blend of traditional medievalism with some new emphases, such as a concern for empirical observation and a desire to construct and replicate nature. As Patrick Curry has correctly observed, any clean, rigorous, abstract modern definitions of these terms are anachronistic and thus meaningless.[16] I hope that instead Yagel's understanding of these categories "will grow out of sensitive analysis of texts in their contexts,"[17] so that the three terms used in the title of this book and their perfect kinship in the mind of Yagel will have emerged clearly by the end.

1. The Ordeals and Rewards of Living: A Biographical Portrait of Abraham ben Hananiah Yagel

Behold I am seventy years old and my strength has waned . . .
I also am without money today . . . For forty years I have been
involved in these kinds of [financial] controversies.

—*Bat Rabim*, fol. 174a

FIFTEEN FIFTY-THREE, the year in which Abraham Yagel was born, marks a watershed in the history of the Italian Jewish community. In that year all copies of the Talmud were burned throughout Italy by papal decree. Only two years later the infamous anti-Jewish edict, *Cum nimis absurdum*, sweepingly reversed the relatively tolerant papal policy toward Jews during the heyday of the Renaissance. In the emotionally charged atmosphere of the Counter-Reformation, Pope Paul IV (1476–1559) and his successors imposed new restrictive legislation leading to the increased impoverishment, ghettoization, and expulsion of Jews, especially in the Papal States themselves. These setbacks were accompanied by severe conversionary pressures: the enforcement of compulsory Christian preaching in synagogues; the proliferation of the *domus catechumenorum*, an institution designed to facilitate the large-scale conversion of Jews to Christianity; and the intensified Christian harassment of Jews, including the censorship of Hebrew books and the wide diffusion of anti-Judaic literature.[1]

These measures stood in sharp contrast to the relatively benign treatment of Jews by the church and secular authorities in Italy throughout previous centuries. Jewish loan bankers had initially been attracted to northern and central Italy because of the generous privileges offered them by local governments eager to attract adequate sources of credit for local businesses and especially for small loans to the poor. As a result of the granting of such privileges to individual Jews in the thirteenth, fourteenth, and fifteenth centuries, small Jewish communities grew up throughout the region, totally dependent on the recipients of these legal contracts (*condotte*), who also carried the primary burden of paying taxes to the authorities. By the sixteenth century, Jewish merchants and artisans joined these communities, until eventually the moneylenders were no longer in the majority. In the relatively tolerant conditions of Jewish political and economic life up until the mid-sixteenth century, the cultural habits and intellectual tastes of Italian Jews were stimulated by their proximity to centers of Italian Renaissance culture. A limited but conspicuous number of Jewish intellectuals established mutually fructifying liaisons with their Christian counterparts to a degree unparalleled in earlier centuries.[2]

The legislative measures of the mid-sixteenth century thus threatened to undermine the significant progress of Jewish-Christian rapprochement during much of the Renaissance. And along with the worsening political atmosphere, by the late sixteenth and early seventeenth centuries there was also a general decline in Jewish banking activities. As capital became more readily available to the Christian population, fewer merchants and artisans used the services of Jewish loan bankers. The latters' clients were increasingly the urban poor, who offered greater risks and more modest profits. With greater restrictions on Jewish moneylending, with the constant pressures to reduce the interest rate, and with the inevitable uncertainties involved in reclaiming the full value of loans, Jewish banking operations suffered accordingly. Some banks were forced to close; others competed fiercely for the diminished revenue available.[3]

Abraham Yagel's intellectual world, his activity as a physician, and his accomplishments as a religious thinker and scientific writer thus emerged in a context of declining political fortunes and diminished economic resources in the Italian Jewish community. And his own economic situation was even more precarious than that of other Jews. Above all, he knew intimately and acutely the treacherous business world of moneylending. Prominent and relatively affluent Jewish loan bankers constantly interacted with Yagel as patrons of his specialized learning, as patients in his medical practice, and as supporters or competitors during his own brief and tempestuous career in banking.

Yagel complained bitterly at every opportunity about the economic indignities to which he was constantly subjected. A highly detailed autobiographical sketch of a few critical years of his life in his *Gei Ḥizzayon* (A valley of vision), his letters, and his notes provide a vivid picture of acute financial burdens, lack of professional independence, and personal degradation by those less intellectually gifted than himself. As he readily acknowledged, despite his great literary promise and academic accomplishments he remained trapped in the misery of bad business ventures, poor financial management, and insufficient income.

Yagel's sense of being trapped is most dramatically conveyed in his partial autobiography, in *Gei Ḥizzayon.* Yagel situates himself as narrator incarcerated in the municipal prison of Mantua. Visited by the spirit of his recently deceased father, he unburdens himself with an extraordinary account of his blundering and painful experiences as a pawnbroker that led to his present confinement. Only when he is led out of the prison cell, under the trusting care of his father's soul, and allowed to roam the heavens in search of the sublime mysteries of the divine world is Yagel relieved of his pain, cathartically released from his pressures, and spiritually rejuvenated. Thus for Yagel the prison is emblematic of his life struggle and his constant effort to escape the stark realities of his material existence by writing, reflection, and spiritual inquiry.[4]

The same dialectical relationship between Yagel's economic failures and frustrations and his compulsion to flee into the world of the mind is captured in a revealing comment he wrote as a young man:

> I am twenty-six years old today . . . and I did not penetrate the secret of this wisdom [dream interpretation] because men rose up and exiled me from our house on numerous occasions. Thus we went and wandered on the mountains until we arrived in this region of the Mantovano. Even there we were not left alone, for God's hand was upon us. He took from me the crown of my head, my father, while I still walked in my innocence, a lad among the sons of the scholars who would go to school together . . . But then the times changed for me, and from the place where I ascended, I descended. I became weary but was not left alone nor did I find rest. I was forced to leave a lovely woman and a graceful gazelle [meaning his life of study] in order to earn a living, to go here and there to bring food to my house. Men not only arose to annoy me but they even took my store [his

bank in Luzzara] from me, leaving me desolate. And only because of God who was with me . . . my soul was uplifted. I have set the Lord always before me and I prayed to Him in His house, to gaze at His gracefulness and to visit His books written for us by those who fear him and do his commandments . . . It was thus my custom, day or night, whenever I could turn from my burdens, especially when I was heartsick, to see and study the books of our ancestors, to make myself markers and to write down the summaries of what I had learned so that the things which I understood would not escape nor be uprooted from my heart.[5]

Thus Yagel alludes to personal misfortunes, exile, and wandering even before the events described in the *Gei Ḥizzayon*, and even before the unexpected death of his father, which forced him to assume the operations of a pawn bank in the town of Luzzara, a task for which he was obviously unsuited. His life of study was prematurely interrupted and he yearned constantly to return to his books. Even this early he underscores the contrast between the burdens of earning a living and his desire to embrace "the lovely woman and graceful gazelle" of study and reflection. His intellectual journals, which he compiled by jotting down passages read in moments of free time, eventually became a kind of therapy, liberating him from the tribulations of poverty, the demands of ruthless creditors, and the pressures of an active medical practice. Although our concern with Yagel is primarily "the lovely woman and graceful gazelle" of his mind and imagination, we cannot ignore entirely the ugliness of his material world, which provoked his spiritual ruminations.

ABRAHAM YAGEL was born in 1553 in the small town of Monselice, located south of Padua and north of Rovigo in the area of the *terra ferma* (the mainland possessions of the Venetian government).[6] That his birthplace was Monselice can be inferred from the way he usually signed his name: "Abraham b. Hananiah Yagel of the Gallico family of Monselice." Although almost nothing is known about his father or his family origins, it is obvious that Gallico was his real family name and that he took the name Abraham Yagel from the Hebrew liturgy of the afternoon service for the Sabbath.[7]

Nothing is known of Yagel's early childhood in Monselice. It appears that he arrived in Luzzara, near Mantua, sometime in the early 1570s with his father, and perhaps with at least one brother. In a fragmentary work written in this period, he mentions his father as still being alive.[8] However, his father must have died before 1578, when Yagel began his *Gei Ḥizzayon*; his death is also mentioned in the introduction to Yagel's encyclopedic work, *Beit Ya'ar ha-Levanon* (House of the forest of Lebanon; cf. 1 Kings 10:17, 21), written in 1579.

It is possible that Yagel arrived in Luzzara as early as 1571–72, when Venice temporarily expelled many Jews, who sought refuge in the Mantovano.[9] He was certainly in Luzzara by 1575, for he describes a plague that swept the city then.[10] In the *Gei Ḥizzayon* Yagel provides a detailed account of the next few years,[11] beginning with the crisis engendered by his father's death: "For after coming to this city, God's spirit swept you up and took you from me . . . I remained a young man without a teacher in business skills since I had never assumed the responsibility of earning a living . . . I came here and from the first day, troubles and tribulations surrounded and passed over my head from human illnesses and injuries. At the time of my coming to the city, there was also a famine in the city, a lack of food and drink."[12]

Yagel immediately sought a partner to help him run a bank that he had inherited from his father. He attempted repeatedly but unsuccessfully to gain ducal permission for such a partnership. Eventually he agreed to an informal arrangement with a woman named Rina, the wife of a Jacob de Lecairo.[13] The terms Rina demanded were most unfavorable to Yagel, but he claimed he had no better option: "I was then like a person sinking in the river, who, even if a sharp sword was held out to him, would hold on to it and would not feel it if it cut his hand, for all of his body was like a sieve . . . The terms [offered by] Madam Rina seduced me and overcame me because of the pleasantness of her words, that money offers a solution and I would never again lack funds. I could also use the money for other business ventures." So he signed the agreement even though he had been warned about her unreliability.[14]

Rina soon reneged on the agreement and offered Yagel a year to find someone to replace her and return to her the money she had already invested in the bank.[15] During that time Yagel entered into negotiation with another banker, Samuel Almagiati.[16] But Rina would not accept the terms of payment in installments that he offered her. The negotiations collapsed, and in the interim Samuel died. His sons reopened negotiations with Rina, but they, too, failed to conclude an agreement with her.[17]

Matters related to the bank soon came to a standstill with the outbreak of plague in the environs of Mantua.[18] At great danger to his own life, Yagel eventually secured for Rina safe refuge at an estate near Luzzara. He then attempted to reopen negotiations with her and with the Almagiati sons. After repeated visits to Mantua to effectuate a final agreement, Yagel discovered to his dismay that neither party was willing to come to terms.[19] He sought the intervention of several distinguished Jews—Azariah Finzi,[20] Barukh Senigo,[21] Reuven of Perugia,[22] Uziel of Camerino,[23] and Barukh Finzi[24]—to whom he testified about these exasperating negotiations, but they apparently had little influence on the two parties in the dispute. Returning to Luzzara, he tried to carry on as best he could. His credit soon evaporated; he could not lend money to all the Christian poor who requested loans; he was slandered and thrown into jail in Luzzara. After a week he secured his release, but not before discovering that the elder Almagiati brother, Eliezer (Lazzarus), was clearly intent on hurting him: "With his loud voice in the markets and streets, he slandered me, saying that I had reached the end of the line, so that even the credit I still had, he caused me to lose."[25]

Realizing that his relationship with the Almagiati had soured, Yagel sought out arbitrators to intervene in his behalf and settle the dispute. He first sent Gershon Porto to speak to Almagiati, but the latter arrogantly snubbed him.[26] He then enlisted the support of three other distinguished Jews of Mantua: Isaac Cohen Porto;[27] Azariah Finzi, who had been involved in the controversy at an earlier stage; and Judah Ya'aleh of Colonia.[28] But Almagiati also vilified them. Porto and Finzi were thrown into prison; Colonia barely escaped by bribing the jailer. The dispute soon involved the governor of Luzzara and even the duke himself.[29] Later, two more arbitrators were appointed—Judah Moscato and Gershon Katz-Porto.[30] The controversy ended when Yagel was ambushed by Eliezer Almagiati and an associate and imprisoned on the charge of having in his possession a small dagger, a right extended only to citizens who had lived in the region for ten years or more. At this point Yagel ends his autobiographical account in the first part of *Gei Ḥizzayon* with the sentiment: "If babes weaned from milk knew of all these happenings from beginning to end as little as I have told you, since it is impossible to tell everything, they would cry on my behalf for the great wrong done to me."[31]

In the second half of *Gei Ḥizzayon*, written sometime later, Yagel covers the period between his first imprisonment in Luzzara and his ultimate imprisonment in Mantua. After ninety-one days he was released from jail in Luzzara. Two months later he was ordered to report to the authorities in Mantua. He traveled to Mantua in the company of a Christian man from Luzzara. Since it was late when they reached Mantua, he accepted his companion's invitation to spend the night in the home of a Christian citizen. Sitting at his host's table, he ate only bread and dried figs. But apparently Eliezer Almagiati had observed his every move; he surprised him at midnight with "the men of the cardinal," who arrested him and locked him up in the fortress of Mantua.[32] He was brought before a judge who informed him of his crime; "Didn't you know that Hebrews cannot eat bread with Christians under the same roof by order of the king and his nobles?" Yagel had been unaware of this decree.[33] He eventually paid his bail and was released but was returned to the same prison when slandered again by Eliezer Almagiati.

Yagel's extraordinarily detailed account of his misfortunes during these years was intended to justify himself to his detractors and to facilitate his own healing process through the very telling. Such an account by a pre-modern Jew is unprecedented in Hebrew literature.[34] It reflects a growing awareness of the self among Jewish writers in this and later eras.[35]

Besides Yagel's own account of this early period of his life, some additional data are available. Yagel indicates in passing the existence of his family, especially a dead brother and a mother-in-law. The colophon of a poem written by Yagel's friend Mordecai Dato reveals the identity of Abraham's wife as Dina, the daughter of Batsheva Fano and Hosea (Salvatore) da Colonia.[36] The latter was a banker in the area of Viadana and Luzzara.[37] Yagel had apparently married Dina soon after his arrival in Luzzara in the 1570s and sometime after her father had died.[38] Yagel's notebook contains a copy of a 1567 public announcement concerning the disposition of Hosea's estate.[39] During the height of Yagel's financial problems Batsheva had become ill, perhaps because of the plague, and may have died soon afterward. Yagel also had at least one brother who also died and apparently had children, who remain unnamed in the sources. The only additional information about Yagel's sojourn in Luzzara is a passing reference to a sick woman he had observed in 1581 and an undated reference to a conversation with a Christian traveler.[40] Yagel wrote his *Gei Ḥizzayon* while he lived in Luzzara, completing at least the first half in 1578. One year later he began his encyclopedia,

Beit Ya'ar ha-Levanon, which he worked on for many years but never completed.

WE KNOW considerably less about Yagel's life and career following the period described in his autobiographical account. Throughout the remaining years of the sixteenth century and into the first decade of the seventeenth, he visited a number of Italian communities, mostly in the vicinity of Mantua and Modena, including Pesaro,[41] Revere,[42] Ferrara,[43] Carpi,[44] Correggio,[45] Reggio,[46] and Modena.[47] He seems to have left Luzzara by the early 1580s, settling eventually in the town of Rubeira, in the province of Reggio nell'Emilia, under the political rule of the Este house. He was in Rubeira as early as 1585, and in 1593 he was given the right, in the absence of Christian physicians, to care for both Christian and Jewish patients.[48] His unsuccessful experiment with banking in Luzzara probably convinced him to earn his living through his other skills, especially medicine. Although he retained ownership of his property in Luzzara and received some income from renting it out, his major occupation was that of a physician and a tutor in the home of some affluent Jewish banking families. Thus during this period he corresponded with a number of distinguished Jewish patients who obviously valued his medical opinion highly.

He also established close ties with some of the most influential Jewish bankers in the region, especially Joseph Fano, the most powerful and politically well-connected Jew in Reggio nell'Emilia. Abraham visited Fano at his summer home outside Ferrara in 1587 and dedicated his second book, *Lekaḥ Tov* (Sound learning; cf. Proverbs 4:2), a summary of the principles of Judaism written for children and published in 1595 in Venice, to him.[49] Yagel clearly taught at least one of Fano's children and probably used this small volume in his teaching.[50] A small earlier book on the treatment of the plague, *Moshi'ah Ḥosim* (Savior of those who take refuge; cf. Psalms 17:7), was published in Venice in 1587 and dedicated to another banker, Or Shraga Sanguini of Venice. Yagel also nurtured a long-term relationship with the Modena banking family of Sassuolo. As early as 1604, he carried on an intense correspondence with Daniel Modena over the illness and eventual death of his son.[51] This family obviously employed him, at least periodically, over the next ten years.[52]

Yagel's residence in the Reggio area coincided with that of the famous kabbalist Menahem Azariah da Fano, who lived in Reggio in the 1580s and returned there in the first decade of the seventeenth century.[53] The two were on intimate terms and corresponded frequently. A letter from Abraham in Rubeira in 1600 asking an unknown rabbi whether he could perform the *pidyon ha-ben* (the ceremony of redeeming the firstborn son on the thirty-first day after birth) of his grandson in the absence of the child's father (Yagel's son), who was out of town, was probably directed to Fano.[54] Yagel's ties with Fano were not only intellectual or spiritual. In 1605 Yagel dedicated his third book, *Eshet Ḥayil* (A woman of valor), a short commentary on Proverbs 31 in praise of women, to Rachel, the wife of Hezekiah ben Isaac Foa, who was the wealthy brother-in-law of Menahem Azariah. This gesture was an obvious expression of his attempt to establish an economic relationship with a very well-to-do family that also supported Fano's mystical and intellectual pursuits.[55]

Yagel lived in the same region of Modena, Reggio, and Sassuolo during the remaining years of his life. In 1613 he was in Modena at the trial of a Jew named David Riko.[56] About a year later, in the fall of 1614, Yagel was in Sassuolo, employed by the wealthy banker Raphael ben Bezalel Modena, probably as a teacher, personal physician, and adviser.[57] A document written by Modena relates an unusual story involving himself and Yagel.[58] Modena had been invited to participate as godfather (*sandek*) in the ritual circumcision ceremony of his sister's newborn infant in Luzzara. The brother-in-law, Elhanan Yedidiah Rieti, and the grandfather, Hananiah Eliakim, were also trustees of the property that Yagel still owned in Luzzara. Yagel apparently accompanied Modena on the trip from Sassuolo to Luzzara either as his employee or more likely, as a personal friend of the Rieti family with ties to the community of Luzzara.

On their way home to Sassuolo after the ceremony, Modena and Yagel were stopped by four armed robbers outside Reggio, taken captive, and brought to an inn in the mountains overlooking Reggio. One of the robbers took Modena's carriage for a ride and was spotted by some police of Reggio, one of whom recognized the carriage because he had once lived in Sassuolo. They pursued the robber until he abandoned the carriage, his weapons, and Yagel's coat and hat. The kidnappers then moved their captives to the high mountains of Lucca. Throughout this time, Modena emphasized later, "they never caused us to transgress the Jewish religion." The two Jews prayed three times a day with phylacteries and prayer shawl; they ate only permitted foods, "and the words 'How pleasant are the songs of Israel' were always on our lips."[59]

During their captivity the Jewish communities in Modena, Luzzara, Sassuolo, Reggio, Mantua, and Ferrara recited prayers and mobilized their resources to secure their release. In Reggio prayers were initiated by Menaham Azariah da Fano and his famous student, Aaron Berakhia of Modena. Finally the kidnappers sent Yagel to the city of Modena to bargain for the release of his valuable patron, for whom they requested a ransom of 10,000 ducats. The duke's militia finally intervened, surprised the captors, and freed Modena. Modena describes the reception of himself and Yagel, led on horses through the streets of Modena together with the captured criminals. The description underscores the importance of this affluent banker from Sassuolo, whose captivity appeared to be of great concern to some six Jewish communities and to the duke himself. At the same time, the narrative portrays Abraham Yagel in a most uncomplimentary light: he is referred to as only "Abraham Yagel Gallico"; he appears to be only a servant and lowly companion of Modena; he is deemed so unimportant that he is soon released to negotiate the terms of Modena's ransom. It is hazardous to infer too much from this portrait.[60] It seems likely, however, that Yagel, who had recently passed his sixtieth birthday, was dependent on Modena for his economic support and that Modena treated him with little respect despite his age and his status as a learned physician and scholar.

Our knowledge of Yagel's whereabouts over the next nine years is incomplete. In Modena in 1617 he witnessed another trial of Jews accused of political crimes against the state.[61] In 1619 Yagel again visited Pesaro but returned to Modena in the following year.

The last documents regarding Yagel's life were written by Yagel himself in 1623 from San Martino, probably San Martino dall'Argine, near Gazzuolo in the Mantovano.[62] The fact that Yagel had left the Modenese region to return to the Mantovano indicates, at the very least, the economic instability of his life even after the age of seventy. Yagel had had previous contact with the household of Joseph Ḥazak of that city and may have returned there on that account.[63] In the first of a series of letters to Hananiah Rieti of Luzzara,[64] he acknowledges his economic situation and the poor business deals he has made over the years: "Behold I am seventy years old and my strength has waned. I no longer am able to go out and come as before. I am also without money today because of the excessive expenditures in which I became entangled during the past several months and because of my negligible income due to the rise of the price of food in this region . . . For forty years I have been involved in these kinds of [financial] controversies.[65]

Yagel had written to Rieti about the status of his house at Luzzara, which the Rieti family apparently had managed for him over the years, sending him the rent to which he was entitled. Yagel's portion of the rent had been withheld and he had first written four times to Raphael Modena, his former employer in Sassuolo and the brother-in-law of Rieti's son, regarding the money owed him. Raphael "responded to me as a mocker before his slaves."[66] In desperation, Yagel turned to Hananiah Rieti, then an old man who died later that year. He recalled the promises made by the Rieti family to pay him a certain amount of the rent from the property. Despite an additional letter to Elhanan, Hananiah's son, Yagel's demands seem to have remained unfulfilled.[67]

The fact that this correspondence represents the final documentation of Abraham Yagel's life is in itself bitter testimony that Yagel's financial problems plagued him to the very end. Framed by the painful feud with the Almagiatis in the 1570s and this last controversy with the Rietis of 1623, Yagel's life was marked throughout by financial failures, unreliable business partnerships, constant anxiety, and severe loss of time. His experience provides a rare glimpse of the more unsavory business world of his Jewish contemporaries. His books, his writing, and his scientific and kabbalistic pursuits provided him the only liberation from his constant economic concerns.

NONE OF YAGEL'S major works was published in his own lifetime, and even today most remain in their original manuscript form. He did, however, publish three small books of limited scope and importance. Of these, his Hebrew "catechism," *Lekah Tov,* is the most interesting. It obviously was written as a kind of pedagogic experiment, adapting for Jewish usage the standard Catholic text of Peter Canisius. Although such "borrowing" might appear audacious to modern readers, it met with ready acceptance by contemporary and later Jewish readers. Clearly oblivious to the book's Catholic overtones, various publishers printed it in numerous Hebrew and Latin editions, and it came to occupy a modest place in the history of Jewish educational texts.[68]

In contrast, Yagel's autobiography and heavenly journey, *Gei Ḥizzayon*, and his massive encyclopedias, *Beit Ya'ar ha-Levanon* and *Be'er Sheva*, probably never left his possession. Some of his close friends may have read them, but not until the nineteenth century did anyone consult them or bother to publish excerpts from them. Similarly, *Bat Rabim* (Daughter of many), his collection of letters and other notices, displays the character of a personal diary and journal for its author's private use.

Nevertheless, Yagel's lack of audience should not obscure the genuine novelty and uniqueness of his literary output. All his works break new ground in both their form and their content. *Gei Ḥizzayon* is unique in Hebrew literature both because of its autobiographical sections describing the mundane affairs of a miserable banker and because of its indebtedness to the literary traditions of Boethius and Boccaccio.[69] In this work Yagel consciously experimented with a new genre in contemporary Italian culture and successfully adapted it for his own didactic purposes. Similarly, his two giant compendia of knowledge, *Beit Ya'ar ha-Levanon* and *Be'er Sheva*, drew their inspiration from the form and content of the medieval and Renaissance encyclopedias. Yagel clearly hoped to classify all knowledge, to reveal the interconnectedness of all learning, and to disclose the path of an intellectual journey that would lead ultimately to the source of all truth, to the revelation at Sinai as understood through the kabbalistic mysteries. In recalling in the title of *Beit Ya'ar ha-Levanon* the name of Solomon's Temple (cf. 1 Kings 7:2), he may also have had in mind the image of Solomon the magician; thus like several of his Jewish and Christian contemporaries, his magical concerns may have motivated him to undertake such literary projects. Above all, he hoped to integrate Jewish and general learning in order to demonstrate the superiority and priority of Judaism within Western culture.[70] His remaining works were also relatively novel. His *Bat Rabim* is a kind of intellectual diary, epistolary collection, and social encyclopedia all in one. His medical *consilia* (discussed in the next chapter) introduced a new secular form of writing relatively uncommon in Hebrew letters.

Yagel wrote no biblical commentaries, no sermons, no legal glosses, and only one insignificant rabbinic *responsum*.[71] He was a Jewish writer whose choice of literary genre was inspired totally by the literary tastes of late Italian Renaissance culture. Perhaps precisely because his writing was so unconventional and untraditional, it went relatively unnoticed by later generations of Hebrew readers.

ALTHOUGH his major writings were relatively unknown, Yagel was still recognized for his intellectual stature by members of his own community, and he maintained close and lasting relationships with several of the Jewish cultural luminaries of his day. A close examination of these personal and intellectual ties, based primarily on the evidence of his own writing and correspondence, allows us to situate Yagel within a well-defined intellectual and literary circle of Italian Jewry and to ascertain his singular role within that circle.

Abraham's closest friend was surely Hananiah Finzi, a rabbi and banker who lived in Gazzuolo, Dosolo, Viadana, and Mantua.[72] In the opening chapter of *Beit Ya'ar ha-Levanon*, written in 1579, Yagel indicates that Finzi had been the one to encourage him to undertake this challenging intellectual project: "One day a most learned sage and rabbi, Hananiah Finzi, a resident of Gazzuolo, passed through this place where I live in Luzzara. He passed by me as a man whose soul is connected with mine; he saw these written homilies neglected in a corner and he liked them very much. Thus he declared that it would be good for you if you made them for the benefit of many . . . therefore, I responded to his words."[73]

In *Be'er Sheva* Yagel seems to refer to Finzi again: "A spiritual friend from childhood, we would walk together to school, and his soul is connected with mine. He saw the words of this book and its intention and also read aloud all the words of the previous chapter from beginning to end . . . for, in my estimation, there is . . . a covenant of love connecting us."[74] If this second passage does indeed describe Finzi, it seems likely that his special relationship with Yagel included reading the manuscripts of his compositions and encouraging him to pursue his writing. In one instance Finzi even secured a manuscript for Yagel to study.[75] He was also a witness to a bizarre incident in the home of Joseph Ḥazak of San Martino: he informed Yagel, who was then in Reggio, that the soul of Ḥazak's deceased daughter-in-law had returned to the household. Yagel did not doubt the veracity of Hananiah's testimony, calling him "a gem without any imperfection in his heart."[76]

When Finzi wrote to Yagel in 1604 regarding the illness of his own brother-in-law, he too recalled their special friendship: "Lying in my bed in the evenings, I remembered your honor. I remembered you with a spiritual love, out of the beds of the night watches; I reflected on your image, which was engraved in my mind. I placed it with a stamp on my heart, with a stamp on my shoulders, for now it is like our love from the days of old and from former years."[77]

Yagel also had a relationship with Azariah Finzi, Hananiah's brother and banking partner. Azariah served as an arbitrator in the dispute with the Almagiatis. Yagel also copied into his journal the correspondence between Azariah and two rabbis regarding the murder of Azariah's daughter by her brother Ishmael because she was a whore. The incident took place in Azariah's house in Ferrara in 1577, at the same time as Yagel's banking troubles in Luzzara. In trying to defend the innocence of his sons, Azariah revealed a sense of his own importance, a sense undoubtedly shared by his brother and other members of the banking class: "It is inappropriate for one who calls himself a Jew," he writes, "especially one with standing, to suffer a veil of shame on his face . . . for the divine presence shines only on noble families."[78] Through his intimate relationship with Hananiah Finzi, Yagel had gained the confidence and respect of one "noble family."

We have already noted the contact between Yagel and Menahem Azariah da Fano, especially the relationship Yagel forged with the wife of Menahem's brother-in-law, Hezekiah Foa, to whom he dedicated his book. Fano's connections with Yagel were based, however, on solid intellectual grounds. On several occasions he solicited Yagel's advice on medical or astronomical matters, such as the astrological background of the prophecies of a Spanish Jewish lad named Nahman;[79] the illness of Hillel of Viadana and the case of a young woman too frightened to enter a ritual bath;[80] and the case of a couple who could no longer live with each other.[81] Referring to Yagel as "unique in our generation in the knowledge of the spheres and expert in all fields of learning,"[82] Fano turned regularly and repeatedly to his resident expert in the sciences of medicine and the stars.

In *Beit Ya'ar ha-Levanon* Yagel records an extremely involved discussion between Fano and himself on astronomical matters.[83] What is interesting about this prolonged inquiry is not the specific issues discussed but the manner in which Fano sought to gain from Yagel "scientific" corroboration of specific statements in kabbalistic literature. For example, Yagel confirms Fano's impression that a specific constellation is hinted at in the *Sefer Yeẓirah;*[84] elsewhere Yagel argues for the plausibility of a lunar eclipse at the moment of creation, substantiating a statement found in Moses Cordovero's *Pardes Rimmonim.*[85]

The intellectual relationship between the two was reciprocal. Yagel was familiar with at least one of Fano's works; he had certainly learned through him of Cordovero's stature among kabbalists.[86] Both were interested in finding correlations between natural and kabbalistic wisdom. Fano was the major Italian kabbalist in Yagel's day, and his writings evince little interest in sources and ideas outside the realm of mythical kabbalah, especially that associated with Isaac Luria.[87] Thus the mutual respect between Yagel, the physician and astrologer, and Fano, the pure kabbalist, is all the more fascinating. It reveals a broader interest in natural and astrological learning on Fano's part, to the extent that this learning enhanced his kabbalistic insights. It also indicates an ability in Yagel to assimilate kabbalistic texts and concepts into his broader intellectual vision. Despite their differences, "the noble *gaon*" (= genius, learned; the title Yagel gave Fano) and "the expert in all fields of learning" shared a common intellectual and spiritual agenda.

Another of Yagel's close associates was Mordecai Dato, the kabbalist, preacher, poet, and messianic enthusiast.[88] Dato not only dedicated a poem to Abraham's wife, Dina; he also composed one in honor of Yagel himself.[89] Yagel often refers to Dato's opinion on a given subject. In one instance, when discussing the secret of the small and large letters of the Torah, he cites a tradition of the scribe Meir of Padua, who was in Mantua, and then the view of Dato.[90] Dato wrote Yagel a letter supporting his position on metempsychosis and offering him additional sources.[91] He also composed especially for Yagel a commentary on a section of the *Pirke de Rabbi Eliezer*, which he later incorporated into his *Migdal David*.[92] After Dato died, Yagel was in contact with his widow, who sought his assistance regarding an invasion of her house by demons (discussed in Chapter 3).

Like his relationship with Fano, Yagel's friendship with Dato was based on mutual respect and admiration, despite the obvious dissimilarities in their intellectual interests and literary accomplishments. Dato's *Iggeret ha-Levanon* and Yagel's *Beit Ya'ar ha-Levanon* share a superficial resemblance.[93] But the manifest divergences between the two are more prominent. With the exception of one conventional chapter in his entire literary corpus, Yagel showed little personal involvement in messianic activity.[94] Fano's and Dato's involvement in Lurianic kabbalah is nowhere reflected in Yagel's writing (see Chapter 9).

The key to the intellectual basis of the two men's friendship is a series of letters in the 1570s from Dato to another kabbalist, Ezra Fano, the teacher of Menahem Azariah da Fano, about the relationship between the kabbalah and other sources of knowledge.[95] In Dato's view, it was a positive step for the kabbalah to seek external substantiation from other sources: "I have known that they ride coupled in my response—the kabbalah and the reason—for this is an eternal supposition that nature, the senses, and philosophy acknowledge it [the kabbalah], so I do not doubt saying . . . that the words of the *Sefer ha-Zohar* are kabbalah."[96] Dato cautioned that one should not expect to find a rational explanation for everything in the kabbalah; nor should one establish an equivalency between naturalistic and kabbalistic truth, since the latter is clearly superior to the former. Nevertheless, he was convinced that naturalistic explanations can often buttress kabbalistic insight.[97] If Yagel had seen these letters, he would have been most comfortable with their conclusions. As we shall see, he, too, considered his naturalistic investigations as confirming kabbalistic truth; nor did he doubt the priority of the kabbalah in establishing truth. Dato probably appreciated Yagel for reasons similar to Fano's. He was their resident authority in naturalistic learning and, like them, believed "that nature, the senses, and philosophy acknowledge" the kabbalah.

Besides these three primary associates, Yagel was acquainted with or knew of several other prominent figures of Italian Jewish culture. Yagel was on intimate terms with Judah Sommo Portaleone, the well-known dramatist and director of Mantua. Despite Sommo's more secular pursuits, the two engaged in a discussion of metempsychosis, and Sommo showed Yagel a detailed model of the Temple that he had built in his own home.[98] Yagel was also familiar with the opinions and writings of the great rabbi and preacher Judah Moscato and probably knew him personally.[99] In 1582 he came to the assistance of Moscato's wife when her husband had been called away from home and she required economic support.[100] Whether he had personal contact with the other luminary of Italian Jewry, Azariah de' Rossi, the historian and author of the *Me'or Einayim,* is impossible to say. It is clear, however, that Yagel consulted Azariah's work on several occasions and quoted it without acknowledging its author.[101] Finally, an author who died years before Yagel was born but who exerted an enormous influence on his thought was Yohanan Alemanno, the kabbalist-philosopher, physician, and magical writer. Yagel repeatedly cited his works; he even owned a manuscript of Alemanno's collected notations, to which he occasionally appended his own comments.[102]

In sum, Yagel's best friends were the leading cultural figures of their generation. They apparently welcomed Yagel into their circle and appreciated enormously his professional and intellectual achievements, which supplemented their own. This reception stands in sharp contrast to his shabby treatment by several Jewish bankers in his youth and by Raphael Modena and the Rieti family at the end of his life. Yagel's stature was assured among these intellectuals primarily because of his specialized knowledge of medicine and natural philosophy. This dimension of Yagel's professional life must be the first topic of our inquiry into his intellectual world.

2. The Art of Healing

Who is greater in knowledge and in love for us than you, master? . . . For from you is the source of life, the virtue of angels, and in your light we shall see light in the divine deliverance of life.

—Solomon Forlì to Abraham Yagel,
Bat Rabim, no. 48, fol. 82a

A wise man will know that if we follow this path, we will have trodden a path of the steps of nature, for wisdom turns toward the mode of reality. There is no wisdom and no true intelligence that can turn in another manner.

—*Bat Rabim*, no. 52, fol. 88a

DESPITE his literary and business interests, Yagel saw himself primarily as a physician. His distinguished contemporaries in the Jewish community of north-central Italy knew him both in this capacity and as an authority on astronomy and astrology. As we saw earlier, no less a religious authority than Menahem Azariah da Fano acknowledged him as "unique in our generation in the knowledge of the spheres" and as an "expert in all fields of learning." Yagel's patients were no less generous in their praise of his intellectual gifts and professional abilities. Solomon Forlì, in requesting Yagel's medical intervention, proclaimed: "Who is greater in knowledge and in love for us than you, master? . . . For from you is the source of life."[1] On another occasion he wrote: "I have known you for some time by the name of one who is wise and discerning, a master of numerous fields and qualities."[2] Daniel Modena, another of Yagel's patients addressed him as "noble of the doctors";[3] Hananiah Finzi, one of Yagel's closest friends, panegyrized him as "a wise man preferable to a prophet," to whom "God bestowed wisdom in his heart to know how to find a cure for a blow."[4] For Finzi, Yagel also represented the Solomon of his generation: "I refer to you in this generation: 'He was the wisest of all men' [1 Kings 5:11]."[5]

No doubt Yagel appreciated such adulation. His voluminous scientific writings, his encyclopedic interests, and his bold educational plan offering to his Hebrew readers a vision of the overarching unity of all knowledge all testify to the seriousness with which he viewed himself and his prodigious accomplishments. Although he rarely referred to himself as "doctor," in one instance he signed a medical prescription in Latin characters with the name "Doctor Yagel."[6] His medical title clearly provided him with intellectual status and spiritual authority among his coreligionists, a situation he earnestly sought and one that partially compensated for his incessant financial difficulties.

Unfortunately, we do not know where Yagel received his medical training.[7] The erudition displayed in his medical writings strongly suggests that he attended a medical school, and we now have corroboration in the form of a recently discovered document. On February 4, 1593, Yagel was given the right, in the absence of Christian physicians, to care for the Christian sick in "Terra Ruberie," probably Rubiera, a town between Reggio and Modena. This right was granted to Yagel explicitly because he was a university-trained physician (*artium et medicine doctore*) and because he had studied and practiced for a long time.[8]

Because Yagel's writings assign so prominent a place to both the theory and the practice of medicine, his role as a physician needs to be considered in relation to other medical practitioners of the sixteenth century as well as to the social and cultural concerns of his own Jewish community. Since medicine was seldom studied or practiced in this period in isolation from a variety of other disciplines, including natural philosophy, mathematics, astrology, magic, and even theology, a brief look at Yagel's medical activity allows us to perceive even larger cultural forces shaping his religious attitudes and intellectual priorities.

YAGEL'S POSITION of respect in the Jewish community was attributable to a great extent to the obvious human needs for which he claimed to offer remedies. Jews of the sixteenth century lived in constant insecurity not only because they were a beleaguered minority but also because, like other human beings, they were constantly subject to pain, illness, and premature death. As Keith Thomas and others have shown, the hazards of coping with limited food supplies, bubonic plague, overcrowded living quarters, and poor sanitation affected all sectors of the population.[9] Despite the high ratio of doctors practicing in northern Italy by the sixteenth century,[10] the region was no less immune to the daily tragedies of life and death than the rest of premodern Europe.

Yet the claims and self-image of medical practitioners far outstripped their ability to effectuate reliable cures. Physicians, despite their sincere intentions, had little control over sanitary conditions. Even in dire emergencies such as plagues, they faced insurmountable difficulties in influencing public health policy. Their quarantines were bitterly resisted; they could not control the accompanying violence and looting; nor could they adequately cope with the putrid conditions of urban squalor that facilitated the virulent spread of the disease. Most important, they lacked appropriate conceptual knowledge. Most graduates of university medical schools were still trained according to the Galenic principles of humoral physiology, principles perfectly logical and internally consistent but unfortunately wrong.[11]

According to the Galenic system, pathological conditions stemmed from abnormalities in one or more of the four humors—blood, choler, melancholy, and phlegm. Curing a patient involved restoring a normal balance or *complexio* of the four through various purges or emetics or bloodletting. In addition to prescriptions limiting diet, a regimen of sleep, and emotional tranquillity, the physician could offer little more than purgative drugs for evacuating the supposed injurious humor from the veins. In the very best circumstances, the patient survived such ineffectual remedies. More often than not, the course of treatment was either useless or harmful. Particularly in times of plague, the Galenic etiology of disease proved itself hopelessly ineffectual.[12]

Although the Galenic system continued to dominate medical learning throughout the sixteenth century because of the sheer weight of its authoritative tradition and appealing logic, it clearly required supplementation and refinement. The patient could be treated conventionally according to the principles of humoral physiology and simultaneously exposed to other forms of therapy—astrological medicine, magical healing, clerical counseling, or a combination of them all.[13] In an intellectual universe structured by correlations and analogies between the corporeal, social, and cosmological, the appeal to supernatural forms of healing therapy appeared intellectually justifiable and self-evident.[14] Medical science was holistic; the physician attempted to integrate his remedies within the cosmic reality he assumed to exist. He thus could prescribe natural remedies of diet control, evacuation, clean air, exercise, and sleep while charting the patient's horoscope and examining his religious and moral behavior.

This "therapeutic eclecticism," as MacDonald has called it, could prove effective where Galenic medical theory and practice could not. By ascribing a variety of causes—natural, astral, and divine—to the patient's ailment, the doctor appeared less vulnerable or culpable if the patient failed to be cured; for although the physician was clearly responsible for the specific natural remedies he prescribed, he could hardly assume total responsibility for a condition astrologically determined, nor could he expect to be blamed for illness engendered by divine intervention. Moreover, as medical science was seen to encompass an astrological, magical, and religious dimension, the physician might prove more effective than his finite and faulty medical knowledge would ordinarily allow him to be. As an interpreter of the heavenly design, as a pastoral counselor, as a magical healer with a grab bag of prayers, charms, and talismans, the physician assumed a critical role as a kind of psychotherapist. Though generally helpless in the face of disease, he could offer psychological and pastoral care; he could heal by the power of suggestion; and he could help alleviate the anguish of his patient by relating an individual's particular pain to a cosmic or divine source. Thus the physician—part scientist, part occultist, part clergyman—assumed a vital role within a society in constant urgent need of the services he purported to offer.

Yagel's medical practice thus can best be understood in relation to those of Christian practitioners such as Girolamo Cardano and Levinus Lemnius of the sixteenth century or Richard Napier and Simon Forman of the seventeenth.[15] All of these had attempted to reconcile their scientific learning with their magical and religious beliefs so that if "natural" methods proved insufficient, they could be corrected or alternated with magical-astrological or divine healing. For all of them, the interlocking character of the universe—the triadic cosmos of spiritual, astral, and material planes of existence, formulated within the Neoplatonic tradition and commonly assumed in the sixteenth and early seventeenth centuries to reflect reality—provided the most reassuring confirmation for their eclecticism. As a Jewish physician caring primarily for Jewish patients, Yagel understood his calling in a similar manner, with one added dimension: he came to his practice fully armed with the rich

traditions of rabbinic medical wisdom and the imaginative speculations of kabbalistic theurgy and magic.

YAGEL'S THEORETICAL and practical writings on medicine proclaim his indebtedness to the Galenic system. In treating both physical ailments and mental disorder he refers constantly to humoral
imbalance, especially that of melancholy, and prescribes remedies
in accordance with the conventional Galenic therapy. However, his
experience persuaded him that Galenic medicine was insufficient
for treating many serious illnesses: "For experience will prove and
confirm what our eyes see daily, that difficult, harmful, and formidable illnesses afflict the human body, and the more the doctors increase their cures and purgations, the more things get worse and the
natural forces are weakened."[16]

Yagel even points out that Galen himself, despite the fact that "he
was a distinguished physician, a wise man in all the secrets of medicine and the father of physicians," was incapable of curing one
young patient.[17] Thus Yagel is not reluctant to utilize and to recommend other cures deemed more efficacious by him: "One should
not be surprised if well-known men possess wonderful amulets . . .
to cure sick patients and to perform wonders in the heaven and on
earth."[18] Proclaiming the wonders of healing through the power of
the stars, he enlists a formidable group of Christian authorities
to support his position—Peter Abano, Francesco Giuntini, and
(Pseudo-) Albertus Magnus—as well as Jewish experts ranging from
talmudic and kabbalist authorities to contemporary medical practitioners—Ishmael Ḥazak and Judah da Revere.[19] But the most significant hidden cause of illness, declares Yagel, is "transgression and
sin before God, for which he [the patient] must pay his debts and
defray his credit." In this case the physician need not prescribe medical treatment but rather should teach the patient "words of repen-
tance and tears," for which this healer appropriately assumes the
title of "a doctor of souls."[20]

Since Yagel regards pathology as the study of divine, astral, and
natural causes of illness, some revealed and some hidden, the physician must function with all three kinds of causes in mind. In a
chapter of *Beit Ya'ar ha-Levanon* devoted to general remedies for
illness, he offers specific guidelines for the patient and the physician, based mainly on a Zoharic text.[21] When one becomes ill, he
should first ask God's forgiveness, but then seek out a physician to

effectuate a cure. The physician, in turn, should offer prayers to God, by whose agency the doctor is able to heal. Then the physician should examine his patient and offer his diagnosis. After determining what ails his patient, he should take blood from him, "since the majority of human illnesses arise from the increase of the blood when bloodletting is not performed at the appropriate time," attempt "to weaken the power of the illness through liquids and other [purgative] drugs," and "protect him [the patient] by a good regimen of eating and drinking" in order to diminish the patient's pain. The physician must also "marshal his words prudently according to the conventions of medicine" in order to put his patient at ease, taking into account the quality of the patient's natural composition, his disease, and the specific conditions that led to the illness.[22] Yagel also cautions against excessive bloodletting. If the patient becomes weak, he must be nourished immediately to restore his strength. Thus far, Yagel's interpretation of the *Zohar* text accords with the conventions of Galenic medicine.

What follows, however, surpasses the parameters of conventional Galenic treatment. The physician must record the details of the patient's horoscope, noting especially the precise time and circumstances of the beginning of the illness. He should also place around his bed substances that emit smoke; herbs and fragrances "will oppose the nature of the patient's constellation, since it is explained to masters of occult knowledge that smoke emissions engender miracles by bringing down the effluvia of the stars, influencing the higher forces, and changing the nature of the stars and conjunctions from evil to good."[23] If the strategy is of no avail, the physician must then prepare his patient to accept death.

Yagel also points out three cardinal errors of physicians recorded in rabbinic literature. A physician might not suspect that the illness is attributable to sin and might consider "that everything evolves only from nature and the increase of the elements." Or he might jeopardize his patient's life "in his wish to do experiments on the bodies of human beings with his wisdom," or he simply will make mistakes in failing to be conscientious in his treatment.[24] Finally, he might show favoritism in treating the wealthy and ignoring the poor.

Yagel's ultimate cure of illness lies in the realm of divine healing. He emphasizes that patients are sometimes cured by various charms, and for this opinion he enlists the authority of the author of the *Sefer ha-Zohar* regarding a mysterious Jewish medical book that contains, in Yagel's phrase, "words of medicine supported by the secrets of the Torah": "For some holy names emerge from verses written in the prophetic books that are employed by masters of amulets to heal known illnesses. Moreover, it [the book] contains medical advice that should be performed only by a sin-fearing person."[25]

These procedures, Yagel explains on the basis of the *Zohar*, are similar to those employed by Balaam the magician, "whose entire strength was in his mouth and in the spirit of his lips" in curing the ill through miracles.[26] He is careful to warn, however, that many such charms are diabolical and can be performed only by "a person fearful of sin and clinging to God."[27] All other charms, performed by less worthy practitioners through black magic, are prohibited. Yet the distinction between acceptable and forbidden charms is not clearly elucidated. The leap in Yagel's instructions from purgation and good diet to reciting holy names in the manner of Balaam from a mysterious Jewish source is both sudden and surprising.

THE MOST COMMON and consistent thread through Yagel's medical and scientific writings is the theme of the triadic universe, the interconnectedness of the divine, astral, and natural worlds. As we shall see later, the theme is also central to Yagel's understanding of magic, which he ultimately derived from his close reading of Henry Cornelius Agrippa's *De Occulta Philosophia*.[28] No doubt Agrippa's three categories of magic—natural, celestial, and ceremonial—were indebted to earlier Neoplatonic sources of antiquity as well as to more recent writings such as Giovanni Pico della Mirandola's *Heptaplus*. For a physician, the infinite possibilities this unified structure offered for correlations between apparently disparate entities and events were especially appealing; for he could impute significance to a particular symptom of a patient by claiming that it reflected a condition visible in both the celestial and divine worlds and by offering a cure related to both these elevated planes of existence.

Yagel devoted most of the first section of his *Beit Ya'ar ha-Levanon* to the subject of sleep and dreams.[29] The work survives in two separate and incomplete drafts and apparently was never finished.[30] However, the conceptual order Yagel constructed in his presentation of the subject is clear. He elucidates six causes of dreams, three known and three hidden, one of each category pertaining to one of the three worlds.[31] Relying heavily on humoral physiology, he analyzes the natural cause of dreams, next considers astrological causation, and concludes with divinely induced dreams. On this last variety, he declares: "Regarding those dreams deriving from the last cause, it is impossible for a philosopher to evaluate them unless he is a divine kabbalist or a sorcerer or a magician who knows how to distinguish the impure from the pure."[32] As in his theoretical remarks on the practice of medicine, Yagel seems to imply that the most exalted physician is one who is also a divine kabbalist or at least one who practices a morally licit form of magic.

Yagel adopts a similar approach in analyzing the birth of Siamese twins to a Jewish family in Venice in 1575.[33] Several other observers considered this monstrous birth a portent signaling the beginning of a plague that swept the entire Veneto region in the same year. In Yagel's dialogue among these children, Yagel, and his father in *Gei Ḥizzayon*, the twins explain their origin in terms of the same three-pronged causation: natural (the mistakes of creation and procreation), astral (unfavorable conjunctions in the skies), and divine (the moral depravities of the citizenry of Venice).[34] Yagel relies on the same conceptual structure in explaining the cases of a young woman and the son of Daniel Modena (discussed later in this chapter).

In his first published work, *Moshi'ah Ḥosim* (Savior of those who take refuge), a plague tract printed in Venice in 1587, Yagel developed his threefold analysis in a comprehensive manner. At the outset he anchors his general approach in rabbinic wisdom: "Every wise-hearted person knows that reality is generally divided into three parts: elementary, heavenly, and intellectual. Every lower part is moved by and receives force and influence from the higher, as the rabbis hint in *Bereshit Rabbah:* 'There exists no blade of grass from below without a constellation in the sky that beats it and tells it to grow.'"[35]

When the ancient philosophers noticed this concatenation of the three worlds, they devised, according to Yagel, various methods of lowering the divine effluvia by natural and talismanic magic, including some sinful practices. Nevertheless, it is incumbent on a "wise-hearted person" to investigate the source of everything, "its principle and cause and the cause of its cause until the investigation culminates in the root principle of the matter," for by knowing "roots" one can grasp more easily the cure of the "branches" and can "strengthen the pillars." "The root of everything" undoubtedly rests on "the manner and rotation of the three worlds we have mentioned."[36]

On the basis of this universal construction, Yagel examines the causes of the plague. He begins with the earthly cause, the emanation of poisonous vapor from the ground, which infects all living beings. People with humoral imbalance are particularly susceptible to this venomous air.[37] The celestial cause is related to the air's condition, which is produced by changes in the stars and their conjunctions, especially that of Saturn and Mars.[38] Yagel explains the divine cause as revenge against the enemies of the Lord "who disturb the law and break the covenant and commit transgressions that are liable to the death penalties of the rabbinic court."[39] Only the righteous still possess the power to reverse the evil decree from bad to good.

After elaborating on the causes of the plague according to each world, Yagel provides a detailed prescription for resisting the disease on each respective level. On the material plane, he offers a long inventory of practical advice, ranging from proper diet, to purification of water and air, to avoidance of "overheating" through excessive sexual activity and rich foods.[40] On the celestial level, he provides a detailed procedure for burning incense in order to bring down astral power, whereby "the higher clings to the lower and allows its spirituality to appear."[41] Yagel's ambivalence in elucidating this pagan procedure is especially transparent. On the one hand, he readily admits that it was practiced by ancient idolators and is forbidden to Jews. On the other hand, this procedure "constituted the wisdom of Abraham, our father, by which he proved [the truth] and emerged victorious over the ancient wise men," informing humanity that these practices were vain deceptions and ultimately would lead to its destruction.[42] Presumably, the method of catching the heavenly effluvia by burning incense is appropriate when the person does not practice idolatry.

On the divine level, the victim is required to ask God's forgiveness through prayer and fasting. The Thirty-sixth Psalm is deemed especially appropriate in the time of plague, and Yagel presents a line-by-line interpretation.[43] Yet the focus of the plague tract remains the extraordinarily detailed instructions for the incense ceremony, the use of talismanic stones and metals, and the prayers and incantations accompanying the procedure. We are left again with the distinct impression that the physician armed with only Galenic medical prescriptions is no match for the virulent plague. For Yagel, the only solution is to employ methods of astral sympathetic magic once practiced by pagan idolators, though now purified and perfected by Jewish practitioners, especially the author of the *Sefer ha-Zohar*.[44] As if to highlight the pragmatic value of his handbook, Yagel appends an "order of incense" composed by the kabbalist Joseph ibn Shraga.[45]

Yagel's published text accords with its contemporary intellectual and scientific context, especially his tripartite explanation of the plague. Paolo Preto's exhaustive study of the plague of Venice in 1575–1577, which contains a detailed summary with large selections from numerous plague tracts written in Italian and Latin at about the same time and in the same locale as Yagel's, provides a ready comparison with Yagel's Hebrew composition.[46] Like Yagel, none of the authors examined by Preto has any real understanding of the plague's causes. Their medical knowledge is eclectic and imprecise. They speak ambiguously about "the corruption of the air and the water," about humoral imbalance, and about the location of the heavenly bodies. They shuttle back and forth between natural, astral, and divine causes.[47] Gerolomo Donzellini, for example, devotes most of his treatise to celestial and natural factors but concludes succinctly: "The cause of all the plagues is the will of God"; thus the helpless plague victim's only recourse is "prayer to the highest and greatest God."[48] Similarly, Leonardo Fioravanti catalogues the causes as corruption of the elements, the putrefaction of the air, the decomposition of human bodies, and divine wrath.[49] In contrast, Giambattisti Cavagnino emphasizes the importance of astral intervention.[50] Yagel's medical recipes are readily found in the treatises of the other writers. His attempt to explain the genesis of the plague from multiple perspectives is also reminiscent of most of the others. He differs strikingly from them, however, in his conscious accentuation of the structure of the three worlds and in his ultimate appeal to incense potions and incantations located primarily in the kabbalistic and folk traditions of Judaism.

THE MOST EXTENSIVE and most revealing information about Yagel's medical practice is found in passing comments of medical interest interspersed throughout his encyclopedic *Beit Ya'ar ha-Levanon* and, more prominently and directly, in his rich collection of short essays and letters, *Bat Rabim*. The latter is particularly valuable because it contains a number of Yagel's *consilia*, letters of professional advice written in response to individual requests for medical counsel. Like Christian doctors, Yagel did not necessarily examine his patients physically before recommending treatment;

nor was his primary purpose to record his observations, but only to prescribe.[51] Yet in a number of cases Yagel did record more detailed observations of the patient's condition by a relative or friend who had petitioned Yagel for advice. This correspondence is particularly useful in exploring the social context of Yagel's practice, in evaluating the specific treatments available, and in assessing the personal relationships between physician and patient. Yagel's special fascination with mental and psychological disorder is apparent from the cases he chose to copy. Reminiscent of the large casebooks of contemporaries such as Napier, Lilly, and Forman,[52] Yagel's medical notes and correspondence present an aspect of Jewish cultural life revealed in Hebrew manuscript sources still largely untapped by modern historical research.[53]

The passages of medical interest in *Beit Ya'ar ha-Levanon* deal primarily with the unusual and the bizarre. Like other doctors and naturalists of his day, Yagel was fascinated with such issues as the restoration of youthful vitality to the old immediately before their death,[54] the danger of drinking water during the equinox,[55] and the willingness of some individuals to starve themselves to death. Thus Yagel describes a man who believed he was dead and subsequently refused to eat. He eventually was cured by a doctor who threatened to bury him.[56] Levinus Lemnius reported a similar case.[57] Yagel also offers testimony about his own experience in Luzzara in 1581 with an apparently anorectic girl who expired after starving herself for twenty-one days.[58]

Yagel devotes an entire chapter to the subject of human will and imagination, one reminiscent of similar discussions in the writings of Cornelius Agrippa and Robert Burton.[59] His insight into the force of suggestion and imagination in healing helps to explain his reliance on the use of amulets and charms: "For our eyes see that sometimes a jester in the eyes of the faithful will tell them negligible things that have no credibility whatsoever. Yet the fools will write and sign and place them in their hands and believe in them. For according to the power of belief and the strength of the desire, they will gain great benefits from the medical recipes and other things."[60]

Another personal experience related by Yagel substantiates the formidable influence of medical charlatans over the masses. He describes the sale of an amulet to a prostitute by a peddler "who did not know the difference between his right and left hand." The peddler wrote a magical formula on a piece of paper and inserted it in the amulet, offering it to her to wear as protection against injury.

The woman, who had been suffering from high fever, was instantaneously cured. When the account of the incident reached the authorities, they interrogated the woman, inspected her amulet, and located the peddler, who readily admitted his deception. Yet when the amulet was destroyed, the woman again became sick. Thus Yagel could not take lightly the psychological efficacy of such seemingly useless remedies when treating his own patients.[61]

Also of interest to Yagel was the explosion of information regarding newly available natural and artificial drugs.[62] The attempts of Yagel and other naturalists of his time to relate the classical zoological and botanical descriptions of Pliny, Dioscordes, and others to the new and often contradictory data now available generated considerable confusion, as we shall see in chapter 4. Yagel devotes considerable space and energy to describing new plants, especially their medicinal use. In one instance, upon curing a patient from a salamander bite, he ponders whether this small creature is identical with the miraculous creature that withstood fire, described by both the ancient philosophers and the rabbis. He concludes that there are two distinct creatures, although he remains skeptical about the wonderful qualities attributed to the legendary reptile. He adds only "that the truth will follow its own course."[63]

Yagel is neither confused nor agitated by the revolutionary pace of the new pharmaceutical discoveries, for it is the divine prerogative, he concludes, to determine when and how new dimensions of the natural world are revealed: "He [God] watches well over all the great things He created in revealing to us in our days things that nature covered from them [earlier generations] for thousands of years, even when He had disclosed them in other lands. For everything God does, He does in his own time, for there is a time for every desire and every act of creation, and according to the need for things and the time, God reveals them."[64] As in the case of Yagel's fascination with other aspects of the natural world, the extraordinary discoveries confirmed and animated his belief in God's omnipotence and omniscience. Thus he proclaims: "For blessed is the wise man of secrets [God], to whom all mysteries are revealed."[65]

Yagel's faith was tested more profoundly, however, by the severity of some of the cases he treated. His correspondence with his patients reveals the existence of a personal bond between physician and patient. The relatively small sampling of *consilia* preserved by Yagel is insufficient to indicate whether the patients and cases they describe were typical of his practice. They provide little sense of the volume of his case load, of the proportion of Jewish or Christian patients he treated, and, like most *consilia* of other physicians, of the outcome of the treatment. The few cases Yagel copied were probably some of the most interesting he had treated, both from his perspective and our own. His patients, in the main, were well-to-do, respected members of the Jewish community. A number were learned in their own right in rabbinic and secular disciplines, such as Menahem Azariah da Fano and Hananiah Finzi. Yagel also treated the wife of Mordecai Dato and once assisted the widow of Judah Moscato.[66] One of his most notable cases was the son of Daniel Modena of Sassuolo, the wealthy banker who apparently offered Yagel employment late in his career. In short, the patients Yagel describes were well connected, forming an interesting cross-section of the Jewish intellectual elite and the affluent from Mantua and Modena.

Almost all of Yagel's recorded cases concern some form of psychological disorder, which he usually subsumes under the general category of melancholia.[67] In a letter to Menahem Azariah da Fano, for example, he describes the illness of Hillel of Viadana as a black, charcoal-like bilious humor affecting the brain and the heart that distorts the imagination and results in the patient's morbid depression. He prescribes soothing liquids and a tranquil atmosphere of prayer and personal support.[68] Yagel also diagnoses the disease of Daniel Modena's son as a form of melancholia. Despite the special pleadings of the father to effectuate a cure, Yagel is soberly realistic about the slim chances for successful treatment. Yagel honestly informs his patron: "A man should know and be prepared for difficult illnesses that are sent [from heaven], which the doctor is not given permission to heal until the time of their order [to heal] arrives."[69]

Nevertheless, Yagel prescribes a full regimen of purgatives and bloodletting. He prepares a chart for his patient listing the recommended order of purgations as well as supplementary astrological data. He orders his patient to hold in his hand a specially crafted copper amulet immediately after the purgation. He also offers an abundance of herbs and drugs as well as "hands outstretched to heaven" in prayer.[70] Yagel's final letter to the father offers consolation on the son's death. In a remarkably compassionate and personal tone, Yagel laments the loss as his own and decries the misery of an old father who is obliged to mourn for his young son's premature death, whereby "the world is overturned and the order of creation is changed." Armed with an unwavering belief in divine justice, he consoles his friend with words of spiritual comfort even after having failed to save the young man's life: "For high upon the high is the righteous judge; with scales and balances of justice, he weighs everything and will act with justice concerning everything that is hidden, for good or bad."[71]

In another case Yagel encourages an unnamed patient to reduce his medication: "I saw your tears regarding your prolonged illness on your sickbed. You doubled and tripled your medication and still [the way] is long." He gently recommends limiting the number of purgations "and letting nature perform its function, since it is a wise worker." He soothes his patient with an entertaining story and encourages him to concentrate on his diet, to seek the support of his wife, and to pray.[72]

YAGEL'S CORRESPONDENCE offers a fuller view of his treatment of psychological disease in two unusual cases. The first involved a young man of Mantua whose symptoms an anonymous observer carefully and clinically described to Yagel:

> Mordecai Ongri . . . of Mantua, twenty-one years old. In the winter, after midnight, when he was alone by the fire looking at a small holy notebook, he claims he heard a sound in the room above as if something had fallen. The young man made a loud and frightening noise. A tremendous fear overcame him and he cried loudly for his father and brothers. When they searched the room above, they saw nothing and told him that it was the sound of cats running from one house to the next and that it was a natural occurrence. Yet from that moment, he remained like a man traumatized and petrified, lying down and incapable of getting up. He continued in this manner until they dressed and washed his face and hands as if he was a small infant . . . The doctor-bloodletter performed purgations and bloodletting on him . . . and this helped him somewhat [in curing] his disease, so that, when threatened, he returned to eating by himself and to taking care of his own bodily needs . . . He also did not trust himself to venture out alone from the house even during the daytime . . . Sometimes he reaches out his hand to take an object but his arm remains extended, for he claims that he is unable [to withdraw it], as if another person's hands restrains him and does not allow him to take the food or clothing. So with great force and threats, he is encouraged to get up, to dress himself . . . to eat and drink. Also, in the beginning of his ill-

ness, he cried a lot. He presently is not alert as he was during the beginning of his illness, when he prolonged his prayer by weeping, made confession, and found satisfaction by standing in the corners [of the room] afraid, alone, like a person who is astonished, surprised, and silent.[73]

Yagel's relatively brief response to this inquiry transparently reveals his inability to offer adequate advice to effectuate a cure. He diagnoses the condition as melancholia. He prescribes sweet foods, chicken soup, and various purgatives. To these he adds Torah, worship, and charitable acts, the ultimate rabbinic prescription. He also suggests an arrangement of prayers with pleasant melodies and songs, all intended to calm the delirious soul. He obviously cannot promise any dramatic remedy for the young man's phobia.[74]

Yagel's best-documented case of psychological illness, recorded in a relatively large number of letters, occurred in 1600. It involved the future wife of the grandson of a most distinguished doctor named Judah (Leone) Portaleone. Both Menahem Azariah da Fano and Solomon Joseph Ḥayyim Forlì initially solicited Yagel's counsel. Months later, Menahem Terracini questioned him on the same matter and Solomon Forlì requested further clarification. Yagel's responses to Fano, Forlì, and Terracini are included with transcriptions of their letters.[75]

The initial letters from Solomon Forlì and Menahem Azariah da Fano describe the young woman's illness. Solomon writes: "May your eyes be attentive to the sound of our supplications . . . regarding the affliction of that daughter, Hannah the daughter of . . . who is married but not permitted to her husband. For her spirit is bitter and she cries and is unable to perform the functions of a wife for her husband in purity, in Torah, and the commandment [of intercourse]."[76] Menahem's letter, as summarized by Yagel, is more specific: "Regarding one woman from a noble family who cannot consummate her marriage because of her impurity, and immerse herself in the waters of the *mikvah* [ritual bath] because of a fear she has of dying. She is stricken with spasms and trembling." Yagel also supplies an astrological observation that he obviously considers significant in diagnosing her condition: "I noticed that in her astrological history, the moon circulates in the constellation of Aquarius."[77]

Yagel's brief response to Fano addresses all three causes of the woman's affliction in accordance with his customary threefold division of the natural, celestial, and divine worlds. He advises that a

liquid potion consisting of a kind of crawfish found in rivers be prepared for her to soothe "the distorted imaginative force" and that
she wear around her neck both a seal in the shape of the moon and
an amulet containing Isaiah 43:2: "When you pass through water, I
will be with you." If these remedies fail, he admits, only God will
have the power to cure her.[78]

In his response to Menahem Terracini Yagel elaborates on his initial letter to Fano. His diagnosis again follows the order of the three
worlds, as he explicitly explains: the natural potion made of crawfish; the astral remedy of a seal representing the moon, "which is
the star that afflicts her and causes her illness"; and a divine cure
based on the combination of the letters from the verse in Isaiah.
Yagel also requests more astrological data regarding the exact time
of the girl's birth, so that "from the stars of her soul I can arrive at
the reason for the illness."[79] He even offers to prepare the amulet
and at the same time encourages the family and friends not to lose
hope. He remains confident that he will ascertain the true cause of
the illness and therefore strongly cautions against seeking the advice of diviners and soothsayers, who are incapable of penetrating
"the mysteries of nature." He implies, no doubt, that his own prescriptions are on a considerably higher plane. Finally, he orders them
to treat the young woman with gentleness and with soft words,
"since her soul is bitter and she deserves compassion."[80]

Some time later, Forlì wrote again to Yagel, indicating that his
advice had been followed and that the young girl's condition was
improving. The family had discovered an "expert" in combining the
letters of the verse Yagel had prescribed. They also had avoided any
consultation with soothsayers. Forlì praised Yagel's formidable abilities and asked him for only one additional clarification: if the astrological history of the girl had previously been stable, why was her
illness first noticed only when she became engaged?[81]

In his answer to Forlì[82] Yagel expresses pleasure at the woman's
progress. He then offers a lesson in astrological prognostication: the
young girl's astrological proclivity was activated only when two
planets within her sign aspected in conjunction, causing her phobia.
However, he emphasizes, such conjunctions are not totally decisive
in determining a person's fate, for human initiative can sometimes
overturn the heavenly decree. The ability "to oppose and to control
the conjunctions" is part of an esoteric tradition conceived originally by Solomon, called "the Wisdom of the Book of Cures."[83] It
was hidden by Hezekiah but never obliterated and was placed in the

trust of the wise men of secrets (kabbalists). Yagel emphasizes that only a select few, chosen by God, retain this power, from whose number he modestly excludes himself.

Then Yagel abruptly breaks off this tantalizing digression and returns to more practical instructions. Yet his passing comment has profound significance. This medical astrologer and natural philosopher had paused to volunteer a most mysterious bit of information regarding the existence of a secret magical tradition still practiced by the esoteric few "whom God calls." Their divine magic is so powerful that it can even overturn the force of an astral conjunction.[84]

Returning to his main purpose, Yagel gives detailed instructions for making the lunar seal, a recipe he had failed to send earlier because the time of the full moon had not yet arrived. He describes the seal's materials as gold inlaid with a variety of precious stones. He mentions the Aramaic letters to be engraved and the exact width of the seal so that water can pass through and not interfere with the ritual ablution. He offers to have the seal made if Forlì is unable to find a Jewish goldsmith, "for in Reggio [where Yagel is living] there is a Jewish man who works with gold and silver."[85]

Yagel's final instructions refer to the influence of the stars on the young woman's humoral imbalance. He returns from Solomon's secret magic to conventional Galenic therapy. Nevertheless, Yagel reiterates the need "to hold a shield and breastplate," which the seal and special preparations he has offered represent, "so that the star will no longer harm her." He concludes: "And a wise man will know that if we follow this path, we will have trodden a path of the steps of nature, for wisdom turns toward the mode of reality. There is no wisdom and no true intelligence that can turn in another manner."[86]

This epistemological statement explains both Yagel's scientific methodology and his elevated status as a Jewish doctor. For Yagel, knowledge is synonymous with following the steps, the signs or markings of natural reality (see Chapter 4). The person most suitably trained to decipher those markings through his broad education as a naturalist, astrologer, and divine occultist is someone like Yagel. The case of the young woman and the ritual bath illustrates the multiple approaches Yagel had at his disposal for treating mental illness. It also indicates quite dramatically his intellectual status in the Jewish community. He was consulted by wealthy Jewish bankers, rabbis, and the most prominent kabbalist of his generation because he was better trained than they to fathom the signs of nature both on earth and in the sky. He regarded common soothsayers with disapproval but was not averse to using his own amulets, seals, and incenses. He further titillated a client's interest by cryptically divulging the secrets of a higher magical tradition, originating with Solomon. Although he disclaimed any knowledge of the latter, he allowed himself the privilege of disclosing its existence, thereby enhancing his own intellectual stature. He gained the trust and confidence of his patients by speaking to them not only as a naturalist and astrologer but also as a Jewish scholar. His charms and prognostications were cast in the traditions of the rabbis. He made expertise as a medical astrologer credible by integrating it with Judaic learning, especially that based on esoteric sources. This creative blending of medicine, astrology, and Judaism marks Yagel's special attraction. He was more than a mere physician and *magus;* he was a thoroughly Jewish one, a sixteenth-century Solomon who demonstrated to his patients that his exploration and penetration of the secrets of nature were wedded to the sources of their own revelatory tradition.

3. Demonology and Disease

Nevertheless, they are emissaries of God, for through everything the Holy One, blessed be HE, sends his emissary, even
through a snake, a spider, or a frog.
　　　　　—*Beit Ya'ar ha-Levanon*, pt. 4, chap. 99, fol. 228b

I noticed the words of one wise doctor . . . who wrote that as
long as the aforementioned humor increases in a human
body . . . and no one hastens to cure it, then . . . a spirit will
attach itself to it that matches it, for one type finds its same
type.
　　　　　—Bodleian Ms. Reggio 8, fol. 42a

SOMETIME AFTER 1613 a messenger reached Abraham Yagel's
home with a bizarre story, one sure to test his skills as a physician
and natural philosopher. It concerned the widow of Mordecai Dato,
who was now living in Rubiera, near Modena, where Yagel had once
lived. She complained of having heard strange noises in her house,
especially the clatter of dishes, while sleeping in her bedroom. Upon
awakening she discovered that dishes, kitchen utensils, and articles
of clothing were missing. After several days she discovered them
outside her house or in the trash heap. Her house keys also seemed
to have disappeared. The members of her household were so frightened by these incidents that they went to sleep in a neighbor's
house. Upon their return, however, they noticed that their beds were
unmade as if someone had slept in them.[1]

Yagel's response to these strange occurrences was immediate and
resolute: "There is no doubt that these are evil spirits living in the
house. If they had been invisible to the people who originally had
lived there . . . for whatever reason, they now revealed themselves to
us, since they came to wander from one place and changed their
location; and the reason for this incident is unknown." Yagel classified these creatures as *mazzamaurielli*, a kind of field demon or

poltergeist that inhabited the earth.[2] They were composed of one or more elements but shaped from fine material that made them invisible. Although they caused harm to human beings, "nevertheless, they are emissaries of God, for through everything, the Holy One, blessed be He, sends his emissary, even through a snake, a spider, or a frog."[3]

The case of Dato's widow reminded Yagel of a similar occurrence several years earlier that had been related to him in detail by an eyewitness. This incident took place in the home of a wealthy Jewish banker, Solomon ben Vita Segal Ostiglia, in Mantua.[4] The reporter was the children's tutor of religious studies, Reuben Jare, who was living in the house at the time.[5] Yagel emphasizes that he has faithfully copied Jare's words so that "important people" might evaluate them and attempt to fathom the wonders of creation:

On a Sabbath day, in the month of Ḥeshvan, 5342 [1582], I was in the house of the noble Solomon Segal Ostiglia, teaching his sons, standing in my usual place while supervising my students. Suddenly, on Saturday evening, a sandal from the foot of the older son fell off. I searched for it throughout the room as best I could, but I could not find it. I then announced that if the demon called a *mazzamauriello* had taken it, I would warn him and declare publicly that his disturbances [should cease] and he should no longer harm, as one says to a hornet.[6] The next day a hat was taken from the oldest son's room while he slept, and the day after that a sandal disappeared. I stood shaking until I spoke to a certain sage, may God preserve him! He made me an amulet for the oldest son. Because of God's compassion, may His name be blessed, no more damage was done.

After fifteen days had passed, however, when I was with my blessed student named Ḥayyim, a lad twelve years old and the oldest son of Solomon Segal, the boy stood near the fire, and suddenly a sandal was snatched from him. And from that day on, the demon would take his clothes and utensils and would do horrible things to him that are too lengthy to tell . . . Once, while the boy was eating roasted meat, it was taken from his hand. On numerous other occasions, as I sat around the table with the members of the household, similar incidents would transpire unseen and unknown to anyone. For miraculously, the boy [once] was missing his underclothing while his upper clothing was still on. And thus he [the demon] would take his stockings and shoes from him, truly more than a hundred times . . .

One morning the boy arose from his bed. He dressed himself only in a patched robe during the winter days in order to distribute charity to the poor. When he finished his work, he announced that he was going back to bed to warm up. But behold, suddenly he arose from his bed dressed from head to foot as a groom leaving his bridal canopy. Yet he did not feel any of this but only [afterward] discovered himself dressed between the sheets. All of this was done while his mother and his brothers were with the boy in the same room. Moreover, many times he would stand on a box or chair in a playful manner as young boys do, while he was fully dressed with all his clothes, and then he would fall to the ground. When he arose, he was naked except for the lower garmet on him . . . The boy also would find sweet candies and fruits in his pockets . . . and once, as he was sitting around the table with his father and the members of the household, he found pieces of cheese and sweet candies under his hat upon his head . . .

The boy's father sent the lad out of the house and out of the city to Viadana to the house of Hillel,[7] may God preserve him! But it did not help at all, for the tormenting spirit pursued him everyplace he went . . . And when I yelled at the boy, the evil spirit would do me harm by sometimes taking my hat, sometimes my shoes, or my rare books. Once when I screamed at the boy and went to sleep, I later discovered scrambled eggs between the sheets and was unable to sleep in the bed . . . These incidents continued for seven months, and after that period the spirit disappeared, thank God, and his location is unknown . . . Blessed [be He] who gave us life and allowed us to reach this time. Blessed [is the One] who makes miracles.[8]

This long, delightfully entertaining, and occasionally hilarious report provided Yagel with an incentive to investigate thoroughly the issue of demonology and its relation to pathology. The problem for a practicing doctor and natural philosopher was a fundamental one. Were the demon stories of credible witnesses such as Dato's widow and the tutor of Solomon Segal's children to be taken as reliable perceptions of reality or to be dismissed out of hand? How was one to understand such mysterious unknown forces apparently seen and experienced by these people? Were they hallucinating, suffering from humoral imbalance like the young woman afraid of the ritual bath? Or could such experiences of Yagel's associates and countless people of earlier generations constitute a significant body of evidence substantiating the reality of these mysterious creatures? And if these spirits did exist, how and where were they to be placed in the divine order of creation? Were they natural or supernatural? Were they genuinely harmful or merely an irritating nuisance to be tolerated but, at least, to be demystified? Finally, did demons enter the bodies of human beings and actually require exorcism? Thus the creature who supposedly pilfered underwear and placed scrambled eggs in teachers' beds was hardly a lighthearted subject. The question of its existence directly challenged Yagel to understand what was rational and what was not, what was real and what was fantasy in the universe in which he lived.

YAGEL OPENS HIS DISCUSSION by quoting Gersonides (Rabbi Levi ben Gershom), the thirteenth-century Jewish Aristotelian philosopher, on the subject of demons. Yagel remarks parenthetically that the text he is using has never been printed but is contained in a rare manuscript belonging to his friend of long standing, Hananiah Finzi, who had made it available to him at the time of the incident in Mantua.[9] Gersonides emphatically denied the existence of demons despite their mention in rabbinic writing and concluded: "If there had been truth to these things, they would not have been hidden forever to the wise men of scholarship."[10] The question hinged, of course, on what constituted a wise man of scholarship and on what criteria such a person was to use to distinguish truth from untruth. Thus Yagel argues:

> Therefore, you see that the intention of this philosopher is to deny that demons have any reality or that spiritual power can be diffused into the heavens and like phenomena, to all of which the senses testify that the opposite [is the case], given the reality of such occurrences that happen to us in every generation . . . For the conclusions of Gersonides are philosophical; however, the senses testify to the contrary of his words. If he actually had seen with his own eyes the incident we described that happened in Mantua, how could he falsify [the impressions based on] his senses and upon his imagination?[11]

Here already is the kernel of Yagel's epistemological argument. Can one uphold a seemingly rational position even when it contradicts the impressions of the senses and empirical evidence? To dem-

onstrate just how subjective Gersonides' rationality was, Yagel jux-
taposes his weighty testimony with that of Abraham ibn Ezra,
another Jewish philosopher and naturalist of equal stature. According to ibn Ezra, demons did exist. They were formed from collisions
of sparks of starlight under the region of the Milky Way while vapor
and smoke ascended from the earth; they clung to human bodies
with matching compositions and entered those bodies. Melancholic
and fearful persons were particularly susceptible to these spirits.[12]

If ibn Ezra could see the problem differently from Gersonides,
then how did Gersonides and "the rest of the sages who follow
Greek philosophy" reach their conclusion? Yagel understands the
essence of their position to be that nothing can be created without
a reason. Since creation must be purposeful, the reality of demons is
logically impossible. Yagel hastens to add that these same philosophers, who denied the existence of such spiritual beings, also had
difficulty in logically maintaining the immortality of individual
souls after the demise of the body.[13] Such "logic," however, failed to
impress Yagel. Here was an obvious instance in which the sheer
weight of human testimony, both Jewish and non-Jewish, tipped the
balance in favor of those who affirmed the existence of demons.

As Sidney Anglo has argued, "the towering edifice of authority"
supporting the existence of demons made it intellectually respectable in the sixteenth century to accept their reality and to acknowledge their magical powers.[14] Such authority began with the Bible
itself, with accounts such as those of Pharaoh's magicians, the
witch of En-dor, and Balaam;[15] through classical writers such as
Homer, Ovid, and Virgil; to the authors of the Neoplatonic-
Hermetic corpus revived by Marsilio Ficino and the Florentine Neoplatonists in the second half of the fifteenth century. Several church
fathers, including Augustine, also believed in demons. Medieval
writers on science such as Roger Bacon and Albertus Magnus readily
accepted their reality, along with the notions of magical correspondences, astral influences, and the existence of other astral spirits.
Then there remained the overwhelming force of popular and folk
beliefs, which clearly took their existence for granted.[16] Added to all
these were two sources—the rabbinic and kabbalist traditions of demonology—that left Yagel no alternative but to assume that demons
were as real as any other part of the universe.[17]

To establish beyond a shadow of a doubt that "the whole world"
believes in demons, Yagel presents a dazzling array of "testimonia"
regarding their existence. He first mentions Socrates and Plato, who

viewed demons as intermediaries between God and man, composed of the elements fire and air. He quotes Apuleius' assertion in *De Deo Socratis* that demons are invisible and made of air.[18] In each case, he characteristically compares the views of his non-Jewish sources with Jewish ones—the Talmud (B.T. Ḥagigah 16b), Nahmanides, and the mystical *Midrash Rut ha-Ne'elam*—pointing out similarities and differences.[19] From this discussion it becomes clear that Yagel's purpose is to outweigh Aristotle's negative view with the positive opinions of Neoplatonic and Jewish scholars.

Although the ancient philosophers had called all good or bad spirits demons,[20] Yagel maintains that a distinction between good and bad ones is necessary. Since these scholars lacked a full understanding of the secret of the harmony of the four planes of existence, available only to the kabbalists, they also could not perceive the hierarchy of the ten levels of angels corresponding to the ten *sefirot*. Lacking this knowledge, they could not have fathomed the existence of an equivalent hierarchy of evil in the ten levels of demons.[21] Some Christian scholars, he points out, were aware of nine groups of demons corresponding to nine groups of heavenly angels.[22] However, they missed the tenth division, "since in those days the tenth sphere was still unknown in the world, whose veracity and vitality is [now] apparent to the latest astronomers."[23] No doubt the discovery only confirmed for Yagel the kabbalists' superior conception of the entire cosmos, one unavailable to either pagan or Christian scholars.

Yagel also refers to other divisions of the legions of demons. Once he speaks of six groups and elsewhere of three levels of demons—spiritual, celestial, and earthly.[24] He subdivides the last into categories corresponding to each of the four elements. He is particularly fascinated by the terrestrial demons that correspond most apparently to the mischievous variety found in Yagel's own neighborhood. Yagel quotes extensively from a Christian author's "history" of the Gothic regions near the North Pole, describing the demons who inhabit that place:

There are so many spirits and demons that the local inhabitants hire them for wages for menial labor in the house and in the field as we use people in this land. For example, if a person comes to his field and notices that it requires planting, reaping, plowing, or some other work, he inquires about their wage for doing his work. Spirits in the form of human beings then approach him. Alternatively, when he hears voices that announce: "I will come for a *selah* or for two, etc., and will do the required work," then he says to that voice: "No, I will give you only a half a *selah* or a quarter, etc." And when the spirit accepts an agreed price, the employer places the money on the ground and leaves. On the morrow, he finds his work completed.[25]

A traveler to those lands to whom Yagel has spoken has confirmed this report. Yagel attributes this phenomenon to the special climate of the place "according to the nature of the climatic zone and its proximity or distance to the Holy Land."[26] Besides this northern variety, he asserts that there are also demons who inhabit toilets and bathhouses, bridges, high walls, other dangerous areas, and generally filthy places. Others have intercourse with humans, are afraid of smoke, and generally evoke fear and panic among people who are suddenly confronted with them.[27]

Finally, to clinch his argument regarding the absolute certainty of the existence of demons, Yagel offers the four Aristotelian causes of demons. The sufficient cause he divides into two: the proximate sufficient cause is the sparks of the stars and the remote sufficient cause is higher angels above the stars; the material cause is the "spirituality" emanating from the elements, particularly from fire and air; the formal cause is their special form distinguishing them from human beings; and their final cause is to be "a rod . . . to judge nations and to bring to them the appropriate retribution according to the divine justice for a [particular] land, a state, or an individual."[28] One wonders whether Yagel was aware of the irony of enlisting the support of Aristotelian causes to disprove an Aristotelian position.

HAVING CONCLUDED that demons do exist and have a rightful place in the hierarchy of created beings, Yagel is ready to take up the more formidable problem of their actual relationship to human illness. To assume credulously that demons are agents of disease, one would have to ignore an entire body of medical literature: "For the sages among the doctors declared that there is no truth [to the assumption] that any evil spirit attacks them or enters their body. Rather the cause is attributable to the activities of the black bile [melancholia] and its accidents."[29]

Yagel knew only too well the alleged self-sufficiency of Galenic medicine in the diagnosis of mental illness. He also realized the obvious limitations of a system that, more often than not, proved inadequate in the treatment of a variety of diseases. As we have seen, it was totally ineffectual in coping with plague. Nevertheless, in his own cases he had often explained disease as a product of humoral imbalance. When linked especially with astrological causation, the theory of the four humors was still the best "science" available. To introduce demonic possession as a cause of illness was to violate the internal consistency of the Galenic system. As a physician, Yagel fully appreciated the power of the imagination, especially of patients in the grips of painful illness; "for then people might think that evil spirits enter their body, but this is not so, for overpowering alien humors are the cause of every ailment."[30] The reconciliation of two obviously contradictory assumptions—that of Galenic therapy and that of the reality of malevolent spirits—thus constituted a real intellectual challenge for him.

His solution was typically eclectic and reflects his characteristic approach of harmonizing conflicting evidence and competing epistemological assumptions: "Afterward I noticed the words of one wise doctor among recent ones who wrote that as long as the aforementioned humor increases in a human body and is left to magnify its strength, and no one hastens to cure it, then, according to its nature and constitution, a spirit will attach itself to it that matches it, for one type finds its same type."[31]

Here, then, was an appropriate strategy for integrating the humoral system with demonology. Yagel illustrates the principle that "one type finds its same type" by the analogy of fire seeking out dry and thin trees. The fire "will desire them [the trees] because they are of the same kind; thus it is immediately energized by them because of its discovery of a matching type." Similarly, Yagel hypothesizes that ash on an unlit candle attracts fire and causes the candle to light, "for one type finds its same type."[32]

Regardless of the fact that Yagel understood the origin of fire as little as he did the origin of disease, he displayed admirably the internal consistency of the scientific theory he was espousing. Like so many other rational thinkers of the sixteenth century, an epistemology of resemblance allowed him to make the kinds of connections his integrative system required.[33] For him, demons plainly revealed the same characteristics as every other part of creation. They sought out and were attracted to creatures with similar characteristics. It was the function of the naturalist-diagnostician to decipher the signs of similitude that revealed the internal consistency and transcendent harmony of the divine creation.

Although Yagel does not identify the literary source of his solution, the general context of this position is not difficult to establish. In the second half of the sixteenth century Johan Wier, Jean Bodin, and Reginald Scot engaged in a well-publicized debate about the existence of demons and witchcraft and their relation to mental disease. Wier took a position similar to Yagel's. In his *De Praestigiis Daemonum*, published in Basel in 1563, this Lutheran physician to Duke William III of Berg publicly criticized the witchcraft trials of his day but asserted that demons were agents of mental disease. Like Yagel, Wier offered a variety of clinical observations of mental cases and a medical explanation for the plausibility of demonic possession. He maintained that mental illness did cause delusions, which in turn rendered their victims more susceptible to demonic interference.[34] Though denying the extreme position of Jean Bodin that witches and demons worked their transitive effects in concert with each other, neither could Wier adopt the totally naturalistic explanation of Reginald Scot, who rejected demonic interference altogether.[35] Wier's middle-of-the-road position lacked the consistency of either of his radical opponents', yet it reflected most clearly the genuine pressures confronting a physician and experimental psychologist who sought to understand mental illness in a culture thoroughly saturated with demonology.

Wier's position also was analogous to that of the Dutch physician Levinus Lemnius, whom Yagel quotes on several occasions (see Chapter 4). Lemnius likewise wrestled with the issue of natural versus demonic causation of disease. Initially he argued that "it is frivolous to refer the causes of these things to ill spirits. For all these things consist in the corruption or inflammation, the quality or quantity of the humours." But elsewhere he was obliged to admit that ill spirits "do not only mix themselves with the humours, but also they entice and urge the minds of men to all wickedness." He eventually concluded "that humours and not bad angels cause diseases, yet the aereal spirits do mix themselves therewith, and increase the disease, by adding fire unto them."[36] Yagel had read the Italian edition of Lemnius' book, so Lemnius may have been the Christian doctor to whom he refers; or he may have been familiar with Wier's equally famous work.[37]

Having adopted the Wier-Lemnius compromise between naturalistic medicine and demonology, Yagel illustrates its applicability with the celebrated case of the biblical Saul's mental illness: "Let us learn from King Saul. An evil spirit did not attack until God turned away from him and directed his heart toward being jealous of David . . . He thus conceived iniquitous thoughts on his bed, saying, 'David will rule.' His jealousy burned in him until he was surrounded by scorched blood and melancholia rose. Then a spirit entered him to beat him, for it found the matter ready with a matching composition. But the individual providence of God [allows] God's eye [to watch over] those who fear him to save [them] from death."[38]

Using the illustrious case of Saul, Yagel cleverly traces the conditions under which demonic possession is possible. First, "God turned from Saul," creating a condition of religious deprivation. Second, Saul, in viewing David's ascendancy, became consumed with jealousy and was psychologically deprived. Third, his jealousy created a condition of overheated blood and humoral imbalance. Then, and only then, was a demon with a compatible nature able to enter his body and disturb him even more. The only cure for his illness, as Yagel comes full circle, was to restore God's beneficent providence and thus alleviate the king's mental anguish.

THE DEBATE over the link between mental illness and demonic possession was not the only instance in Yagel's excursus in demonology that required harmonization between naturalistic explanation and popular cultural attitudes. Two other discussions illustrate Yagel's attempt to accommodate seemingly irreconcilable approaches.

One of the major problems for naturalists such as Yagel was the slippery character of demons. How should they be defined and classified? Were they part of the natural or supernatural world, or might they perhaps claim an intermediate position? In searching for an appropriate scientific heading under which to place these anomolous creatures, Yagel discovered a comparable category, which naturalists called androgyny. The features common to both demons and androgynous creatures, he argued, were their state of imperfection and their intermediate status between God and human beings.[39] Without claiming that androgynous creatures and demons were identical, Yagel elected to treat them analogously in order to establish a precise category for demons.

Quoting Galen's *Ars parva*, Yagel begins by summarizing the classical threefold division of medicine.[40] According to Galen, medicine treats human beings who are either healthy, sick, or in an intermediate, androgynous state. He further distinguishes among three types of androgynous creatures. The first is "devoid of the two extremes" of either health or sickness. The second can be found in a median condition between the two extremes of absolute health or absolute illness. The third is identifiable by a condition that fluctuates between health and illness.[41] So far the analogy to demons is hidden in the cryptic language used to describe the three categories, but Yagel soon clarifies his purpose in citing Galen's analysis.

What Galen meant by the first category, claims Yagel, is a condition of total spirituality. This is the highest status of androgynous creatures and equivalent to that of demons from the uppermost levels of the supernal world and comparable to the category of angels.[42] The second level constitutes an intermediate status sharing qualities of both spirituality and materiality. This kind of androgynous creature is analogous to certain types of air or water demons, which, "because of their closeness to the land, are more inundated with matter and are thus similar in some respects to human beings. But in other respects they possess spirituality as angels, even though different from the first category that we described above."[43] The third type of androgynous creatures is completely corporeal. This status is equivalent to that of "demons of the earth who live in the extreme regions of the north and Gothia." They are creatures with material needs who look like dwarfs, sleep with women, and do menial labor. Yagel has already described them in his account of their activities in the land of Goths.[44] By appropriating Galen's categories of androgynous creatures in his analysis of demons, Yagel hopes to confer a "scientific" status on them and thus validate their existence.

Yagel is less successful, however, in providing similar "scientific" confirmation of the existence of human spirits that hover over cemeteries and even enter the bodies of living human beings. After describing spirits of people "who have died before their time," he adds: "people say that these spirits go wandering in the land, and when they discover a body waiting for them . . . they possess it and depart from it only at the conclusion of their fixed period on the earth."[45] Such spirits, called *dibbukim*, attracted the attention of many of his contemporaries, Jews and Christians alike. Recently Gedaliah Nigal and others have documented numerous cases of *dibbuk* possession among Jews, beginning in Yagel's period.[46] Yagel himself refers to an actual case reported by, among others, his contemporary Gedaliah ibn Yaḥya, regarding a young Jewish woman in Ferrara in 1575 whose body appeared to have been invaded by the soul of a Christian criminal.[47]

Yagel's dilemma concerning such cases was obvious: to accept them at face value was to suspend entirely the laws of nature as Yagel understood them. Although he maintained elsewhere in his writings that a modified purgation of the souls of the dead in other human bodies was possible (see Chapter 8), in the context of this discussion he was unwilling to believe that the voices emanating from people who were allegedly possessed were actually those of souls of the dead. Since Yagel already had demystified demons by providing them with a kind of "scientific" status, he was more comfortable with designating these cases as possession by demons rather than as possession by human souls; the demons only acted as if they were human. Yagel knew that ancients such as Plotinus and Pythagoras had maintained that every human being has his demonic admirers who cry and wail in their affection for earthly individuals; they will even "change their names and call themselves by the names of people whom they love."[48] Yagel had by no means resolved all the problems related to possession, but at least he could argue that the phenomenon was exclusively demonic, and thereby reduce it to a more understandable and thus less harmful category.

An even thornier problem was that of the biblical witch of En-dor, a virtual nightmare to rationally inclined but pious exegetes.[49] For how, in Yagel's words, "was this great thing possible, that the soul of a holy prophet was obliged to obey the voice of a woman known to the gentiles for her whoredom and then disappear because of her sorcery"?[50] Yagel clearly understands the consequences of accepting this story literally; it describes magical practices unambiguously prohibited by Jewish religious law.[51] He also acknowledges having seen this case in a list of prohibited forms of magic in the handbook of his Christian contemporary, Bartolommeo Cocles.[52] He feebly attempts to explain the witch's actions scientifically by quoting, of all people, the thirteenth-century kabbalist commentator on the Torah, Menahem Recanati. According to Recanati, the animal faculty of the soul stays in the body after death, cries in its rotting sanctuary, and can be called up by a witch. Only because of this faculty "do dead people speak in their graves." But fully cognizant that he is treading on the hazardous ground of forbidden black magical practices, Yagel closes the subject by announcing that although these practices exist, they should not be performed by Jews.[53] To label Samuel's soul as that of a demon dressed up in human attire was also a step Yagel was not ready to take; it would have called into question the authenticity of the sacred text itself.[54] The only solution left in this case was to opt for Recanati's interpretation and assume that in most other cases possession by the souls of the dead actually meant demonic possession. For even a good scientist had to admit that some contradictions were not always reconcilable and that an element of uncertainty, incomprehensibility, even mystery still enveloped the marvelous world of God's creation.

AT LEAST TWO of Yagel's coreligionists of the sixteenth and seventeenth centuries made similar attempts to demonstrate rationally what most Jews took for granted, that demons existed and that they were primary agents of disease.[55] Eliezer Ashkenazi (1513–1586), an itinerant exegete and rabbi with broad knowledge of both the kabbalah and the sciences, published his main work, *Ma'aseh Adonai,* a commentary on the Torah, in Venice in 1583. In his discussion of demons he admits his difficulty in accepting their reality, since they cannot be confirmed by sense perception. Since a belief in the reality of demons is neither beneficial nor detrimental to the betterment of one's soul, Ashkenazi cautiously refrains from expressing his opinion on their existence. Nevertheless, he advises against dismissing demons out of hand simply because they are not perceived by the senses or because they were not explicitly mentioned in the biblical description of creation. He then offers his own "scientific hypothesis" to explain how these creatures could possibly exist. Demons and spirits are bodies of evil persons who have died. Their bodies are composed of a fine, invisible hylic substance that envelops the sensitive soul. They are obliged to wander the earth for a limited period until they are called to their ultimate punishment in the fires of hell. The rabbis acknowledged their existence because they constitute a vital part of the scheme of divine retribution.[56]

Ashkenazi also considers the evidence of possession by demons, specifically the case of the woman of Ferrara, reported previously by both ibn Yaḥya and Yagel. Like his contemporaries, he is impressed by the evidence and attempts to offer a scientific explanation of this phenomenon. He explains that under ordinary circumstances these spirits are inaudible to mortals because of the thinness of the matter of which they are composed. However, upon entering the body of a living person, they can be heard because the hollowness of the person's throat allows their voices to project.[57] Thus demonic existence and possession are plausible for Ashkenazi, although he hesitates to endorse them categorically. Yet since the rabbis had long affirmed the reality of demons, and since "science" admits their credibility, Ashkenazi offers little resistance in allowing them a place in the natural order of creation.

Manasseh ben Israel's intellectual arguments in favor of the existence of demons are far less tentative than Ashkenazi's formulation. His *Nishmat Ḥayyim*, published in Amsterdam in 1652, cites the authority of tradition, empirical evidence, and logic to prove that such spirits exist. He presents eyewitness testimonies both of traditional Jewish authorities and of contemporary Christian demonologists to establish through the compelling weight of these accounts that the existence of demons is incontrovertible.

He also refutes the assumption that demons are not real because they are neither seen nor heard. He first argues that, like the element earth, the element air should also be capable of generating creatures, since it "is the cause of vitality and life." He then belittles those who dismiss demons solely because they are not seen. How, then, might one explain "the Infinite, the great, mighty, and wonderful God whose wonder fills all the earth yet no person can see him and live"? Since no one would deny God's existence, one should never assume that "it is appropriate to deny all that is hidden from the eye." As in the case of the divine presence, we perceive the reality of demons from their actions on earth. Were we to deny everything not experienced directly by our senses, he mockingly exclaims, we conceivably could deny the existence of Jerusalem or Venice if we had not personally visited either city. Since such an exaggerated skepticism is clearly unwarranted, Manassah concludes, there is no valid reason to deny the existence of demons, given the abundance of historical and contemporary reports.[58] As in the case of Yagel, the fact that rabbis and kabbalists fully concurred with the latest medical and legal authorities in the Christian world left Manasseh convinced of the truthfulness of his assertions.

By and large, the existence of demons remained unchallenged in Jewish circles well into the eighteenth century. Even so forceful an advocate of the secular sciences as Phinehas Elijah Hurwitz (1765–1821) could not dislodge the well-established view that demons were responsible for certain diseases. In his Hebrew anthology of the sciences, the *Sefer ha-Berit*, he vigorously maintains that many patients who claim to be possessed by demons are actually suffering from natural causes that are curable by conventional medical therapy. However, "there are also [cases] where an evil spirit clings to him [the patient]." These incidents are extremely rare and should be treated by "a master of [the divine] name" rather than a regular doctor. One distinguishes the first kind of ailment from the second, according to Hurwitz, on the basis of the quality of the information emanating from the mouth of the supposedly possessed person. If the message is truly mysterious, if the patient reveals genuinely novel information, speaks in an unknown tongue, or discloses secret knowledge unavailable locally, "it is appropriate to take him to a master of a name . . . for undoubtedly an evil spirit kicks him."[59]

CLEARLY, the scientific enthusiasts in the Jewish community from Abraham Yagel to Phinehas Hurwitz failed to expunge the prevailing belief in demons from either the popular or elite Jewish cultures of their day. In the treatment of disease, the attribution of illness to demonic agents may even have relieved the fears of anxious sufferers, who conceived of demons as somewhat familiar forces in the mysterious dark universe in which they lived.[60] In fact Yagel and those like him reinforced the perception that those banal vexations called demons were neither as terrifying nor as incomprehensible as they might appear. By classifying an entire community of supernatural beings as demons, they rendered a part of the unknown intelligible to mere human beings and susceptible to rational scrutiny. To a greater degree than ever before, because demons were considered a legitimate part of the natural world, they could fall under the naturalists's purview and control.

Stuart Clark has recently pointed out the close affinity between the new sciences of the sixteenth and seventeenth centuries and demonology.[61] The demonologists approached the unknown with the conscious objective of establishing criteria of intelligibility. By defining demons as part of the natural order, as unusual but not miraculous, as annoying but not terrifying, they succeeded in "demystifying and deflating demonic pretensions."[62] Their treatises on demonology were part of a larger epistemological debate about what was real or unreal, what was rational or irrational. By establishing analytic distinctions between miracles, natural wonders, and ordinary occurrences, they contributed substantially to the scientific discourse of their day.

Yagel's discourse on demons should thus be viewed as part of the larger debate on defining the criteria for evaluating the marvelous in nature and on distinguishing the rational from the irrational. What makes Yagel's treatment of the subject more than a mere Jewish echo of the larger European discussion is his inclusion of the substantial testimony of rabbinic and kabbalistic opinions. In their weighing and sifting of contradictory authorities, the Christian demonologists had little or no access to this significant body of evidence. Yet when it too was systematically evaluated and correlated with classical, medieval, and contemporary demonology, the results were no doubt reassuring, especially to the Jewish investigator. The rabbis had long assumed that demons occupied a part of the natural order, that their magic was less ominous than other types of occult activity, and that one who dabbled in demonic magic was less culpable than other practitioners of magic. In short, the weight of Jewish tradition confirmed and validated what contemporary demonologists were now declaring. Once again, the symmetry between traditional Jewish learning and contemporary knowledge was striking. Those detestable spirits investigated and analyzed by the new experts in demonology were none other than the same pesty creatures already familiar to and tolerated by the rabbis for generations. Despite the extensive new literature on the subject, the rabbis still appeared to have the final word.

4. Unicorns, Great Beasts, and the Marvelous Variety of Nature

And in our days, one *re'em* was brought to the land of Portugal from the Indian island . . . it is bigger than the elephant, armed with scales all over its skin, with a thick visible horn on its nose, with which it fights its battles with the elephant and with other animals.

—*Beit Ya'ar ha-Levanon*, pt. 4, chap. 45, fol. 108a

It is not God's will that what he creates for man's benefit and what he has given us remain hidden. . . . He has allowed nothing to remain without exterior and visible signs in the form of special marks—just as a man who has buried a hoard of treasure marks the spot, that he may find it again.

—Paracelsus, *De Natura Rerum*

DEMONS were by no means the only bizarre creatures that Yagel attempted to explain. Several chapters of *Beit Ya'ar ha-Levanon* also discuss the obscure biblical animal the *re'em*.[1] Why did Yagel regard this legendary beast important enough to merit so much attention? Even more curious is the fact that his learned investigation was not self-inspired but was commissioned by a well-to-do Jewish banker, Solomon Fano of Lugo.[2] Fano had concerned himself considerably with the subject, uncovering a wealth of references to the mysterious creature in Jewish and classical sources. Dissatisfied with the results of his research, he turned to Yagel for a more authoritative treatment of the matter.[3]

The prominence afforded fanciful fauna in Yagel's wide-ranging *Beit Ya'ar ha-Levanon* is a promising starting point for considering a number of issues critical to Yagel and some of his contemporaries: the need to reconcile classical, medieval Christian, and rabbinic mythology; the currency of a heated literary debate between doctors and naturalists; the impact of the new geographic discoveries on

Jewish thought; and the elevation of the study of nature, in all its bizarre manifestations, to a fundamental expression of Jewish faith.

THE HEBREW BIBLE mentions the *re'em* eight times with little explicit description except that the animal is majestic, wild, and powerful and possesses at least one horn.[4] As Solomon Fano amply pointed out in his inquiry to Yagel, the rabbis had added their own fanciful details to the biblical portrait.[5] Commenting on the animal mentioned in the book of Psalms, they claimed that its sheer magnitude allowed King David to mistake it for a mountain; he was unaware that he had mounted a *re'em* until a lion startled the creature, causing it to stir.[6] Elsewhere they compared the *re'em* to Mount Tabor and related how the animal escaped the flood by being tied to the outside of the ark. Fano might also have recalled other rabbinic embellishments: the *re'em*'s connection with Og, king of Bashan; its fight with the lion; and Adam's choice of a sacrifice to God.[7] But the precise identity of the animal remained elusive to Fano. Was the animal a clean or unclean beast; did it have one or occasionally two horns on its head; and, most important, was it identifiable with the famous unicorn or with the recently observed rhinoceros first transported to western Europe in the beginning of the sixteenth century?

Fano's confusion derived especially from his difficulty in relating the cluster of rabbinic references he had collected to the overwhelming body of classical and medieval information about the unicorn. For if the *re'em* and the unicorn were indeed the same creatures, as was most commonly assumed, their composite portraits simply did not match. By Fano's time the unicorn had become a multifaceted literary, religious, and iconographic subject deeply embedded in Western culture, represented in diverse and often contradictory ways by numerous writers.[8] Classical naturalists such as Aelian and Pliny had subsumed at least seven different animals under the general category of unicorn: the rhinoceros, the Indian ass, the oryx, the Indian ox, the Indian horse, the bison, and a specific creature—the unicorn proper and par excellence.[9] There was also little unanimity about the texture, color, length, and location of the horn. Why these unicorns were eventually identified with the *re'em*, which is never depicted in the Bible as single-horned, is unclear.[10] Even more problematic was the identification of this strong, ferocious beast with the meek, innocent creature made famous in the third-century *Physiologus*. This composition describes the unicorn as a small animal, likened to a kid with a divided hoof and beard, that falls asleep in the lap of a virgin and thus is captured. The erotic theme of the unicorn with virgin was later incorporated in Christian symbolism, eventually meant to allude to Christ and the Virgin Mary, while the exotic horn was likened to the holy cross.[11]

To any literate person of the sixteenth or seventeenth century, the unicorn, in all its manifestations, was one of the most familiar and attractive animals in European culture, despite—or perhaps because of—the fact that hardly anyone had actually observed what he thought to be such a creature. How startling the news must have been when, as Yagel relates, "in our days, one *re'em* was brought to the land of Portugal from the Indian island, having been ambushed in a trap, and afterward seafarers conveyed the sight of its form, for it is bigger than the elephant, armed with scales all over its skin, with a thick visible horn on its nose, with which it fights its battles with the elephant and with other animals."[12] The subject of Yagel's description, a rhinoceros brought to Lisbon in 1515, suddenly precipitated a direct confrontation between fact and fiction, between the fabled animal of Western mythology and the hideous real creature soon to be memorialized in Albrecht Dürer's famous portrait.[13] Thus Fano had good reason to be perplexed; for "we will not know . . . if some or most of the things said about him [the *re'em*] are fictional or if they actually are real."[14]

Yagel's answer to Fano appears to have been written in two different stages.[15] An initial and apparently tentative answer is followed by a much more comprehensive explanation. Yet even Yagel's initial characterization indicates the significance the *re'em* had for him. He first cautions Fano not to treat lightly the rabbinic depictions of the animal, for hidden underneath them are secrets that men are unable to know; and although Aristotle, Pliny, and all the naturalists failed to describe the *re'em* in the same way, "several degrees of strange beasts will be found in the world never observed by the philosophers nor even imagined by the ancients, and they would regard it as a deception if one told them."[16] Yagel states categorically that the unicorn and rhinoceros are the same and, more tentatively, that they are identical with the *re'em*. The recently discovered rhinoceros leads him to conclude somewhat hesitantly that maybe there are two kinds of *re'emim*: the unicorn-rhinoceros, and the one described by the rabbis in all its splendor and enormity, "the first of the ways of God among the animals of the forest." And even though it is difficult to imagine such a gigantic creature, rabbinic testimony is sufficient to validate its reality, "for if our blessed rabbis told us, are we greater than they in wisdom and number in telling their sons and pupils the greatness of God's acts among all the creatures to which he assigned names in the world?"[17]

Yagel next treats the *re'em* more comprehensively and systematically. He asserts that the *re'em* is always one-horned and that the biblical passages suggesting two horns need to be read metaphorically. The *re'em* symbolizes the greatness and majesty of the Jewish people, a sign of the rejuvenation of Israel's powers over her enemies. Yagel now identifies five different types of *re'emim*. The first is the wild horse, referred to by Pliny and Solinius and made famous elsewhere by its association with the virgin used as a snare to entrap the beast. Yagel pauses to relate the elaborate story of such a unicorn horse befriending a virgin who sat each day by a well until she was raped by a hunter and lost her odor of chastity. The beast then attacked the maiden, who died and was buried beside the well.[18] The second type is a wild ass, found in India and mentioned by Philostratus in his *Vita Apollonii.*[19] The third, referred to by Aristotle and Pliny, is the African wild sheep with a cleft hoof and a large black horn.[20] The fourth is the wild ox of India, possessing a horn in the middle of its head and, though lacking a cleft hoof, nevertheless sacrificed by Adam. Finally, there is the rhinoceros, originally brought to Rome by Pompey, which has its horn on its nose and fights with the elephant.[21] In each of the five cases Yagel carefully integrates the descriptions by the classicists with those by the rabbis, together with the eyewitness accounts of the rhinoceros and the wide variety of horns he had seen or heard of in his own day. Most of his discussion focuses on the horn. Yagel is convinced of its medicinal value for a wide variety of diseases, especially its prophylactic function in detecting the presence of poison. He discusses in some detail the preparation of horn dust mixed with flower water, a formula he apparently had used in his own medical practice. He also refers to the medicinal use of unicorn blood, teeth, skin, and hooves. He briefly explains how to distinguish between real and fake horns. He concludes by reminding his reader that the *re'emim* are "the first of God's ways among those beasts referred to by Job . . . and they are with us in reality."[22]

But in fact the matter is still not settled for Yagel. His lengthy exposition seems to have encouraged him to enlarge the parameters of the discussion to include similar monstrous beasts. He first devotes an entire chapter to the cerastes, a small poisonous serpent of the Sahara and Mesopotamia with two very short proturberances vaguely reminiscent of horns. He describes horned fowl recently displayed in Rome and described by his contemporary Michele Mercati.[23] At last he reaches a subject of great fascination to him: an animal he calls "the great beast."[24] He leaves no doubt that although this animal is of the same sort as the *re'em*-unicorn, he would have required little external stimulus (such as Fano's inquiry) to elaborate on it anyway, particularly on the marvelous virtue of its hooves. In fact he says at the beginning of the fourth book of *Beit Ya'ar ha-Levanon* that he intends to compose an entire essay on the hooves of the animal for inclusion in his collection of other expositions of wondrous manifestations of nature.[25] This chapter is similar in format to the chapter on the *re'em*. Yagel carefully describes the various identities attributed by the ancients to this elusive creature. He dismisses the three categories of identification—ass, goat, and antelope—and asserts instead that the animal is unique by virtue of its special curative qualities. In his detailed description he mentions that it is susceptible to epilepsy despite Pliny's assertion that only human beings and the quail experience that illness.[26] He devotes the rest of his exposition to the beast's medicinal uses, especially those of the hooves.[27]

YAGEL'S SOURCES for his extensive remarks about these fabulous creatures provide some insight into why he concerned himself with such matters. By Yagel's time, the ancient and medieval writers on unicorns and similar wonders had been joined by a large number of naturalists who found the subject of utmost importance and fascination. The issue was no longer only literary, theological, or artistic; the unicorn now became a topic of contemporary scientific investigation, albeit one still largely dependent on literary rather than empirical methods of inquiry. Between 1550 and 1700 some twenty-five discussions of unicorns appeared throughout Europe either as separate treatises or as long chapters in larger works.[28] The catalysts of this renewed interest were the discoveries of hitherto unknown fauna in the Far East and the New World and the bewildering amount of information about them reaching Europe in the sixteenth and seventeenth centuries.[29] Contemporary investigators were confronted with the problem of harmonizing the old and new learning, of reevaluating accepted canons of knowledge in the light of constantly proliferating empirical data.

The *re'em*-unicorn presented such a case. Had the explorers indeed brought back from the Far East a unicorn identical with the fabled beast of literature and tapestries? And what was one to make of all those alleged unicorn horns selling for high prices at fine markets throughout Europe and adorning the tables of so many aspiring to nobility?[30] Did the horns actually detect posion in food and drink, and were they efficacious in curing a wide variety of ailments? The perplexing reality of early modern Europe rapidly transformed the fanciful unicorn lying docilely in virgins' laps into something of a *cause célèbre*. "The battle of the books," as Odell Shepard called it,[31] pitted the champions of the unicorn and the usefulness of its horn against those who questioned the authority of unicorn tradition and found the horn of dubious medical value. The traditionalists included Sebastian Münster, who in his *Cosmographiae Universalis* of 1550 unhesitatingly identified the Hebrew *re'em* with the recently observed beast described by the geographer Ludovico di Varthema.[32] Similarly, the Italian scholar Girolamo Cardano identified the unicorn with the rhinoceros and discussed the beneficial qualities of its horn.[33] Konrad von Gesner's *Historiae Animalium*, the standard sixteenth-century work on the subject, and Edward Topsel's *The History of Four-Footed Beasts and Serpents* likewise treated the unicorn and its horn. They not only quoted Münster's identification of the biblical *re'em* and unicorn but also supplemented the classical sources with reference to the *re'em* in the Hebrew commentaries of Saadia, Rashi, and David Kimḥi.[34] They treated the rhinoceros as an animal separate from but related to the unicorn and added Dürer's famous portrait of the beast. They also included a separate entry on the cerastes, the serpent described by Yagel.[35]

First and foremost in the detractors' camp was the Italian physician Andrea Marini, who published his *Discorso* in Venice in 1566, denying the existence of the unicorn and the medicinal value of its horn.[36] He was followed in 1582 by Ambroise Paré, who published a treatise in Paris cautiously negating the medicinal value of the unicorn horn while maintaining a belief in the animal's existence because it was mentioned in the Bible.[37]

Although Marini's arguments influenced Paré and others, they failed to erode the faith of the unicorn enthusiasts. In the same year that Marini's work was published, another Italian physician, Andrea Bacci, published an apparent rebuttal to Marini's devastating assault.[38] Writing to his benefactor, Don Francesco Medici, who seems to have expired soon afterward from poison undetected by his priceless unicorn horn, Bacci championed the virtues of the horn. Armed with a host of authorities and detailed "evidence" of the horn's utility, Bacci constructed an eloquent defense. His work was republished four times, although Marini's treatise seems to have had greater influence on later sixteenth-century naturalists. By the seventeenth century, however, almost every authority who discussed the unicorn issue firmly supported the Florentine doctor.[39]

All the elements of Yagel's discussion of unicorn lore can be traced, in one form or another, to the contemporary authorities. Yet more remains to be said not only about Yagel's *re'em* but also and especially about his "great beast."

Some fifteen years after Bacci had published his unicorn discourse in Latin, he republished it in Italian with two new compositions, one on the twelve precious stones found on the breastplate of the biblical high priest and the other "della gran bestia."[40] There is little doubt that Yagel was familiar with this small volume and that it played a role in his decision to compose not only his own unicorn and great beast chapters but also a similar elucidation of the stones of the priestly breastplate. A careful comparison of Bacci's and Yagel's accounts of the unicorn and breastplate, however, demonstrates that Yagel neither copied nor relied excessively on Bacci's versions; his exposition of both subjects, especially the priestly breastplate, is original.

On the other hand, in describing "the great beast" he follows Bacci's narrative closely, though without slavishly copying from it. Among his unmistakable references to Bacci's composition are his comment regarding the animal's epilepsy[41] and an obscure quotation from another sixteenth-century naturalist, Levinus Lemnius.[42] When Yagel mentions at the beginning of his chapter that his information came from a book about "the great beast," he is most likely alluding to Bacci's modest composition, which may also have provided him with the initial impetus to write about the hooves of the beast.

YAGEL'S GENERAL INTEREST in unicorns and other strange animals was shared to some extent by his Jewish contemporaries, especially by those with similar medical interests. Amatus Lusitanus, in his famous commentary on Dioscorides, treats the unicorn horn with utmost seriousness.[43] David de Pomis, in his *Dittionario novo hebraico*, printed in Hebrew, Latin, and Italian, even describes a test for distinguishing a true unicorn horn: place it in a vessel with several live scorpions; if the scorpions die, the horn is genuine.[44] Isaac Cardoso, in his *Philosophia Libera*, mentions the unicorn and rhinoceros separately.[45] Abraham Portaleone, in his *Shilte Gibburim*, also discusses the unicorn, citing Ludovico di Varthema's *Itineria* as his source.[46] He also mentions the virgin capture of the beast.[47] But most interesting of all, in a long chapter on other exotic animals, Portaleone provides a detailed exposition of Yagel's favorite creature, the "gran bestia."[48] Although Yagel's presentation is longer, a careful comparison of the two reveals plainly that either both drew from the same source, apparently Bacci's treatise, or Portaleone relied to some extent on Yagel's account. It is impossible to date Yagel's description precisely. His composition of *Beit Ya'ar ha-Levanon* extended from the late sixteenth to the early seventeenth century; Portaleone apparently completed his work in 1607–08.[49] Whatever the precise connection between the two, their parallel descriptions of "the great beast," the one in manuscript and especially the one published, suggest that both authors assumed that Hebrew readers would be keenly interested in their graphic portrayals.[50]

OF COURSE, it takes more than the availability of certain books or the currency of a literary debate to incline a writer to choose consciously to pursue one subject rather than another. What deeply felt needs of this Jewish physician were fulfilled by such seemingly fanciful excursuses on exotic fauna? The answer to this question requires a broader investigation of the basic assumptions and the deeper meaning underlying Yagel's study of nature and the physical world.

A good starting point is Andrea Bacci's writing. When Yagel read Bacci's unicorn discourse, he might have noticed an eloquent passage describing two great secrets of nature.[51] They are, first, that nature contents herself with producing only a few examples of those species especially noted for their beauty; second, she does this so that God may have greater glory in his works. In a carefully crafted argument, Bacci extols the divine glory in every created thing. God may reveal his majesty in his manner of producing beautiful objects such as gems or in the length of time he takes to make them, as in the case of gold or marble. He manifests his presence in nature by creating some animals in great numbers to serve mankind and others, less necessary to man, in limited numbers with instincts to flee from the sight of humans and thus survive. In elephants and whales he reveals the magnificent enormity of creation, and in ants and beetles the distinctive beauty of minuteness in his works. Finally, God and nature reveal their splendor by making certain things rare. The unicorn is wonderful, proclaims Bacci, precisely because of its rareness, and this was the divine intention.

Along similar lines, Levinus Lemnius, Bacci's contemporary and a naturalist also known and quoted by Yagel, offers a quotation from Aristotle in the opening of his *Degli occulti miracoli:* "There is nothing in nature so small or contemptible that may not make men in some things to wonder at it." He continues: "for in the smallest works of nature the Diety shines forth, and all things are good and beautiful." This leads Lemnius to the following conclusion regarding man's reaction to God's universe:

> In therefore so great multitude and variety of things existing, we must not only admire the force of nature and efficience, but His majesty and immensity from which all things are produced and do proceed . . . For the nature of things, which is vast and diffused all over, far and near, when it doth everywhere present itself to our eye and mind, it doth wonderfully affect a man, and directs him into an exceeding great love and adoration of the maker of it . . . So that in the things we plainly see, we must not only look upon the excellent workmanship of nature that is to be imitated, but we must behold the majesty, amplitude, glory, splendor, magnificence of God, and the goodwill of a most bountiful father unto mankind.[52]

Lemnius' sentiment that the divine glory shines through nature's handiwork is at least as old as the Psalmist, but no age before or after the sixteenth and seventeenth centuries has understood better how well the heavens declare God's glory or experienced more movingly the spontaneous exhilaration of uncovering the hidden beauty of nature.[53] Thus Paracelsus wrote at the beginning of the sixteenth century:

> Behold the herbs! Their virtues are invisible and yet they can be detected. Behold the beasts which can neither speak nor explain anything, and yet nothing is so hidden in them that man cannot learn of it. Thus there is no thing on earth or in the sea, in chaos or in the firmament, that does not become manifest at the appointed time. It is God's will that nothing remain un-

known to man as he walks in the light of nature; for all things belonging to nature exist for the sake of man. And since they have been created for his sake, and since it is he who needs them, he must explore everything that lies in nature.[54]

And some hundred years later, Robert Hooke expressed himself in a similar manner: "Tis the contemplation of the wonderful order, law, and power of that we call nature that does most magnify the beauty and excellency of the divine providence, which has so disposed, ordered, adapted, and empowered each part so to operate as to produce the wonderful effects which we see; I say wonderful because every natural production may be truly said to be a wonder or miracle if duly considered."[55]

A huge number of contemporary passages express similar sentiments about nature and God and man's relationship to both.[56] These views were shared with equal conviction by Abraham Yagel. He expresses the same enthusiasm for the study of the most minute aspects of God's creation: "the ancient philosophers and the wise men of every generation passionately desired to seek out and inquire into the details of lowly things regarding beasts, animals, fowl, and fish . . . as they sought out and inquired into the higher eternally existing things." Solomon, Yagel asserts, most clearly demonstrated this aspiration to know the insignificant things of nature and their hidden divine secrets. These secrets were also revealed in every subsequent generation, and "to those who come after us, things that the eye has never seen will still be revealed, for this is a condition of nature . . . for before Him all the secrets of all times, past, present, and future, will be divulged, and He renews each day the act of creation."[57]

The recognition of God's revelation through nature is perhaps the underlying message of Yagel's entire work. He calls his composition on natural history "The Opening of Hope,"[58] as if to suggest that his age and his generation have been blessed in undue proportion with opportunities to unravel God's secrets and thus to appreciate more profoundly his wondrous glory. And thus it is his joyful task to relate profusely "the different phenomena that benefit us and our friends in all the good that God invites to our hands, and from these things your eyes will be opened and your ideas expressed to give praise and exaltation to the producer and maker who makes light and creates that which is completed for us. God, our master, how wonderful is your name in all the earth!"[59] What greater pleasure could Yagel expect than to unveil the hidden divine mysteries of unicorns and great beasts?

Yagel's sentiments about natural phenomena reveal the heart of his entire intellectual enterprise, the essential core of his epistemology and beliefs.[60] Like many of his contemporaries, Yagel understood the quest for all knowledge as a search for resemblance—whether based on adjacency of place or requiring no contact at all, whether based on subtle analogies or on intricate relations of sympathies or antipathies.[61] Meaning in every aspect of human experience thus denotes the bringing to light of a resemblance, a likeness, a sameness of all things. And if all knowledge is so defined, there can be no resemblance without discernible signs or signatures. To appreciate the similarities underlying all things is to identify such signs even when they appear to be hidden in nature: "It is not God's will that what he creates for man's benefit and what he has given us remain hidden . . . And even though He has hidden certain things, He has allowed nothing to remain without exterior and visible signs in the form of special marks—just as a man who has buried a hoard of treasure marks the spot, and he may find it again."[62] If the world is indeed covered with signs to be deciphered and hidden "treasures" to be discovered, then to know is to interpret, and divination is a vital part of knowledge. The natural magician thus functions within the acceptable norms of learning as a legitimate investigator of signs and signatures in nature.[63]

To him who seeks knowledge of the divine world, there is no clear distinction between the visible marks of God on the earth's surface and those on the pages of a divine text. Both kinds of signs reveal the same eternal truths to the persistent decoder. Since language partakes of the same network of similitudes and signs, it must be studied as nature is studied. And of all civilization's numerous tongues, Hebrew contains the most transparent marks of the language of God and of the natural world.[64]

Because things and words had equivalent status as divine signatures of God's vast creation, Yagel and many of his Jewish and Christian contemporaries found the project of writing an encyclopedia especially attractive.[65] The encyclopedia represented an attempt to reconstitute the very order of the universe by determining the way in which words and things are linked together in common space. Since nature depicted "an unbroken tissue of words and signs,"[66] the encyclopedist did not need to distinguish between what he had read about the subject he describes and what he had heard or seen.

Knowledge of anything required gathering the whole dense layer of signs, interpreting them, and relating their languages to one another.[67]

The more bizarre and unusual the sign was, the greater the challenge posed to the investigator to place it within the framework of similitudes he had already classified. The bizarre demonstrated a greater diversity of things than was normally assumed; it forced man to penetrate more deeply the divine reason, holding the promise of more profound signatures still unknown to him. Nature constantly deceives him, but with persistence and with an abiding faith in a coherent and comprehensive divine plan, man remains confident that he, as God's mediator and classifier, can solve the puzzle. To interpet all signs constituted both the painful dilemma and the grandeur and dignity of the human condition. This outlook, together with the profound impact of the discovery of unknown skies and unknown lands, accounted for the unusual interest in monsters and prodigies of nature in Yagel's generation.[68] New plants, new animals, new planets and stars, appearing at a dizzying pace, confirmed anew the overwhelming complexity of God's creation, the unceasing need to classify and unravel even more signs, and a sense of awe and humility before the sheer brilliance of the creator.

Thus for Yagel and his fellow naturalists, theirs was a generation blessed with the good fortune of witnessing the explosion and diffusion of new and vital signs in every area of human experience. God indeed was "renewing every day the act of creation," and theirs was the opportunity to categorize, to interpret the plethora of divine signatures, to bring them together, and to reveal even more deeply the essential unity of all things in the face of the greatest apparent diversity ever known to human civilization. Thus men such as Bacci, Lemnius, Paracelsus, and Hooke approached their investigation of nature as a kind of revelatory experience—as theologians studying scriptural revelation. Every fresh observation, every step in cataloguing new natural data awoke more profoundly in them a sense of religious experience. Approaching the natural world with the unshakable assumption of the Creator's goodness, they were entirely confident that all their discoveries would reaffirm the harmony and majesty in which they confidently believed. The vast and uncharted universe offered untold possibilities for satisfying their religious needs.[69]

That Yagel shared with them the same predilection for discovering signs in nature, the same lack of discrimination between words and things, the same fascination with the bizarre, the same feeling of awe and gratitude for having been selected to live in this particularly eventful era of discovery, and the same sense of religious mission to collect, to classify, to integrate all data and thus to reaffirm God's unity—all of this is apparent from his writings, especially *Beit Ya'ar ha-Levanon* and *Be'er Sheva*. But this is not all. As a Jew conversant with Jewish literature, especially the kabbalah, and strongly affirming the primacy of Jewish revelation, Yagel's attitude toward nature carried additional implications.

In the first place, if all meaning denoted likeness, it became the intellectual task of the Jewish scholar to discover signs embedded in the natural world and in Western civilization analogous to those in the Jewish tradition, and then to integrate them, weaving them creatively into one divine harmony. Thus the announced purpose of Yagel's *Be'er Sheva* is "to pass over the well of learning from nature and astronomy and to collect something from everything, and to make erect and to connect a little or a lot with connections from the splendid sayings of the rabbis."[70] The goal of connecting and integrating receives repeated emphasis throughout his other writings as well.[71] Harmonizing Jewish with non-Jewish knowledge was an aspiration by no means unique to Yagel and his particular community, but given contemporary European scholars' priority of discovering similitude, this undertaking assumed additional significance for Jews. They sought more than ever to translate the language of their own cultural signs into that found in nature and in the European intellectual tradition. *Re'em* and unicorn and rhinoceros could be correlated so that they revealed the same identifiable markings.

This intellectual task was made easier by the new status assigned to Judaic learning by the Christian scholarly community.[72] The secrets hidden in Hebrew letters and words, the profound insights of rabbinic wisdom, and the rabbinic and kabbalistic hermeneutical tools for decoding texts were eagerly sought by an increasingly sympathetic and enthusiastic intellectual world. Offering a new reservoir of divine signatures previously inaccessible to scholars of Latin and Greek texts, the Jewish literary tradition, now available both in manuscripts and in newly printed books, could no longer be ignored. Nor could Christians' new interest in Jewish learning go unnoticed by Jewish scholars such as Yagel. They labored to promote their own signs and to "connect" them with those found in other cultural settings, in order to demonstrate the Jewish contribution to Western civilization and to eliminate the sense of cultural insularity that separated Jews from Christians. Anticipating the obsession of later generations of Jewish intellectuals, Yagel's intellectual agenda and that of some of his colleagues was thus related to their own need for social and political acceptance.[73]

The epistemology of resemblance also promoted the study of nature among Jews to an even greater extent than in previous centuries. The Jewish scholar was expert in reading signs implanted in Jewish texts as well as in nature. The universal search for signatures in all things implied the elevation of naturalistic learning—medicine, natural history, astronomy, and astrology—in the traditional curriculum of Jewish religious education.[74] Among Jews, those considered most intellectually suited for such a task were the physicians trained in rabbinic and kabbalistic learning and also in the ways of nature. More than ever before, rabbis in the sixteenth and seventeenth centuries chose also to be physicians, not only because of the social and material utility of a medical practice and because of practical limitations imposed on them in acquiring any other learned degree—but also because of the new intellectual respectibility afforded their expertise within both the Jewish and non-Jewish worlds.[75] Who besides the Jewish doctor, armed with rabbinic and kabbalistic erudition, was more capable to decipher, to evaluate, and to integrate the multiplicity of God's signs? Thus Yagel's simultaneous training in naturalistic and Jewish disciplines placed him in the advantageous position of being able to undertake his ambitious intellectual plan—an encyclopedia of all knowledge firmly linked with the wisdom of his own culture.

A surprising number of contemporary Jewish scholars, almost all of them physicians, shared the same fundamental assumptions regarding the acquisition of Jewish and naturalistic knowledge. Thus Gedaliah ibn Yaḥya could sing the praises of a medical education for Jews: "For this wisdom of medicine is precious and exalted as a ladder resting on the ground, in order that man might reach the knowledge of God's blessed majesty and His miracles in heaven and on earth."[76] Judah Sommo Portaleone, Yagel's close friend, likewise juxtaposed the importance of the study of the secrets of the Torah with a knowledge of the nature of different creatures, while Leone Modena explained God's rebuke of Job as the result of his neglect of studying nature.[77] Similarly, the writings of Abraham Portaleone, David de Pomis, Joseph Delmedigo, and many other Jewish scholars of the sixteenth and seventeenth centuries reveal a similar intellectual program and a common perception of the purpose and nature of Jewish learning.[78]

For medieval Jewish philosophers, the theoretical study of both physics and metaphysics, when properly integrated within Jewish tradition, became a religious commandment.[79] For Jews such as Yagel, living in a dramatically changing intellectual universe, the empirical study of nature, when properly integrated with Jewish tradition, became, more than ever before, a most compelling obligation. And that is why they could not take lightly the subject of unicorns and great beasts, or, for that matter, the issue of monstrous births.

5. Out of the Mouths of Babes and Sucklings

Our incident . . . had not happened in Venice for a thousand years . . . We came to all the city's inhabitants to tell them that the thing came from God . . . to teach . . . that good things are brought about by good people.

—*Gei Ḥizzayon*, pt. 1, p. 23b

He [the child from Grodek] is accurate in what he says and is consistently wise and knowledgeable . . . he answers correctly as if he were a mature person who had acquired knowledge and possessed heavenly sapience to foretell the future.

—*Bat Rabim*, no. 68, fols. 109b–110a

THE GHETTO of Venice was in a state of great commotion. It was the late afternoon of May 26, 1575, and the daughter of Gabriel Ẓarfati, the wife of a Jew named Petaḥiah, had just given birth to a creature with two heads and four hands but conjoined from the waist down.[1] The news of these Siamese twins quickly spread throughout the ghetto and beyond. The infants, apparently healthy at birth, became an instant sensation to Jews and non-Jews alike. A stream of visitors inundated the family's residence. Under constant pressure and exposure, the infants succumbed some eight days later.[2]

The story of this bizarre spectacle did not end, however, with the death of the twins. In fact it took an even more grisly and macabre twist. Instead of immediately burying the deceased children, the father handed them over to the local *gemilut ḥasadim* (benevolent) society "as a present."[3] The members of the society preserved them in a solution, carried them from place to place, and displayed the corpse to anyone who would pay a price to view it, until they collected "a handsome sum." It is not clear who was ultimately responsible for this profitable but unconscionable capitalist venture—the parents, the heads of the confraternity, or both parties.[4] Whatever the case, the perpetrators had sought to legitimate their actions by appeal to Jewish religious custom and apparently had obtained approval from some questionable legal authorities.[5] Nevertheless, there were those among the Venetian rabbinate who could not countenance such an act, notably Rabbis Samuel Judah Katzenellenbogen and Raphael Joseph Treves, who composed *responsa* disapproving of the sodality's activity and calling for the immediate burial of the corpse in accordance with the dictates of Jewish law.

Largely as a result of the notoriety gained by the confraternity's hawking of the unfortunate children, news of the monstrous birth quickly spread beyond Venice to other parts of Italy and to Germany. To both a popular audience and a learned community of scholars fascinated by the new "science" of teratology, the data on the Jewish twins were of considerable interest.[6] Full descriptions of the twins are found in the monster handbooks of Ulisse Aldrovandi and Johann Schenck.[7] The twins were even memorialized in contemporary German and Italian poems and portrayed alongside the narratives.[8] The coincidence of the twins' birth with the outbreak of a devastating plague in the environs of Venice led many observers to consider their birth as a manifestation of divine displeasure with Venice and its inhabitants.[9]

The most important vehicle of dissemination about the monstrous birth was undoubtedly an anonymous fourteen-page pamphlet in Italian, first published by Giuseppe Gregorio of Cremona in Venice only two days after the twins' death, and reissued the next year in Bologna. The treatise, which includes a picture of the twins and two horoscopes summarizing the pertinent astrological data of the day of birth and the day of impregnation, is titled *Discorso sopra gli accidenti del parto monstruoso nato di una Hebrea in Venetia nell'anno 1575 a di xxvi di Maggio*. The second edition emphasizes the Jewish provenance of the birth by providing the additional title *Dove si ragiona altamente del futuro destino de gli Hebrei*.[10]

After describing the "monster," the author offers a detailed explanation of this phenomenon according to a conventional division of reality into three parts: material, heavenly, and divine. He first considers the immediate cause of the birth as understood by naturalists and physicians: either an excessive or insufficient amount of semen or unclean spermatozoa. Next he considers the astrological factors, concluding with the explanation of the ancient seers (*aruspici*) that such prodigies are omens of heavenly displeasure. He describes other recorded incidents of monstrous births both in ancient times and in the more recent past. He concludes with an offensive vilification of the "perverse and obstinate *sinagoga*," the false Jewish interpretations of the prophecies of the book of Daniel, and the usurious practices of contemporary Jews. After predicting their final doom, he calls for the conversion of the Jews to Christianity. That this oddity of nature had occurred within a Jewish household of the ghetto was an opportunity not to be missed by this Christian author. The ultimate "lessons" of this tragedy were clearly theological.

THREE YEARS LATER, Abraham Yagel composed his imaginary heavenly journey, the *Gei Ḥizzayon*.[11] Sitting in a cell in the municipal prison of Mantua, so he informs his readers, he was awakened by the soul of his departed father, who accompanied him on his spiritual odyssey to the supernal heights of the universe. Throughout his ascent he encountered individuals from all walks of life, each with his own story to relate, each a personification of an idea or religious message. In a manner transparently reminiscent of Boethius' *Consolation of Philosophy*, Yagel's journey to the uppermost heavens was meant to chastise, to enlighten, to reform its narrator as he ascended from the depravity of his material existence in the Mantuan dungeon to the exhilarating freedom and illumination of the secrets of the divine mysteries of the kabbalah.

Among the characters who engage Yagel in dialogue during his celestial wanderings are the notorious twins of the Venetian ghetto.[12] Having learned of their strange appearance from the sensational Italian pamphlet, Yagel recovers the infants from their miserable lot as pitiful oddities of nature, recasts them as majestic prophetic characters in his mysterious romance, and thus affords them a place in the annals of Hebrew literature. Relying primarily on the *Discorso* for his information about the twins, he uses the incident to impart a religious message radically different from that of the Italian pamphleteer.

The twins make their entrance in a highly dramatic fashion. Although attached to each other, they fly toward Yagel and his father, whispering quietly to each other, "their voices sounding like a ghost out of the ground." Their initial pronouncements are prophetic. One predicts "that there will be a war or famine in the land or one of the remaining calamities threatening to come to the world." The prognostication is imprecise, but surely Yagel has in mind the disastrous plague of Venice, which immediately followed the death of the twins. The same child counsels immediate flight from the city as the only solution to the impending disaster. Yet he simultaneously contradicts himself by quoting the rabbinic statement: "If there is a plague in the city, remain where you are."[13]

The opening prophecy of doom is followed by a long discussion between Yagel and his father on the essence of the soul, how it comes into the world, and related issues, all triggered by the strange appearance of these infant souls who had expired three years earlier.[14] Finally, father and son approach the twins and ask them the reason for their being attached. The first responds impatiently that mere mortals have no right to understand such hidden divine secrets. His brother, however, is more forthcoming. Though recognizing the finitude of human knowledge, he considers the quest for greater understanding implicit in their question to be both appropriate and desirable. His answer constitutes the longest part of Yagel's narrative of the encounter.[15]

Following the structure of the *Discorso*'s argument, the infant divides his explanation into three parts corresponding to the order of three worlds. He opens, however, with a strong religious emphasis. Since God is always just, any calamity is caused by human and not by divine failing. Thus, "if He [God] brings about evil, let us search and try our ways, and return to the Lord." He is even more explicit in viewing this birth primarily as a portent of divine wrath:

> For it is taught that the only evil that descends from above is that which our sins caused and that from which our iniquities prevented the good. If the thing which happens in the state is a miracle, transcending the boundaries of nature and accepted practice, as was the case with our incident, which, in our eyes, had not happened in Venice for a thousand years, nor in any of the states adjacent to it . . . it is fitting that we attribute this matter to a general cause. We came to all the city's inhabitants to tell them that this thing came from God, not only to teach specific things but rather to teach the overall general cause that good things are brought about by good people.[16]

The same religious message is emphasized again by a parallel drawn between the biblical incident of the slain body of a beheaded heifer (Deuteronomy 21) and the corpse of the Venetian twins. In both cases, those responsible for ruling the state were ultimately responsible for the welfare of their communities. Although the father's household bears partial responsibility for this disaster, the city's inhabitants and their leadership also are culpable. The fact that the plague took the lives of so many citizens is tangible evidence of their punishment:

> With respect to the city in which we were born, she is also guilty for her sins to have nature distort its ways and actions. . . . For the Lord's hand was upon her. Afterwards, many in her midst died from plagues and bitter illnesses accompanying them. . . . And if out of the mouths of babes and sucklings [Psalms 8:3], they would have learned, as the people of Ninevah did in returning to the Lord, leaving the iniquity on their hands, who knows if God might not have regretted and turned his anger away from them? For God is merciful and forgiving and has no desire for the death of the wicked, but only in the reversal of his ways so that he may live.[17]

Up to this point Yagel has virtually ignored the *Discorso* and has instead underscored the religious message of the monstrous birth and the prophetic function of the twins. However, he now relies increasingly on his Italian source. From the *Discorso* he includes a description of some monstrous births earlier in the century; he also copies verbatim the testimony of the medieval Arab scholar Ibn Abi l-Ridjal (Aben Ragel) and of Xenophon regarding other monstrous children.[18] As we shall see, Yagel valued these testimonies highly and referred to them again and again many years after the incident of the Venetian infants.

When the twin turns to consider the heavenly cause of the birth, Yagel's dependence on the Italian pamphlet is even more evident: he lifts almost the entire first half of the *Discorso*'s astrological calculations.[19] Apparently, Yagel felt that it was sufficient to relate the astrological circumstances surrounding the birth day and not those of the day of impregnation; thus he ignores the entire second half of the *Discorso*'s tedious discussion.

The concluding explication of the natural, material causes of the incident follow generally the outline of the *Discorso*.[20] The infant repeats the primary reasons for this abnormality—the excess, scarcity, or filthiness of the sperm—but he also includes a wealth of additional information drawn primarily from rabbinic sources and from Yagel's own medical experience.[21] The account closes with the children asking Yagel and his father for their prayers. In place of the *Discorso*'s defamatory comments about Jews and Judaism, Yagel offers a powerful moral exhortation to his readers. In Yagel's treatment, the conjoined twins are no longer passive, lamentable objects of pity. Instead they are empowered to offer their own comprehensive explanation of the tragedy of their birth. They are not only competent naturalists and astrologers; they are also divine seers enlisted by God to speak his truth. Thus "out of the mouths of babes" the higher purpose of this divinely ordained malfunction is revealed.

YAGEL'S FASCINATION with the prophetic abilities of young children proved to be lifelong. Some forty-two years later he again reflected on the birth of a child, and in a manner strikingly reminiscent of his ruminations in *Gei Ḥizzayon*.

In 1620, Abraham ben Naphtali Hirsch Schor, the head of the rabbinic court of Satanov, Poland, wrote to Rabbi Mordecai ben David Katz, of the neighboring community of Lvov (Lemberg), about a "great and terrible act of God that I heard and saw with my own eyes here in the holy congregation of Satanov."[22] Rabbi Abraham related the following story:

> Here in the holy congregation of Grodek [Gorodok], three parasangs from Satanov, there lives a man named Rabbi Gedaliah with a small four-and-a-half-year-old son. The youth is a mere boy having no superiority in his studies over the rest of the children of his age. But when his father began to study the Hebrew alphabet and the prayer book with him, he subsequently brought the boy before me to the holy congregation of Satanov to test him. And I tested him several times and more—myself along with my colleagues who were with me—and we saw the work of the Lord and His wonders, for He is exceedingly great. I asked him: "Please tell me the beginning of the *halakhah* learned today." He immediately related the *halakhah*, answering: "Rabbi Ashi said that our *mishnah* states: I can likewise prove, etc."

Rabbi Abraham then questioned the boy about various passages in the *Zohar*, asking the father to have his son quote from specific pages. The child answered correctly even when the rabbi failed to mention a specific page but only placed his finger on a particular passage in the book hidden from the child but apparently not from his father. The boy was even able to read the rabbi's mind, quoting precisely biblical passages that Rabbi Abraham had been contemplating, again through the mediation of the father. In light of such an incredible demonstration, the rabbi could only conclude that "the boy knows what is in the heart of man and this can only be a spirit of prophecy." He was especially impressed by the child's ability because the boy still had not learned to read fluently but occasionally mispronounced words and was generally very shy.

The news of the extraordinary child of Grodek quickly spread to several other Jewish communities in Poland. Quoting Rabbi Abraham's testimony, a Rabbi Joshua of Brest Litovsk wrote to the head of the rabbinic tribunal of Vilna, which then ordered that the story not be told to women and children and especially not to gentiles.[23] The bearer of Joshua's letter, a Jew from Lublin, also carried to the tribunal a second letter from Schor, in which the Satanov rabbi related that he had asked the boy about the redemption of Israel and the boy said: "I do not know," and when asked who had placed such things in his mouth he answered: "God the Lord, the God of Israel."[24]

The source of all this correspondence was Joseph Solomon Delmedigo, the Italian Jewish physician, scientist, and philosopher and younger contemporary of Yagel. In his Hebrew work *Sefer Elim*, first published in 1629, Delmedigo quoted Rabbi Abraham's letter in full, explained how its contents reached Lvov and Vilna, and also reproduced another letter from his own disciple, Moses Metz, addressed to a Karaite, Zeraḥ ben Nissim, describing Delmedigo's role in the affairs.[25]

Metz's letter told how he and Delmedigo had traveled to the town of Grodek to observe firsthand the spectacle of the precocious child, who by that time had become a *cause célèbre*, so that "all the Polish rabbis and with them several thousand Jews feared to see him." But the shrewd Delmedigo proved capable of exposing the deception of the Grodek child prodigy:

> For immediately when my teacher [Delmedigo] saw that he needed his father, he detected a trick whereby he [the father] would give him clues in code. For example, for the letter "aleph," he would say "yes" to him in Yiddish; for "bet," "good"; for "gimel," "right"; and so on. And the questioner had to ask the question through his father, and his father would elicit and answer from him [the boy], placing in his mouth the letters with these pseudonyms so that he would recite the letters without vowels or vocalization and his father would interpret and vocalize them.

Delmedigo confirmed his initial suspicion by testing the child without the assistance of his father, and immediately "the trick was made known to all the congregation." Metz went on to say that the father had made a handsome profit from his guile and that the rabbis excommunicated the father when they learned of his deceitful behavior. The boy died soon afterward; Metz could not ascertain the cause. Metz also acknowledged that even after Delmedigo had publicly exposed the impostor, some ardent followers continued to believe in him, and he strongly admonished those who uncritically accepted such popular superstitions, "for they are the affairs of women and the masses."[26]

Elsewhere in *Sefer Elim*, Delmedigo himself recounted the affair, underscoring the chicanery of the father.[27] In another work, *Maẓref la-Ḥokhmah*, he once more proclaimd: "But as regards the affair of the Polish child from Grodek, it was a trick, as I have shown to all the world when I came to see it."[28]

According to the accounts of Delmedigo and Metz, the matter ended with the excommunication of the father and the premature death of his son, even though they acknowledged that a small number of enthusiastic supporters stubbornly persisted in believing in the boy, "because of their own embarrassment in revealing how ignorant they had been." But both Delmedigo and Metz apparently had underestimated the magnetic appeal of the Polish wonder child. For despite Delmedigo's insistence that he had shown the world the trick of the boy's father, there remained those who either ignored Delmedigo's demonstration or else remained impervious to Delmedigo's claim that he had ever exposed the father in the first place. In fact, Delmedigo's assumption that his disclosure had convincingly closed the case of the Grodek boy was perhaps more wishful thinking than an accurate reading of the responses of the boy's following.

Besides the material collected in Delmedigo's writings, there exists an additional letter about the Polish child, written by Mordecai ben David Katz of Lvov to Ḥayyim Vital, the major disciple of Isaac Luria and the great kabbalistic authority in Safad. Katz, after having received Abraham Schor's first letter regarding the boy from Grodek, recopied Schor's entire letter as quoted in Delmedigo's work and then added the following story:

A female servant had worked for a certain Jew in the holy congregation of Potylicz. When two years had passed, she ran away from the Jew without telling him that she was running away. But immediately after her escape, some hostile gentiles from the same place of Potylicz arose to slander this Jew by saying: "Where is this woman servant who had worked for you?" But the Jew did not know where she had fled. In short, this confusion continued to increase because of our many sins until God gave them the inspiration to say: "Let us go to visit and inquire of this same boy." And behold, when they came to the boy, before they said anything to him, the boy began to speak [of how] these men had come to investigate the whereabouts of the maidservant, and he mentioned her by name, that she was alive, and that they should be relieved of their confusion.[29]

The boy had intended to reveal the woman's whereabouts but was suddenly interrupted by "one wicked man" (a reference to Delmedigo?) who began to argue with the boy's father, causing him to flee from the place. Subsequently the boy would say nothing more. Rabbi Katz asked Vital to examine the entire matter in order to advise him what action to take. He turned to Vital because he had heard that shortly before Isaac Luria had died, he had told his disciple Vital that during the latter's lifetime "one boy would appear in the land of Edom [Christian lands] who would relate wondrous and terrible things of God."[30]

We come finally to Yagel's testimony. Yagel first heard the news of the Polish child in the fall of 1620, while he was residing in Modena. He mentions the boy's impressive knowledge of Jewish law, his ability to answer any question posed to him, and his successful deterrence of "the many who rose up against him to kill him." He also states that the boy heard the sweet songs of angels in his ears but that beyond this it is impossible for him to recount all of the boy's numerous accomplishments. He does, however, emphasize the miraculous dimension of the boy's achievements.[31]

Some months later Yagel added the following details:

Ten Jewish authorities of considerable stature from those regions [of Poland] went and found the boy, met with him in a certain place, and asked him to tell them about the redemption and the transformation and the secret of when the wondrous end will come. But the boy refused to answer until they adjured him in the name of God that he tell what he knew. Then he replied: "Know that you will not be set at peace by my words." But their hearts were most troubled concerning this and the men pleaded with him. But when he began to answer them that on the next [Hebrew month of] Nisan birth pangs will begin and a period of trouble will come to Jacob, he could not manage to say that they would be saved and how the salvation would transpire, for a fire fell from heaven and he departed in a storm and was no longer visible to them.[32]

Upon witnessing this miraculous sight, the entire community mourned and fasted in trepidation. Yagel relates that after some forty days the boy finally returned, to the delight and relief of the community. But this time, the rabbis zealously guarded the child and refrained from asking him any more provocative questions.[33]

THE MOST INTERESTING aspect of Yagel's report of the Polish child is its striking contrast to that of Joseph Delmedigo. Delmedigo apparently derided such wonder-workers as the boy of Grodek because of his own scientific proclivities and rational attitudes. But his contemporary Yagel, an erudite physician and scientific enthusiast in his own right, chose to treat such wonders seriously and credulously.

From both of Yagel's letters on the wonder child, it is evident that he was well aware of the great importance of the motif of the child prodigy in earlier Jewish literature.[34] An exceedingly rich source for this motif was the literature of the Jewish mystics. The stories about young children with wondrous abilities appearing before wise men and other adults with startling revelations of mystical knowledge were especially favorite subjects of the author of the *Zohar*.[35] Yagel himself mentions the parallel between these stories and his Polish marvel.[36]

Of special significance in this regard is the fascinating story of the character of Rabbi Gaddiel, made famous most recently in the writing of S. Y. Agnon and particularly well known in Jewish kabbalistic literature of the seventeenth century. The story concerns a wonder child who possessed divine knowledge and was killed at the age of seven by his enemies but ascended to the Garden of Eden to learn the divine mysteries from God himself. As Gershom Scholem has demonstrated, the midrashic work *The Testament of R. Eliezer the Great* is the original source of this story. Later it was copied by Ḥayyim Vital and incorporated into the writings attributed to Isaac Luria and into later midrashic collections of the seventeenth and eighteenth centuries.[37]

The stories of Rabbi Gaddiel and of the Grodek boy are parallel in several respects, particularly in Yagel's version. Like Rabbi Gaddiel, the Polish child possesses divine knowledge, as the singing of angels in his ears suggests. Both encounter enemies who desire to kill them. Even the background of gentile hostility to Jews, more obvious in the martyrdom of Gaddiel, is intimated in the Grodek boy's involvement in the episode of the Jew and his missing Christian maid.

But Yagel apparently had more than a literary motif in mind when reflecting on the meaning of the Polish child. He also recalls a similar boy prophet appearing in the Spanish Jewish community at the end of the thirteenth century. He had read the well-known *responsum* of Rabbi Solomon ben Adret, describing an unusual child in Avila who, though ignorant and untutored, had experienced angelic visions that inspired him to write a book of biblical commentaries.[38] In suggesting an analogy between the two boys,[39] Yagel could not have failed to note the common eschatological background of their prophetic statements. The visions of the Spanish child were directly related to an inspired Joachimite apocalyptic literature appearing at the end of the thirteenth century. In fact Avila itself had emerged as a conjectured place of origin of the Messiah, who was to appear in 1295. The aura of messianic anticipation was also manifest in the Grodek child, who, according to the testimonies of both Schor and Yagel, was pressed by his contemporaries to foretell when the messianic redemption would come.

The messianic theme was even more prominent in the tale of another illustrious Jewish child prodigy named Nahman, upon which Yagel had already commented.[40] The story of this youthful prophet was traditionally ascribed to David ben Abraham Maimuni (1222–1300), the head of the Egyptian Jewish community who is thought to have written a commentary for the rabbis of Barcelona on the apocalypse prophesied by Nahman. In fact these prophecies were most likely written close to the time of David Maimuni, sometime during the thirteenth century.[41] In 1517 the prophecies of Nahman enjoyed a renewed popularity as a result of the commentary of Rabbi Abraham ben Eliezer ha-Levi, a Spanish émigré and kabbalist, completed in Jerusalem in the same year. Primarily because of Rabbi Abraham's treatment of Nahman, the prophecies were widely circulated among the Spanish Jewish immigrants who had settled in Italy, Turkey, and Palestine. At the end of the sixteenth century, Gedaliah ibn Yahya included the story of Nahman in his historical narrative, and, like the Gaddiel narrative, it was also incorporated into a famous seventeenth-century collection.[42]

In 1598 Yagel responded to two different queries about the prophecies of Nahman from the well-known Italian kabbalist Menaham

Azariah da Fano, with whom he had corresponded on several other occasions. Fano asked Yagel to explain first the astrological circumstances of Nahman's birth and then the prophecies themselves. In answer to the first question, Yagel concluded that Nahman's astrological data suggested a premature and unnatural death for the boy. In his response to the second, Yagel copied the boy's biography as told to him by Fano—the circumstances of his parents, his prophecy at birth, his long silence for twelve years, his final blessing to his parents, and his premature death—and then offered a learned interpretation.

Obviously, in the mind of Yagel, the phenomena of Nahman and the Grodek youth were distinctly connected. Having reflected on both children over a span of some twenty years, he could not have failed to notice the obvious similarities between the two youths—their precocity, their premature deaths, and, most significantly, the messianic theme that infused both their stories. Nahman, it seems, had an opportunity to utter his messianic prophecies, whereas the Grodek boy was interrupted by a heavenly fire before speaking of the redemption. But both stories were the result of the same collective mood of messianic expectation agitating the Jewish community of the sixteenth and seventeenth centuries. Yagel's obvious sense of personal involvement in both stories indicates that he, too, had been affected by that mood.

One other detail of Yagel's explanation of Nahman is worth noting. When Fano asked him whether Nahman was an authentic prophet, Yagel answered negatively. Instead, he placed him in the category of a monster, a species that, he explained, was well known in nature and previously documented by ancients such as Xenophon and by medieval Arabic scholars such as Aben Ragel. Yagel's references in his narrative on the Siamese twins of Venice and in this letter on Nahman are identical.[43] Although twenty years had passed between the writing of the two accounts, he clearly had not forgotten his thoughts on the monstrous birth of Venice when reflecting on Nahman and his prodigious accomplishments. The connection established in his own mind between the Grodek child and Nahman was similar to the one between the Venetian children and Nahman. And in one obvious way all the children were related, he believed: they were all monsters.[44]

YAGEL'S COMPARISON OF the Grodek child with Rabbi Gaddiel, the child from Avila, and Nahman reveals only one side of his fascination with the phenomenon of child prodigies in Jewish culture. There remains the "scientific" side to consider. The tale of the Polish boy, for Yagel, was not a theme unique to the Jewish experience. It was also symptomatic of a condition shared by all human beings, subject to the same universal processes inherent in nature.[45]

In considering the Grodek lad, Yagel is especially struck by the boy's visionary faculties: "according to what has been heard, he is accurate in what he says and is consistently wise and knowledgeable; one asks and he responds; one asks about a given subject and he answers correctly as if he were a mature person who had acquired knowledge and possessed heavenly sapience to foretell the future."[46] Such ability, Yagel concludes, is a universal attribute of certain individuals, both Jews and non-Jews, who are prepared to receive divine inspiration either "according to a natural disposition or a disposition achieved by [their own] effort."[47] After defining this kind of prophetic aptitude, Yagel presents several historical examples. First he recalls Balaam and his prophetic abilities.[48] Then he mentions two child prophets who appeared in medieval Christian society, both of whom were uneducated and simple folk:

Observe what happened to the seventeen-year-old girl who was a shepherdess during the time of Charles VII, the king of France, who was surrounded by the armies of the English king, which almost took from him [Charles] his entire kingdom. But this young maiden arose, aroused herself from her slumber, gathered her strength, left her flock in the field, went to King Charles, and told him what she told him; the essence of her words was that she desired to lead his armies and to be victorious over his enemies. And the king trusted her word and placed her in charge of his army; and she girded her weaponry and fought the king's enemies and was victorious over them with great honor. And chroniclers of that time sang her praises as if she were skilled in war from her youth and knew her enemy's strategy in war.[49]

And who would believe the account of the child born in England named Merlin, who revealed future events and secret things and who transcribed in a document before the kings and nobles all that would happen to them in the end of days, in addition to all the incredible feats he accomplished in the days of his youth, which were recorded in the chronicles of that kingdom?[50]

Yagel concludes his short history of divine seers by mentioning two Jewish visionaries, the child prophet of Avila and the more recent messianic figure, Solomon Molcho.[51] The prophetic gifts of all these individuals, he explains, were transitory, and in some cases, such as those of Joan of Arc and Solomon Molcho, the prophets died an unnatural and premature death. These historical predecents, he considered, were sufficient to lend credibility to the fantastic tale of the child from Grodek.

Yagel's natural explanation of the prophetic gift is similar to the approaches of some learned Christians. Agostino Nifo and Pietro Pomponazzi had presented parallel expositions of prophetic endowment almost a century earlier.[52] More recently, Girolamo Cardano had explained that certain human beings exceeded others in their inborn powers of clairvoyance and divination.[53] In his massive scientific encyclopedia, *De Rerum Varietate,* Cardano claimed that he himself possessed the power to go into a trance whenever he pleased, to see anything he wished by the force of his own imagination, and to foresee his own future in dreams or in his fingernails. Immediately following the description of his own endownments, Cardano presented a catalogue of other unnatural and miraculous phenomena, including descriptions of both Joan of Arc and Merlin.[54] Yagel knew of Cardano's work, quoted him directly on other occasions (see Chapter 6 below), and appears to have been profoundly influenced by this erudite but eccentric Christian scholar.[55] In all likelihood, Yagel, in reflecting on the authenticity of the Grodek child, consulted Cardano's work and used the descriptions of the French and English children that he found there.

Yagel's explanation of the prophetic abilities of Nahman is somewhat different, however. He places Nahman in the category of monsters, a category he had already utilized in describing the Venetian infants and a category that would also fit quite well his portrait of the Grodek child. By referring to this category, Yagel revealed strikingly his knowledge of the popular and scientific literature of his day directly related to the subject of wonder children. By the sixteenth and early seventeenth centuries, books on the bizarre extravagances of nature had appeared throughout Europe. As Jean Céard and others have demonstrated, the prevailing fascination with monsters and prodigies stemmed from the desire to record and measure every abnormality so as to penetrate the order and regularity of the universe.[56] Monsters testified to the fecundity and multiformity of nature; they also functioned as portents of things to come. A knowledge of these signs permitted humans to acquire greater wisdom about the universe, but at the same time they dramatically indicated the finitude of human experience. For nature still chose to hide its face, to deceive mankind. Thus, accompanying the effort to explain monsters in a natural context was a chilling fear that not all had yet been explained. The monster might also represent a sign, an omen, a celestial notice of the potential terror and instability of the yet unknowable future. In the sixteenth century, the "natural sciences" of divination and teratology remained intertwined.[57]

Girolamo Cardano was especially preoccupied with numerous tales of monsters and monstrous births and their relation to divination. That Yagel, his Jewish admirer, was clearly of like mind is demonstrated not only by Yagel's preoccupation with Nahman and the Siamese twins but also by his fascination with psychic phenomena in his medical correspondence and by his systematic treatment of dreams and divination in *Beit Ya'ar ha-Levanon*.

In the cases of the Grodek child, Nahman, and the Venetian twins, Yagel encountered a subject familiar to him from his previous reading on divination and teratology and from his own medical experience. Instead of rejecting such children out of hand, Yagel treated them as matters worthy of psychological explanation. Contemporary science as understood by Yagel, Cardano, and others could not distinguish clearly between the universe as a religious subject and as a scientific one. The Siamese twins of Venice could be explained by material and astrological causes, but they were also prominent manifestations of divine wrath. And in the literary setting of Yagel's *Gei Ḥizzayon* they became remarkable mouthpieces of the divine truth. Similarly for Yagel, Nahman and the Grodek child were concurrently objects of scientific inquiry and omens of messianic redemption, curious prodigies of the natural world who ironically also offered reassurance to a society in anxious search of miracles.

Because prophecy, magic, and the miraculous occupied an ill-defined area often indistinguishable from scientific experimentation in the cultural world of Abraham Yagel, this Italian Jewish doctor came to share a common universe of discourse with the Polish rabbis and with the kabbalistic sages of Safad and Italy such as Vital and Fano. Despite the medical and scientific background he shared with Delmedigo, Yagel would have been uneasy with his colleague's categorical rejection of wonder children. Like his coreligionists, he treated them with the utmost seriousness, responding to their extraordinary behavior with credulity and curious amazement.

6. Comets and the New Heavens

Although it [Girolamo Cardano's view] is against ... Aristotle's view and method, nevertheless, I wrote this view, for it appears correct to me, after seeing [the words] of [the rabbi] Samuel the Babylonian.

—*Be'er Sheva*, pt. 2, chap. 15, fol. 49b

You shall truly see ... the words of a wise gentile man who in our day found several stars from a nebula that the ancients never saw, and he placed their signs and their markings in a book and also spoke of the appearances seen on the moon, and not in puzzles but the true opinion, and what are the analogous figures to the human face [seen] from above.

—*Beit Ya'ar ha-Levanon*, pt. 4, chap. 98, fols. 226b–227b

YAGEL'S FASCINATION with the natural world was not restricted to exotic fauna and flora. Although most of his extant naturalistic writings are devoted to the biological sciences, he was also knowledgeable about the celestial world. As was mentioned earlier, Menahem Azariah da Fano singled him out as "unique in our generation in the knowledge of the spheres"; he regularly used astrological prognostications in his medical practice; and he assumed that everything that happened in the material world was intimately linked to heavenly and divine processes above. For Yagel, knowledge of one world required, at least theoretically, a knowledge of the other two.

Several chapters of his encyclopedic works are devoted to astronomical matters.[1] Moreover, he also composed, or at least planned to compose, a commentary on the *Centiloquium*, a collection of 100 astrological aphorisms attributed to either Ptolemy or Hermes Trismegistus.[2] In the surviving introduction to this commentary, Yagel claims familiarity with Ptolemy's astronomical works and also mentions that he has compared the Greek version of the *Centiloquium* with its Arabic translation.[3]

Yagel's astronomical writings supply new evidence on the Jewish response to contemporary astronomical discoveries and the reevaluation of the Aristotelian cosmos among Christian intellectuals. Although the Christian response to the new astronomy, especially Copernicus' heliocentric theory, has been studied systematically and comprehensively, no similar investigation has yet been undertaken with respect to Jewish thought.[4] The only well-researched Jewish figures to have displayed considerable familiarity with the new astronomy were David Gans (1541–1613)[5] and Joseph Solomon Delmedigo (1591–1655).[6] Both were associated personally with the astronomical revolution: Gans knew Brahe and Kepler; Delmedigo was a student of Galileo. Both were aware of Copernicus' new theories and wrote about them in Hebrew; Delmedigo accepted the Copernican cosmology without reservation. Although it would be tempting to conclude from this small sample that Jewish thinkers were more open-minded than some of their Christian counterparts in accepting the assumptions of the new astronomy, the current lack of documentation makes such a conclusion unwarranted.[7]

Yagel's testimony offers an interesting contrast to Gans's and Delmedigo's, since his information appears to have been derived primarily from his reading. Two examples illustrate his awareness of and reaction to the astronomical discoveries of his day: his response to a new astronomical theory on comets that openly challenged the Aristotelian cosmogony, and his reflections on the discovery of the telescope, the most significant technological discovery of his generation, which offered dramatic support for the Copernican hypothesis.

In *Be'er Sheva* Yagel devotes a relatively long chapter to comets.[8] The theory of the origin of comets dominant from antiquity until the sixteenth century was that of Aristotle, described in his *Meteorology:*

> We have laid down that the outer part of the terrestrial world, that is, of all that lies beneath the celestial revolutions, is composed of a hot dry exhalation. This and the greater part of the air which is continuous with and below it are carried round the earth by the movement of the circular revolution: as it is carried round its movement, it frequently causes it to catch fire, wherever it is suitably constituted, which we maintain is the cause of scattered shooting stars. Now when as a result of the upper motion, there impinges upon a suitable condensation a fiery principle which is neither so very strong as to cause a rapid and

widespread conflagration, nor so feeble as to be quickly extinguished, but which is yet strong enough and widespread enough; and when besides, there coincides with it an exhalation from below of suitable consistency; then a comet is produced, its exact form depending on the form taken by the exhalation.[9]

Inextricably tied to Aristotle's view of the universe, his theory of comets rested on the basic distinction between a perfect celestial realm, where motion is eternal, circular, and not subject to change and decay, and a terrestrial realm, where motion is transient, moves in a straight line toward the center, and is subject to continuous change and decay. Since comets were clearly observable as transitory phenomena, it was impossible for Aristotle to locate them in the celestial realm; he was obliged to define them as fiery exhalations rising from the earth, carried around by the motion of the sky, and catching fire when ignited by that motion. To challenge Aristotle's cometary theory thus required challenging his entire cosmology.[10] For that reason, cometary theory in the sixteenth and seventeenth centuries was a central feature of the new assault against the Aristotelian universe, launched by a swelling number of astronomers now armed with more sophisticated tools for calculation and observation.[11]

One of the earliest of this group to contest openly the Aristotelian view of comets was the Italian scholar Girolamo Cardano.[12] Cardano was a distinguished physician and naturalist who held chairs of medicine at the universities of Pavia and Bologna and composed over two hundred works on medicine, mathematics, physics, philosophy, religion, and music. Multiple editions of his works appeared throughout the sixteenth century, and he was cited by numerous authors. In his two encyclopedias, *De Subtilitate* and *De Rerum Varietate,* Cardano argued that comets he had observed in Milan could not be formed of earthly vapors, because vapors could not rise far enough or burn long enough to account for how they looked. He suggested instead that, because comets appeared to move more slowly than the moon, thereby indicating that they were farther away, they were celestial phenomena. He also proposed using the method of parallaxes to determine whether comets were above or below the moon, although he did not provide calculations of such observations.[13] However, Cardano concluded that comets were globes formed in the sky and illuminated by the sun; the sun's rays shining through the comet accounted for the apparent beard or tail.

Because comets are seen best when the air is dry and when there are winds, Cardano understood them as portents of drought, corruption, famine, and death. Although he failed to make the necessary observations and computations later supplied by Tycho Brahe (1546–1601) and many others who described the comet of 1577 and those of the early seventeenth century, Cardano did openly deny the Aristotelian doctrine and at least suggested the use of parallax measurement.

In his own treatise on comets, Yagel apparently was more impressed by Cardano's writings on the subject than by any of the other sources he had consulted. He was familiar with the Aristotelian view of comets, for he defines it precisely at the beginning of his chapter.[14] However, upon examining "the words of the wise great doctor of his generation, Girolamo Cardano, whose opinion is different regarding their [the comets'] composition, location, appearance, largeness or smallness, motion, orbit, and duration," he discovered "proof and support for some of his arguments from the words of our great sages of sacred memory and from the words of Ptolemy and Abi l-Ridjal [Aben Ragel]."[15] Support from the latter two authorities was already available to Yagel in Cardano's own arguments, especially in his commentary on Ptolemy's *Quadripartitum*.[16] But Yagel on his own initiative supplies rabbinic support for his thesis. This appeal to Jewish authority constitutes the most original part of Yagel's composition and the most revealing testimony on why he preferred Cardano's view of comets to Aristotle's.

As we have seen, Yagel was indebted to Cardano for much more than his views on comets. He quoted him on other occasions and appears to have relied on his views on divination, monsters, and bizarre fauna.[17] Most important, Yagel may have used Cardano's two encyclopedias as models for his analogous Hebrew compositions. Both men were fascinated by the wonders of nature, the occult, and the new discoveries in astronomy and geography, and both approached science from a profoundly religious orientation. Although Yagel consulted a wide variety of sixteenth-century writers and never relied on one source, Cardano's broad intellectual plan as well as his specific views on individual topics unquestionably made a lasting impression on him.

Yagel, however, did not hesitate to disagree with his Italian mentor when the latter's views contradicted what for Yagel constituted well-established truth. Thus he challenged Cardano's emphatic rejection of Aristotle's doctrine of the four elements, despite his admiration for the Bolognese doctor.[18] In opening his discussion of the elements, Yagel remarked:

> In the days of our fathers, one wise man arose from among the Christian scholars who held the opinion that the elements were three. His name was Girolamo Cardano, a philosopher, astronomer, and great physician, who, on the basis of the wondrous strength of his wisdom and the written words in his many books, cannot be dismissed so his name be forgotten. For behold in his book . . . he concluded that the elements were three and they were earth, water, and air. And he did not mention fire, saying that fire is never an element in the universe but only the heat from the sun. And since the sun heats especially the uppermost region of the air, the ancients thus considered that a fourth element derived from fire is located there, a view that is not his view.[19]

After summarizing Cardano's innovation, Yagel seems to express admiration for its simple logic; though predisposed to maintain his belief in the theory of four elements, he readily admits that even a false assumption can yield correct conclusions.[20] But in this case, good logic is not enough to countervail the weight and time-honored authority of all previous generations:

> What further justification is needed when every sect of scholars, ancients and moderns, [accepts the thesis of four elements] and the matter is publicized in the world and everyone has accepted [the reality of the four elements] as a primary proposition? If the natural philosophers built their entire philosophies on them [the theory of the four elements]; if the doctors who came after them established and inquired regarding changing compositions on the basis of the truthfulness of the four elements; if the astronomers similarly assumed their reality . . . Also the rabbis of sacred memory mentioned the four elements in an accepted and publicized manner for anyone . . . thus who are we to enlarge upon a matter that even schoolchildren know, and anyone who disputes this fact is like one who disputes the senses and that accepted by all authorities? For these wise sages did not count the four elements as kinds of mixtures so that we might consider whether to increase or decrease them, but rather they established by observable proof that there are four, no less and no more.[21]

Yagel's emphatic rejection of Cardano's position in the name of a universal community of scholars—natural philosophers, physicians, astronomers, rabbis, and even recent kabbalistic authorities, including Moses Cordovero[22]—leaves no doubt about the limits his traditional thinking imposed upon him when he considered unusually novel and even logically coherent ideas. Since Yagel could discover no authoritative precedent for Cardano's unique viewpoint or any apparent deficiency in the regnant Aristotelian doctrine, he ultimately could not accept such a novelty.[23]

This rejection of Cardano's theory about elements makes Yagel's ready acceptance of his novel departure from Aristotle regarding comets all the more intriguing. Yagel familiarized himself with Cardano's cometary theory by consulting both *De Subtilitate* and *De Rerum Varietate*. He carefully summarizes the discussions there regarding the location, composition, and motion of comets and why Cardano could not accept the Aristotelian position.[24] Yagel also copies or paraphrases major sections of Cardano's commentary on Ptolemy's *Quadripartitum*, in which Cardano demonstrated that Ptolemy's view supported his own and contradicted that of Aristotle.[25] Here Yagel summarizes Cardano's discussion of the three kinds of comets, the description of comets seen in the times of Josephus and Charles Martel, and the specific influence exerted by the various planets on comets coming into proximity with them.[26]

Yagel interrupts his synopsis of Cardano with a discussion of the planetary influences on comets that he claims to have taken from a work by the thirteenth-century Italian astrologer Cecco D'Ascoli.[27] Cecco is best remembered for a small didactic poem called *L'acerba*, which includes a short section on comets. The Venetian edition, printed in 1560, includes a commentary by a fifteenth-century Italian named Niccolò Masetti. Yagel used this edition, translated the commentary almost word for word, but attributed it to Cecco D'Ascoli himself.[28] Apparently impressed by Masetti's colorful narrative, Yagel inserted this text into his discussion because of its clear relevance to the subject under discussion.

Then Yagel returns to Cardano's commentary, reproducing his lengthy discussion of astrological prognostications based on the observation of comets. Cardano had listed ten general factors in making such predictions: the comet's size, type, light, location, its relation to the place from which it is seen on earth, its relation to other planets, its location within the four parts and the twelve astrological houses of the sky, its shape, duration, and movement. Yagel takes up each of these factors, occasionally inserting his own observations.[29] Cardano had provided numerous examples, especially of comets portending religious change. He had mentioned in particular the comets accompanying the Magi at Christ's birth. Yagel delicately passes over the event but nevertheless recalls: "The matter [of comets' portending religious change] is substantiated by scholars regarding the origin of the Christian and the Muslim faiths and that of the heretics [Protestant reformers] who have recently appeared."[30]

At this point Yagel allows himself a digression on the astrological consequences of the appearance of a comet during the birth of a child according to the comet's precise location in the sky.[31] His primary source for this section was Leopold of Austria's chapter on comets in *Compilatio de Astrorum Scientia*.

Having exhausted the subject of the astrological impact of comets, Yagel has still to resolve the central issue dividing Cardano from Aristotle. As if to allow Aristotle one more hearing before resolving the matter, Yagel devotes the remainder of his treatise to a detailed summary of the views of one of Aristotle's major supporters, Albertus Magnus. In his commentary on Aristotle's *Meteorology* Albertus had recapitulated and refuted the views of every major opponent of Aristotle known during Albertus' lifetime.[32] But despite the comprehensiveness of Albertus' arguments, Yagel remains unconvinced: "But you, nice reader, know and believe that for every argument Albertus can make and for the proofs he brought, we are able as well, from our side, to present other proofs and other rebuttals to affirm every view of the ancient philosophers whom he disputed and ridiculed, despite the fact that he was a great wise man and philosopher in his generation who was committed to the truth."[33]

What encouraged Yagel to resist Albertus' demonstrations so firmly and to support instead Cardano's bold departure from Aristotle? He writes:

If it [Cardano's view] is against the opinion of wise philosophers who follow Aristotle's view and method, nevertheless, I wrote this view, for it appears correct to me after seeing [the words] of [the rabbi] Samuel the Babylonian . . . regarding meteors [*zikin*], earthquakes, thunder, winds, and lightning, one says: "Blessed be He whose strength fills the world. What are *zikin?* Samuel said a *kokhva deshavit* [a comet]." And Samuel stated: "The paths of the heavens are as familiar to me as the streets of Nehardea with the exception of the comet of which I am ignorant.

What is it? For it was taught that [no comet] ever passed through the constellation of Orion, for if it passed through, the world would be destroyed. But has it not appeared to have passed through? Its splendor passed through, which made it appear to have passed through."[34]

Yagel proceeds to explain that Samuel's *kokhva de-shavit* can refer only to a comet. Despite the fact that Samuel "was a great wise man in the science of astrology," he still confessed his ignorance of the origin of comets: "For there is no doubt that he had learned much wisdom from the writings of the Greeks who had preceded him by some five hundred years, and if he had been inclined to accept their words, he would not have asked: 'What is it?'"[35] However, Yagel explains, Samuel's answer is totally consistent with Cardano's position. Samuel had no idea of the comet's essence because it is only the gathering place of light rays from the stars and assumes no definable form. Furthermore, when he taught that a comet never passes through the constellation of Orion, Samuel was simply stating that comets move away from the Equator toward the North Pole (near Orion). When he suggested that the world would be destroyed if a comet passed through Orion, he was indicating that a comet moving past the North Pole becomes stationary, since the pole is stationary. Thus the motion of most comets is usually below the pole; yet if they enter the vicinity of the pole, they engender drought, famine, and earthly destruction.[36]

However forced Yagel's exegesis of Samuel's words might appear, it seems to have provided him with sufficient support of Cardano's position. Cardano had adequately demonstrated to him the insurmountable problems related to Aristotle's theory. He also had observed that Cardano had enlisted the authority of Ptolemy and Abi l-Ridjal on his side. All Yagel required was a familiar rabbinic precursor whose view seemed to approximate that of Cardano, and this he found in Samuel. And if any doubt lingered about the reliability of this novel approach, he always could take comfort in the fact that even Samuel never fully understood the nature of the comet: "For we are not haughty enough to believe that we better understand what Samuel, of sacred memory, understood, for the secret things belong to God."[37]

OF ALL THE INVENTIONS of the seventeenth century, Galileo's telescope certainly was the most important, and of all the publications of that era, his *Sidereus Nuncius* undoubtedly generated the most enthusiasm.[38] Initially printed in Venice in 1610 in a limited edition of 500 copies, it rapidly became a best-seller. The full title of the work already conveyed its feverish pitch of excitement: "The Starry Messenger, revealing great, unusual, and remarkable spectacles, opening these to the consideration of every man, and especially of philosophers and astronomers . . . with the aid of a spyglass lately invented by him, in the surface of the moon, in innumerable fixed stars, in nebulae, and above all, in four planets swiftly revolving around Jupiter . . . and known to no one, before the author recently perceived them and decided they should be named the Medicean Stars."

In a crisp, engaging style Galileo announced to his countrymen the remarkable revelation of peering through his lead tube fitted with two glass lenses and focusing on the surface of the moon, the constellations of Orion, Taurus, and the Pleiades, the Milky Way, and the moons of Jupiter. The impact on European culture was almost instantaneous. The spyglass stirred the imagination of poets, prose writers, philosophers, and theologians to new heights, dramatically underscoring the vastness of the universe and the minuteness of human beings.

Yagel shared this sense of excitement. In *Beit Ya'ar ha-Levanon* he opens a short chapter on Galileo's discovery in the following manner:

> Our words were sincere, that in every generation things will be revealed to humanity that never were imagined by the ancients . . . For behold you have seen among the fruits of the earth and the animals of the forest what we wrote in previous chapters of our composition, and also now in this chapter, you shall truly see that my witness which is in heaven and my work which is on high[39] will appear regarding the words of a wise gentile man who in our day found several stars from a nebula that the ancients never saw, and he placed their signs and their markings in a book and also spoke of the appearances seen on the moon, and not in puzzles but the true opinion, and what are the analogous figures to the human face [seen] from above.[40]

Paraphrasing the Talmud's characterization of Samuel, which he has already quoted in connection with comets, Yagel expresses his intense admiration for Galileo: "The paths of the heavens are as familiar to him as the streets of Florence where he dwells."[41]

Yagel's Hebrew report on the *Sidereus Nuncius* was probably written soon after the book first appeared.[42] Yagel was not the only Jew to describe Galileo's observations through the telescope; Joseph Delmedigo had known of the instrument and had even looked through it on many occasions under the supervision and guidance of Galileo himself.[43] But Yagel's chapter is of historical interest as the spontaneous reaction of a Jew who first learned of the spectacular disclosure simply by reading Galileo's book.

What most impressed Yagel about Galileo's book was its description of the construction of the telescope itself and its manifold uses. His first inclination was to understate the novelty of the instrument by locating Jewish precursors. His search yielded two analogous inventions. He describes the first as "what is found in the words of our rabbis of blessed memory in the [talmudic tractate] *Eruvin*, regarding the same tube that was in the hand of Rabban Gamaliel, which allowed him to see as far as two thousand cubits within the Sabbath boundary."[44] The second he discovered in the tenth-century commentary on the *Sefer Yeẓirah*, written by the Italian Jewish physician Shabbetai Donnolo. In the introduction to this work, Donnolo described his teacher in astronomy, an Arab named Bagdash, whose teaching agreed with that of the ancients and that of the Jews, especially the homiletic work on astronomical matters, the *Baraita de-Shemu'el*, and who taught him how to use an instrument that Yagel considered to be the same as Galileo's spyglass. "And thus the secret of the instrument in which the paths of heaven are seen was covered up, for our forefathers never imagined it and now it has been revealed, for there is nothing new under the sun."[45]

But the fact that the instrument had previously been discovered by Jews in no way diminishes Yagel's gratitude to Galileo for his "rediscovery": "For we are to praise this emissary selected for this, by whose words the moderns are capable of seeing the paths of the firmaments and things that were hidden from their eyes. And also this instrument can be used by them in sea passages, to estimate boundaries, fortified cities, and towers."[46] Thus Yagel also noticed, beyond its scientific value, the economic and military utility of so useful an invention. He then describes the materials of the instrument, its construction, and precise directions for its use. He briefly relates the sight Galileo beheld while looking through the telescope: the surface of the moon, the cluster of small stars making up the Milky Way, and other clusters never before visible to the naked eye.

Most important, Yagel is noticeably aware of the revolutionary impact of these discoveries in relation to the Aristotelian cosmos:

> For in this [the discovery of the new star clusters], he shocked all the traditional astronomers, forcing them to augment the heavenly spheres and totally upsetting the applecart regarding the theory of the ancients, which was held tenaciously until this day. For in his judgments and arguments he will destroy all the wisdom of Ptolemy and his associates if one does not answer him with the words of the philosophers. For Maimonides wrote in the *Guide* [1.73] that the senses will deceive us, for already authorities of our generation, great in learning and in number, have arisen to write libelously against him, presenting counterarguments against him.[47]

For Yagel, the intellectual commotion stirred by Galileo is parallel to that engendered by the twelfth-century Arab astronomer al-Biruni, who openly attacked the astronomical edifice of Aristotle and Ptolemy. This Arab, too, "sought to destroy the foundations of learning in astronomy, and his words have remained as a closed book until the present generation."[48]

What precisely Yagel had in mind in describing Galileo as a destroyer of the foundations of astronomy is not clear. Did he truly appreciate that Galileo's evidence could now be used to confirm the Copernican universe, that Jupiter's moons as celestial bodies are subject to the same laws of motion as bodies observable on earth, that the planets appear to revolve around the sun, and that the earth is "a wandering body surpassing the moon in splendor"?[49] Nowhere in his writing does he mention Copernicus. Unlike David Gans and Joseph Delmedigo, Yagel makes no explicit reference to the heliocentric theory; on the contrary, his usual descriptions of the universe offer no traces of deviation from the Aristotelian cosmology.[50] Nevertheless, as his enthusiasm about Galileo confirms, he knew more than he chose to describe here. Elsewhere he referred to Giovanni Antonio Magini of Padua, who in 1589 published a work titled *New Theories of Celestial Orbs Agreeing with the Observations of Copernicus*.[51] Yagel also was familiar with the writings of Francesco Giuntini, another Italian who had presented the Copernican hypothesis in a favorable light.[52]

Even more revealing is Yagel's knowledge of the popular Prutenic tables, which followed Copernicus' calculations but were silent on his heliocentric cosmology: "[Some scholars] will not hesitate to assume a false hypothesis in order to uphold a truthful corollary. See what Niccolò Prutenco did, who hastily conceived tables of the stellar movements . . . they are considered to be the most truthful calculation of their latest scholars . . . but they are based on silver foundations from a well-known false assumption that the constellation stands while the earth moves. There is no doubt that he was exceedingly wise and intelligent and didn't believe this thing."[53] Yagel leaves little doubt that he does not believe "this thing" either.

Yagel's silence regarding Galileo's support of Copernicus seems to betray a lack of confidence in the new theory and also a note of discomfort. How could this Galileo, he writes, so bombastically pronounce the death of the traditional system with so much assurance and arrogance: "For who is this man who comes after the 'king' who established the foundations of learning followed by all scholars in every generation? He is no other than a man precipitate in his work, haughtily rising up to proclaim: 'I will rule over all in riddles and guileful secrets . . . ' but his associates will not listen to him."[54]

In the end, however, Yagel's annoyance is tempered by a calming sense of security that God will reveal in due course what he chooses to reveal. The disclosures of this turbulent era, no matter how startling, are to be understood from the perspective of faith in God's bountiful goodness. So Yagel concludes: "There is nothing new under the sun, and what will be, will be, in controversies, in differences of opinion, in the order of all degrees and fields of learning, secret and hidden . . . for the truth will follow its course and God sits in heaven laughing, for to Him all the mysteries will be revealed."[55] The discomfort and insecurity induced by the new disclosures are only temporary. Ultimately, Galileo's conclusions will be judged one way or the other, while humanity's vision of God's omniscience and purposefulness remains firmly intact.

YAGEL'S RESPONSES to Cardano's comet theory and to Galileo's telescope reveal a familiarity with current astronomical literature that is especially impressive in one who was not a trained astronomer. He not only cites classical and medieval sources but also has read a leading sixteenth-century theorist on comets and reports on Galileo's famous tract only a short time after its publication. When viewed in the context of his notable erudition in medical, botanical, and zoological literature, as well as in rabbinic, kabbalistic, philosophical, and magical sources (discussed further in the following chapters), the encyclopedic character of Yagel's scholarship in scientific matters compares favorably with that of Delmedigo, Gans, Portaleone, and other distinguished Jewish scholars of his generation.

Yagel's reaction to scientific novelty was cautiously skeptical but never closed-minded. The implications of Galileo's findings evoked in him noticeable unease but not anxiety. The sanctified authority of Jewish sources remained a dominant element in his thinking. When a new theory such as Cardano's could be linked successfully with an earlier rabbinic statement, the theory was made credible, even against the weighted authority of the Aristotelian tradition. Similarly, Galileo's telescope, when viewed as a "rediscovery" of an invention known to a Jewish authority centuries before, also appeared more plausible to him. Yagel's religious convictions did not appear to obstruct his ability to admit the new. By locating precedents within Jewish tradition, he was able to make the new more comprehensible and more compatible with his own experience. Yagel's testimony thus offers an interesting example of the distinctive capacity of Jewish thought to reorient itself to a new cultural situation while retaining a continuous bond with the past.

7. On Stretching the Permissible: The Place of Magic in Judaism

Seeing there is a three-fold world, Elementary, Celestial, and Intellectual, and every inferior is governed by its superior . . . it should be possible for us to ascend . . . through each world, to the same very originall world itself, the maker of all things and first cause.

—Henry Cornelius Agrippa,
Three Books of Occult Philosophy, bk. 1, chap. 1

It [magic] is a noble discipline, which is the act of creation . . . Not only are its actions and matters permissible, but it is a commandment, a commandment to understand and learn it.

—*Beit Ya'ar ha-Levanon*, pt. 4, chap. 107, fol. 244a

BESIDES LINKING medical and naturalistic concerns with magic, Yagel devoted several chapters to magic alone. Most unusual is a chapter at the end of the second part of *Beit Ya'ar ha-Levanon* that bears no apparent relation to the thirty preceding chapters, that breaks off in the middle of a sentence, and, unlike most of Yagel's other discourses in his expansive compendium, whose meaning is obscure.[1] One anonymous reader found the chapter so enigmatic that he filled in the empty space left in the manuscript with his own comments.[2] Although the announced topic was the secret of *Shi'ur Komah* (The measure of God's body),[3] this reader could provide little more than an expression of piety regarding the finitude of human knowledge and experience and the dangers of attempting to penetrate the sublime mysteries unavailable to human beings. The chapter was significant, claimed this commentator, because the author, although intending to interpret the mystery of God's measurements, "had begun to speak about it but did not finish. The wise man should listen and learn a lesson [from this]."[4]

Yagel's message, however, may be more transparent when situated in the larger context of other themes discussed elsewhere in his writings. It is my contention that Yagel's real purpose was the opposite of what his reader had imagined: not to warn his reader to be careful "of things that are above us," but rather to encourage him to overcome the old limits, "to dare to know" more and to utilize his human capacity to the fullest in being creative as God is creative.[5] Moreover, the content of the chapter is emblematic of some of Yagel's major concerns in all his writings regarding the role of magic: the comprehension of nature and the application of its powers for human benefit, and the legitimation of his occupation and self-image as doctor, occultist, and natural scientist within the religious traditions of Judaism.

Yagel opens the chapter by establishing the connection between knowing the measure of God's body and mastering the secret of the four worlds, a connection long assumed by many earlier kabbalists.[6] For Yagel, the study of the divine body was not mere anthropomorphic speculation but was actually synonymous with mystical illumination in general and the secret of the concatenation of the multiple levels of existence in particular. We have already seen how Yagel constantly emphasized the importance of the secret of the three worlds, which for him were essentially identical with the kabbalistic formulation of four worlds.[7] In this chapter, however, the theme is presented in a highly distinctive manner. Yagel opens with a pastoral story:

There was a man who had been a shepherd from his youth until his hair grew white. He led his flocks in deserts, in mountainous regions, and in faraway hills very distant from city folk. This was the case either because he had been taught by his forefathers to remove himself from robbery or because he realized himself and was afraid, for in the profession of shepherdry, it is good to be solitary and not to mix [with other] flocks [in order] to lessen controversies among shepherds. This desert person was bright and thoughtful. Not only did he ruminate about subjects related to his flock and herds; he also comprehended the course of the sun in its inclination, the length of days and their shortening. He would devise a scheme to know the divisions of the hours so that close to the time of the sunset he would gather his flock with a whistle. Also at night he would awaken himself to observe the stars Pleiades, Orion, and the Great Bear, and from them he would know the parts of the watches of the night, on either long or short nights.[8]

The shepherd finally decided to leave his flock in order to visit the city. There he observed the customs of urban life, especially a judge meting out justice. He compared the judge to a shepherd who directs his flock with righteousness and with the fairness of his intelligence. He absorbed calmly everything else he saw until he heard the sound of a clock coming from a high watchtower in the center of the city: "The man was astonished by the object and asked: 'How can this instrument, lacking the spirit of life in it, keep its orderly path correctly, swaying with equilibrium so that one hears its sound every hour in all the city?' He asked to ascend to the top of the tower to observe it, but the guards would not allow him to go, since it was the king's rule that no outsider could enter there."[9]

The shepherd then left the city still fascinated by the wonderful creation he had seen there from a distance. While watering his flock near the bottom of a waterfall he conceived the idea of creating something similar to mark the changes of time,

> to shape instruments from various articles that would make a sound when water passed through them, divided up at fixed times as exemplified by the sound he had heard from the tower. And so he did, connecting one instrument to another from those shepherd's basins made of hollow wood and dry and empty gourd husks. He erected them by the waterfall and established a line of measurement between them. But he saw that it did not work because the heavy stream of water broke the gourds. So then he placed the broken pieces between each instrument to temper the force of the waterfall.[10]

He succeeded in creating an instrument similar to the one he had seen and heard in the city. Some time later, a man from the city associated with the king passed by the shepherd's invention, saw it work, and reported to the king what he had observed. He praised this man's work, his native intelligence, and his extraordinary ability to create so sophisticated an instrument without proper materials or tools. For "he made the instrument like the one in the tower with only his own hands, and he brought to light with his own intelligence a small object related and similar to the big one."[11]

Yagel finally reaches the point of the parable:

Our fathers were always shepherds and cattlemen. They led their flocks in the desert, distancing themselves from robbery. Because of their righteous nature and sharp intelligence, they recognized and knew the wisdom of nature and reality and the rules of political organization and its magnificently built foundation . . . for they heeded the way of God to do righteously and justly . . . and with their intelligence, they tried to recognize "the Head of the citadel," blessed is the One who spoke and the world came to be, the living God who bestows life, strength, and sustenance to every living being, until their yearning brought them to the point where "the Head of the citadel" was revealed to our old father [Abraham] in a dream, in a prophetic vision.[12]

God thus revealed his righteous and wondrous ways to his people, his manner of creation without the aid of any other agency, and the complex variety of things—good and bad, light and darkness, heat and cold—all from one simple cause. The gift the shepherd had been given was also that of the Jewish people. In the case of the shepherd, "he remained astonished and silent to fathom the ways of the instrument in the tower whose acts and results he heard and understood, even though he had not observed the manner of the construction and the work in it."[13] Similarly, the wisest scholars prove incapable of penetrating all the secrets of creation, all of nature's variety and apparent contradictions. Some hypothesize that the world was created from inert matter upon which forms were stamped. Others maintain a universal duality such as "the belief of the Mani." But our forefathers, Yagel argues, negated all such beliefs and upheld one cardinal principle, that "from one simple cause HE created in the beginning everything in the heavens above and on the earth. The belief was established by prophecy and there is no doubt that it is proper and correct, a truth and a faith."[14]

Only the precise manner of creation remains unknown; some maintain that the variations and contradictions evolved as humanity became more distant from "the original source." Finally, Yagel concludes: "And just as the desert man attempted to level out the broken pieces by measurement in order to bring about the effects of the water so that the sound of the water was heard from a distance every hour and from these [effects] gained the virtue of the instrument in the tower that he had not seen, so, too these perfect people with us . . ."[15]

The crucial sentence remains unfinished, and Yagel's precise prescription to the heirs of the prophetic tradition is never spelled out. What indeed did Yagel have in mind in constructing an analogy between the creative shepherd and the Jewish people? What seems clear is that, like the simple shepherd, the Jewish people possess the natural faculties to be creative through the revelation received at Sinai. They need not rely on philosophic speculations, which are ultimately baseless, but only on their authentic legacy of understanding the divine. Although they have never witnessed the act of creation (as the shepherd never inspected the watchtower), they are endowed with the power to invent and to replicate God's creation.[16] The question remains, however, what are they to generate? Can they recreate objects of the natural world? Can they create other human beings? Do they actually have the power to imitate the creative divine act? Does the gift of Torah enable the Jew to assume a role usually assigned to God, that of supreme maker? Is the uniqueness of the Jewish prophetic tradition ultimately defined as the quality that enables its recipient to become a supermagician? And what does all of this have to do with the divine secret of *shi'ur komah*, the alleged subject of Yagel's chapter? The aborted narrative does not furnish a conclusive answer to any of these questions, but it is sufficiently suggestive to allow us to approach Yagel's extended discussions on magic and its place in Judaism with these intriguing questions in mind.

Yagel takes up the subject of magic and its related fields in the context of defining activities that are forbidden or permitted by Judaism. He had already addressed, at least indirectly, the permissible limits of human activity both in his excursus on the practice of medicine and its appropriate procedures and in his discourse on demonology.[17] In these discussions, Yagel had treated the proper function of magic in therapy and in demonic exorcism. He later treated the general subject of magic more directly in several chapters near the end of *Beit Ya'ar ha-Levanon*.[18] In an earlier chapter, however, he first raised the subject in considering the suitable criteria for reading and studying books of an allegedly harmful character.

YAGEL FIRST MENTIONS MAGIC in *Beit Ya'ar ha-Levanon* in connection with whether Jews are allowed to read from the books of the Apocrypha, especially the Wisdom of Ben Sira.[19] Yagel obviously was favorably disposed to reading these extracanonical writings.

Elsewhere he had even translated from the Greek a passage from 4 Esdras.[20] His discussion of the rabbinic passages on reading Ben Sira is reminiscent of a similar and more extended discussion by his Italian contemporary Azariah de' Rossi, in his *Me'or Einayim.*[21] De' Rossi probably composed his chapter earlier, and Yagel may have had access to it. Yet Yagel did not copy slavishly from de' Rossi, and it is certainly possible that he treated his subject independently. Whatever the case, both authors arrive at essentially the same conclusion after analyzing the key statements of the rabbis, especially B.T. Sanhedrin 100b. Although they claim that these ancient texts were not composed under the influence of "the holy spirit," they acknowledge that they contain worthwhile and morally beneficial statements and should be consulted and studied, albeit discriminately.[22] De' Rossi argues that the rabbis perused even heretical and magical books in order to assess the truth or falsehood of their opponents' positions.[23] Both authors regard the apocryphal writings as on a clearly higher level than the magical and heretical books; they recommend the reading of them by recourse to Maimonides' famous dictum: "Accept the truth from whoever states it."[24] Yagel adds that we should approach these works "as we do any book from the writings of a wise author whereby permission is granted to separate the food from the refuse."[25]

On the basis of this discussion, Yagel finally offers three general categories of "books that have been and will be written until the final day" that should be excluded from the overwhelming majority of titles a Jew is permitted to read. First are heretical writings that contain atheistic and dualistic views of God, works "that are against the faith of God that Moses established and against the rabbinic tradition."[26] Second are all writings that offer instruction in human activity that is expressly prohibited (in the Bible), such as "occult activity and [that of] a *magus* performed through the agency of Satan and destructive angels, or one who inquires by necromancy, soothsaying, and communicates with the dead [also] called 'necromancia'; and similarly, books written about fields and matters that harm human beings."[27] Third are humorous writing, poetry, and fictional histories "that arouse the passion of love." However, Yagel quickly adds that books on the natural, mathematical, astral, and divine sciences and true historical writings of kings and states "can be read when one has time," for anyone can learn from them "moral lessons and will understand the boundaries of nations and seas and will orient [himself] to the times, past, present, and future . . . One should find no difficulty [in mastering] historical events, for what was will be, and one should compare a similar thing to its counterpart."[28]

Yagel's approval of good history as distinguished from bad fiction was a sentiment undoubtedly shared by many of his contemporaries.[29] What is more interesting, in the context of the subject of magic, is his linkage of histories with books of science. Their common feature is that they "compare a similar thing to its counterpart."[30] As we have seen earlier, Yagel appealed to an epistemology of resemblance for determining truth and as a rationale for his investigations in medicine and the natural sciences. Like many of his contemporaries, Yagel understood the quest for knowledge of the natural world as a search for likeness or sameness; the study of history constituted part of the same quest.

The other writings excluded by Yagel from the canon of permitted books are not unexpected. We shall return later in this chapter to the second category, the books on satanic (black) magic and related fields subsumed under the category of necromancy. But first we shall consider Yagel's more comprehensive discussion of magical writings and practices, which elicits the following questions: How does he distinguish between works that are strictly forbidden and related works on natural, astral, and divine science that are permitted? Are they mutually exclusive categories? Is Yagel consistent in separating the two? And are there instances in which magic is not only permitted but enthusiastically endorsed by the Jewish religious tradition?

YAGEL TURNS AGAIN to the subject of magical practices permitted and forbidden in Judaism immediately after considering the subjects of demonology, the biblical witch of En-dor, and several morally repugnant practices of natives of the New World in the lands recently discovered by the Spanish.[31] Having pointed out what is unambiguously forbidden, Yagel next considers magical practices that can be considered acceptable and even morally beneficial.[32]

He bases his remarks on the classic rabbinic discussion of the problem in B.T. Sanhedrin 67a. There the rabbis differentiate between various kinds of magic, some forbidden and some permitted.[33] Yagel focuses on the conclusion of the discussion, where two rabbis are engaged in an activity called "the laws of creation," which enables them to create a young calf for their Friday night meal.[34] Quoting a similar passage only a few pages earlier, where the same incident is described as "the Book of Creation" (*Sefer Yeẓirah*),[35] Yagel attempts to ascertain in what kind of activity the rabbis were engaged. For in both cases, their actions testified to the fact that according to Jewish law, they were permitted to do what they did.

To answer the question, Yagel considers the responses of earlier interpreters of the rabbinic text. Rabbi Yeruham had argued that "the Book of Creation" was equivalent to practices that used the aid of demons and that were permitted by Jewish law. Rabbi Joseph Karo, however, contended that the activity described did not refer in any way to demons; it indicated only that, just as demonic activity is permitted, so too are practices related to "the Book of Creation." Karo, following the earlier interpretation of Rashi, argued instead that "the Book of Creation" should be identified with the ancient book attributed to Abraham "on the subject of [Hebrew] letter permutations by which the world came into being."[36]

Yagel's reaction to Karo's interpretation is mixed. On the one hand, he is favorably disposed to the view that "the Book of Creation" and demonology are two unrelated entities. On the other hand, he cannot support Karo's identification of the book and laws of creation mentioned in the Talmud with a specific book attributed to Abraham and considered a classic of the kabbalist tradition among Jews and Christians. For why would the rabbis include this activity with other explicit magical practices if they had meant Abraham's book, a work ostensibly unrelated to magic?[37] Another explanation was required.

Accordingly, Yagel himself offers a definition of magic. He begins with the definition of the rabbis found in B.T. Sanhedrin 67b together with Rashi's commentary: "Magicians [*kashafim*] are those who deny 'the household of heaven,'" to which Rashi added: "they kill that which was decreed to live." Yagel adds the following clarification: "[The term] magician [*mekhashef*] includes all the fields that the Bible explained; all of them are deceptions and lies regarding the order of the act of creation which is 'the household of heaven' and by which God in ten sayings worked and produced and ordered nature and the substances."[38] The magicians attempt to displace the natural processes by hastening the act of creation and thus distort the natural order, causing "iniquity and evil in their midst. Through their poisonous substances, they cause bodily harm, illness, and even death, and that is why the biblical text declares: 'The sorceress should be put to death.'"[39]

However, not all magicians perform the same functions, nor are all their activities forbidden. Yagel divides magic into three categories "according to the order of creation and reality": elemental or material, heavenly, and intellectual or divine. The triadic division is a familiar one in Yagel's writings. The threefold division was the major theme of the second half of his heavenly odyssey, *Gei Ḥizza-yon,* as well as the primary conceptual framework in his method of healing and his view of reality in general; moreover, Yagel had illustrated the secret of this triadic (or fourfold) universe, which he called *shi'ur komah,* by the shepherd parable.[40]

Yagel examines a number of places in rabbinic literature where the term *mekhashef* appears and he demonstrates that the term is synonymous with the Latin term *magus*.[41] But because it is a generic term, the word can be understood in different ways, referring to both the permitted and forbidden types of occult activity. The former type, which includes the activity of the physician, is called natural magic:

> For the wise man in the science of nature who is a doctor, craftsman, and fine philosopher who knows the substances and natures is called a *magus*. Because of his ability, he understands the composition of the elements, their active and passive sides, and he recognizes the best substances to use and to change them from good to evil and from evil to good through the virtues of herbs, their squeezing and their diffusion, until the fifth element is taken from them. [This individual] works immediately with materials according to the definition of their composition, which nature defined at the beginning of their creation. He knows when a composite substance is of a certain type and what matter is ready to receive a certain form, etc. This is a natural *magus,* and all his activities are permitted.[42]

There is no doubt that Yagel was profoundly influenced in his definition by Cornelius Agrippa's tripartite division of magic, which forms the basis for the three-part structure of *De Occulta Philosophia.* In his opening chapter, for example, Agrippa wrote: "Seeing there is a three-fold world, Elementary, Celestial, and Intellectual, and every inferior is governed by its superior, and receiveth the influence of the vertues thereof, wise men conceive in no way irrationall that it should be possible for us to ascend by the same degrees through each world, to the same very originall world itself, the maker of all things and first cause."[43]

Similarly, Agrippa defined magic as "a faculty of wonderful vertue, full of most high vertue, full of most high mysteries, containing the most profound contemplation of most secret things, the knowledge of whole nature, and it doth instruct us concerning the differing and agreement of things amongst themselves whence it produceth its wonderful effects, by uniting the vertues of things through the application of them one to the other, and to their inferior sutable subjects, joyning and knitting them together thoroughly by the powers and vertues of the superior bodies." [44] The rest of Agrippa's first book is devoted to analyzing all aspects of natural magic.

But Agrippa was not the only source of Yagel's definition. Yagel was also familiar with Bartolommeo Cocles' *Chyromantie ac Physionomie Anastasis*, whose introduction discussed the various categories of magic. [45] He may also have known Ficino's definition of the magician as "a contemplator and expositor of divine things . . . a wise man and a priest" [46] or Pico's assessment of magic as "the sum of natural wisdom, and the practical part of natural science, based on exact and absolute understanding of natural things." [47] He could have discovered a similar definition of magic in Martin Del Rio's treatise as "an art or technique, which by using the power in creation rather than a supernatural power, produces things of a marvelous and unusual kind, the reason for which escapes the senses and ordinary comprehension." [48] Even more accessible to him was Giambattista della Porta's famous handbook on natural magic, whose opening chapters on the nature of magic and general instructions for the magician were widely read and quoted. [49] Francesco Giuntini had also offered a similar definition of magic in a book well known to Yagel. [50] In short, Yagel followed not only Agrippa but a growing company of doctors, natural scientists, and occultists who considered the form of magic they practiced both licit and ennobling, morally correct and spiritually uplifting. As long as their magic was not harmful to humanity; as long as they refrained from distorting and corrupting "the household of heaven"; and as long as they pursued what was natural and beneficial, their function was religiously significant. As Ficino had suggested, they were both wise men and priests.

YAGEL HAD YET to offer an alternative to Karo's and Rashi's explanation of the rabbis' calf. And even before another explanation could be suggested, there remained the astonishing puzzle of the young calf itself. Did the rabbis actually create animals to butcher for Sabbath feasts? How was it that their actions were legitimate whereas other, more conventional forms of magic were not? Yagel certainly must have asked himself that question with respect to either the calf or the mute person formed by Rava, mentioned on the same talmudic page.[51] In either case, he could offer a rational answer. Upon concluding his definition of natural magic, Yagel adds:

> And even if he creates "a third-grown calf" or another animal or [even] a man, [it is permitted] as the scholars told us. For a man will be able to do this through the wisdom of nature; he only will be unable to give him the spirit of life in his nostrils . . . as Giulio Camillo wrote in his book; also the wise man, the author of *De Occulta Philosophia:* and Roger Bacon, along with other scholars, both recent and ancient, who offer instruction among themselves and their disciples to people [so that they] can change their initial nature and produce things and new creatures, removing and replacing forms according to the composition of the different kinds of substances.[52]

Yagel's lack of hesitation in pronouncing that the creation of life, even human life, was a licit practice of the natural magician, reflected a convergence in his thought of two authoritative traditions—the rabbinic-kabbalistic and the hermetic-magical—both of which spoke approvingly of the human act of creation. On the one hand, the rabbinic legends established a legitimate precedent and exemplar of appropriate human behavior. Creating life was seen not as a perversion of nature but as a pure and holy act in which man could confirm that he was created in the divine image and endowed with the divine creative powers. Whether "the Book of Creation," attributed to Abraham, was initially intended as a manual of magical practices or not, it was certainly considered as such by its major commentators.[53] Certainly Rashi and Joseph Karo, as Yagel had pointed out, had conceived it to be the instructional handbook the rabbis had used to make the calf. A tradition among the German pietists had also claimed that Abraham had created beings by a magical process suggested in "the Book of Creation."[54] Eleazar of Worms even offered instructions for creating such a being (a *golem*).[55] Kabbalists who lived at about the same time as Yagel—Meir ibn Gabbai, Moses Cordovero, and Abraham Azulai—also mentioned Jewish traditions of *golem* making. By the sixteenth and seventeenth centuries, accounts of producing artificial human beings were diffused throughout the Jewish community, especially in eastern Europe.[56]

The other legitimating authorities for creating artificial beings were the medieval and Renaissance traditions of magic and Hermeticism. Foremost was the *homunculus* of Paracelsus, the artificial embryo created by alchemical procedures from blood, sperm, and urine.[57] Other scholars had written about the artificial production of human beings, and Yagel offered a representative sampling of three of them—Roger Bacon, Henry Cornelius Agrippa, and Guilio Camillo. The first two are not surprising choices. Both Bacon of the thirteenth and Agrippa of the sixteenth century were considered magicians par excellence; if any sorcerers of the western European tradition were empowered by popular opinion with such abilities, it was most certainly they. By the sixteenth century, the legend that Friar Bacon had constructed an artificial head of brass but could not make it speak had gained wide currency.[58] Agrippa had referred to the magical statues of the Hermetic work the *Asclepius* in his *De Occulta Philosophia.* At one point, in speaking about talismans imprinted with celestial images, he had written: "But who can give soul to an image, life to stone, metal wood or wax? And who can make children of Abraham come out of stones? Truly, this secret is not known to the thick-witted worker . . . and no one has such powers but he who has cohabited with the elements, vanquished nature, mounted higher than the heavens, elevating himself above the angels to the archetype itself, with whom he then becomes cooperator and can do all things."[59] Understandably, Yagel would have associated Agrippa's *magus* with the wondrous powers to create life.

Yagel's mention of Guilio Camillo is more unusual. Giulio Camillo Delminio was one of the most famous people of the sixteenth century, primarily because of his construction of a life-size model of a theater.[60] His *Idea del theatro* (Venice, 1550) was published in ten editions by 1584. As Frances Yates has shown, Camillo belonged to the Hermetic-kabbalistic tradition initiated by Pico della Mirandola. His theater was actually a memory building representing the order of eternal truth and depicting the various stages of creation, from the first cause through the angels, the planetary spheres, and down to man. The theater's basic planetary images were talismans receiving astral power that could be channeled and operated through the agency of the theater. By mastering the proportions of universal harmony whose memory was preserved in the theater's structure, the operator could harness the magical powers of the cosmos.

That Yagel had read Camillo's writings, especially his *Idea*, is beyond doubt. Elsewhere, he had related one of its principal anecdotes:

There is a story told about the sage Guilio Camillo who was employed as a scholar by the king of France and who composed the *theatro*, which conceived of a design of the heaven and earth through astronomy and through the law of creation. He was a scholar for the king of France. Once several lions entered the street in front of the royal palace, for the doors of the enclosure in which they stood had been destroyed. Everyone fled from their sound while Guilio Camillo stood before them. The lions became submissive before him as a student before his teacher until he motioned them by raising his hand and yelling [at them] until they returned to the lion den. They said he did all this because of the intensity of his natural constellation in its ascendancy, which was Leo ... Also the sun was at its full strength.[61]

The lion story was known in a number of versions. In the version of Giuseppe Betussi, "it was thought by all that he [Camillo] remained safe and sound because he was under the planet of the sun."[62] Similarly, in Camillo's own version of the story, the one apparently known to Yagel, "the animal recognized that there was much of solar virtue in him." On the basis of this story, Yates has concluded that the author of the *theatro* was a solar *magus*.[63]

Camillo's connection with the creation of artificial beings appears to be similar to Agrippa's. He, too, referred to the magic statues of the *Asclepius* and the process of infusing them with life and magical power.[64] A later writer, Pietro Passi, had also specifically mentioned Camillo's description of the artificial production of human beings.[65] It is also worth noting that Yagel devoted a large earlier section of *Beit Ya'ar ha-Levanon* to memory systems reminiscent of Camillo's memory building.[66] One wonders whether Yagel's massive encyclopedia, named after Solomon's house of wisdom, bore any resemblance in its overall plan and magical functions to those of Camillo's theater, also called "Solomon's house of wisdom."

HAVING DEFINED natural magic and its licit functions, including the artificial creation of human beings, Yagel also underscores the significance of the talmudic passages for the rabbis' production of the calf and the human being. He also emphasizes that from this discipline emerge a variety of ancillary ones "for the benefit of people and the masses," including pharmacology, medicine, meteorology, and the study of vapors, wind patterns, comets, and tides.[67]

Fundamentally, he is referring to his own profession and his own multiple talents and specialties. In the strongest terms possible, he emphasizes the significance of this field and its honorable place within Judaism. His own personal stake in this formulation is transparent:

> The conclusion is that with anything under the lunar constellation until the center of the earth, their compositions and varied virtues, our actions are sincere and it is a noble discipline. This is the act of creation and the laws of creation because it is the law and judgment on natural matters and their activities. Not only are its actions and matters permissible as long as no harm befalls any human being . . . but it is a commandment, a commandment to understand and learn it. For from it, one will note the design of the Lord [cf. Isaiah 5:12], who created everything with hidden knowledge, who put wisdom in the hidden parts [Job 38:36] as the creator of everything together according to their varieties. From this knowledge, he will ascend to the heights of other disciplines intertwined with this one, for it is a ladder to ascend to the *Ma'ase Merkavah* [the mystical speculations on the divine chariot], all of which God also created and formed in order that [we] will know his ways.[68]

Like the pious rabbis who created the calf, Yagel, as Jewish *magus* of his generation, was engaged in an activity that "no religion or norm would ever prohibit,"[69] and certainly not Judaism. On the contrary, Yagel's preoccupations followed the supreme Jewish commandment to understand "the design of the Lord" and to know his ways.

Thus in Yagel's view "the laws" and "the Book of Creation" in the Talmud referred neither to demonology nor to the mystical work ascribed to Abraham, but to instructional manuals in natural magic, works equivalent to such popular texts as those of Agrippa, della Porta, and Cocles. Certain that the books he has studied have been sanctioned and sanctified by Jewish tradition, he lashes out at Rashi and Joseph Karo for missing the point of this rabbinic passage: "What credentials do these scholars have [in defining] the precise differences in the meaning of *magus* . . . for one is a commentator and one is a codifier and neither has any expertise in these [magical] disciplines."[70] The implication is clear. Only an expert (such as Yagel) in "calf making" and its related disciplines can make sense of the passage and extract its real significance: the legitimation and ennoblement of the natural magician-scientist within Jewish normative tradition.

Yagel had to establish only one more bond between rabbinic teachings and the study and praxis of natural magic. This he found in a rabbinic discussion of David interpreting 1 Samuel 16:18: "I have observed a son of Jesse the Bethlehemite who is skilled in music; he is a stalwart fellow and a warrior, sensible in speech, and handsome in appearance, and the Lord is with him." From this verse the rabbis deduced that David knew how to ask and how to respond, how to give and take in "the war of Torah," how to expound the law, and how to understand one thing from another; they also deduced that the law was to be determined according to his view.[71]

The rabbis had transformed King David into a super-rabbi, a supreme master of Jewish law. Yagel's intention was different; he would make him into a Jewish *magus* following the same lines as the rabbis. Thus, in Yagel's opinion, David demonstrated the following qualities: he was able to ask about natural change and to be knowledgeable in offering both a proximate and ultimate cause for the change; he could reason analogically and could distinguish between truth and falsehood; he could ascertain something from something else; he did not accept a conclusion only on the basis of someone else's authority but only with rational proof; and, finally, God was with him in his search for knowledge.[72]

To clinch his argument that David's qualities, as understood by the rabbis, really applied to the natural magician-scientist, Yagel attempted to find their parallels in a work dealing with natural magic. In the *Summa Perfectionis* of the medieval Arabic scholar Jabir ibn Hayyan, called Geber in the Latin West, Yagel found what he was seeking. This work on the principles of alchemy included an introductory chapter on "the qualifications of the artificer." Among these Geber listed not only good skills, natural industry, knowledge of the principles of the art, an ability to search for causes, and fear of God but also, Yagel notes, the disposition to live modestly and with self-discipline.[73] Geber's qualities were far from a perfect match with those of the rabbis, even when adapted by Yagel. Yet this observation would certainly not have troubled him. He had again proved to his satisfaction that the ways of the rabbis and natural magicians were equivalent. Nor was he hesitant to employ the work of an Arab alchemist. He had already stated that the extraction of "the fifth element" and similar activities were clearly the province of the wise natural magician. So he believed that King David and Geber truly had much in common.

THE REMAINING PARTS of Yagel's discussion treat celestial and intellectual magic. Again, Yagel borrows the categories from Agrippa's *De Occulta Philosophia* and is indebted to Agrippa's analysis throughout. Like Agrippa, Yagel, with his strong interest in astrology, appreciates the function of mathematics in celestial magical operations.[74] However, he quickly turns to the general categories of talismans imprinted with celestial images.[75] But Yagel is more careful than Agrippa in delineating what kinds of talismans are religiously permitted and which are not. According to Yagel, there are three major types of talismans. The first, shaped in the image of a person or celestial figure, draws down the celestial effluvia with the aid of a corresponding vaporous smoke, which activates the talisman. This talisman is idolatrous and is forbidden to Jews; use of it is punishable by stoning. The second type is made of square or round tables on which are inscribed letters or calculations. This type is also forbidden but is not necessarily punishable by stoning. The third type consists of amulets, which can be used without penalty. Clearly, Yagel had used this type in his own medical practice.[76]

In his discussion of intellectual magic, which uses the names of divine intelligences or demons, Yagel again follows Agrippa's general outline but distances himself from its Christian overtones. Yagel follows the rabbis in distinguishing the harmless magic associated with earthly demons from the kind described by Agrippa as illicit magic that involves calling up impure demons and aerial spirits. This magic is most harmful and is punishable by stoning.[77] Clearly uneasy about discussing these last two categories, Yagel provides few details and minimal commentary on them. His uneasiness may have been exacerbated by Agrippa's conspicuous use of kabbala and Hebrew divine names along with the name of Jesus.[78]

Having exposed the formidable dangers of dabbling in these higher levels of magical activity, Yagel might have been expected to add some strong words of caution regarding the pitfalls of exceeding the boundaries of human potentiality. At the very least, he might have underscored again the distinction between white and black magic, between the magic that was his stock in trade and the kind that appeared to exceed the limits of propriety and permissible religious behavior. To reinforce that distinction, he might have enlisted the support of additional rabbinic passages readily available to him. But he does none of these things. In the end, the demarcation between licit and illicit, permissible and forbidden, is far from his thoughts. Although he notes that the ancient philosophers in pursuit of their astral magic "erred in reaching the habitation of the twisted serpent who stands around the place of the king's treasures,"[79] this fact does not deter him. The magical quest fascinates and energizes him. Such a quest, which aims to penetrate all secrets and gain control of all the hidden powers of creation, cannot be easily abandoned at the point where the natural limits have been passed.

If there are no limits to the magical quest, the qualifications, both intellectual and moral, of the practitioner of magic must assume an even greater critical importance for Yagel. Although the ancient pagan philosophers erred, there were others, fortified by their own religious esoteric tradition, who did not:

> And the sage, the wise kabbalist like Abraham our father and Rabbi Akiva, and others like them among the rest of the sages and prophets controlled them [the celestial forces] all and knew the orders of the worlds and how they connected one to each other . . . and they did not err in reaching the place of the serpent who guards the king's treasures. For they knew the hidden things there and [they ascended] from height to height until they reached the One who created everything together in such a way that their hands controlled all parts of the worlds and everything was created to obey them.[80]

Like Cornelius Agrippa, Pico della Mirandola, and Pico's Jewish mentor Yohanan Alemanno, Yagel believed that the best magic possible was Jewish magic, especially one practiced by Jewish kabbalists.[81] According to Pico, kabbalah and magic were interrelated; in fact kabbalah was the highest and most efficacious form of magic. And for a Jewish *magus* such as Yagel, the Jews' traditions in magic were their supreme badge of honor. Jews were the beneficiaries of an occult-mystical tradition to which all other nations and cultures had aspired in vain. Only the Jewish magician was fortified by his religious teachings to enter "the royal palace" and unravel the mysteries of the interlocking worlds. The archetypal magician was Abraham "our father":

> Abraham our father . . . followed, observed the ways of judgment of the orders of creation and the categories and types. Then he

united them by their essences according to the level of the worlds. God revealed to him and informed him of the orders of the higher and lower existences and he observed the sight of the levels. For the Most High is above "the world of making," "the world of formation," "the world of creation," and "the world of emanation," for their sound is the sound of falling water in a waterfall whose end is in its beginning and cleaves one to the other.[82]

When Abraham died, Yagel adds, his posterity lost the knowledge he had possessed; moreover, it was forbidden to them.[83]

Nevertheless, Abraham was the true supreme magician who heard "the sound" of the four worlds, "the sound of falling water in a waterfall." D. P. Walker informs us that hearing sounds was a critical dimension of the magic practiced by Marsilio Ficino. Sounds move and animate the air and thus affect the human spirit. Hearing puts us in more direct contact both with external reality and with the aerial movements that occur in our spirits. Sound is movement, whereas vision is static.[84] Thus Abraham mastered the most profound secret of the world by hearing. In addition, he heard a waterfall whose beginning was indistinguishable from its end, like the interlocking levels of creation.

We have returned finally to the parable of the solitary shepherd. The shepherd never saw the clock in the watchtower; he only heard it. He was inspired to replicate the act of creation upon hearing a waterfall. The instrument that he produced was made from broken pieces of gourds flattened to take advantage of the impact of the falling water "so that the sound of the water was heard from a distance . . . and he gained the virtue of the instrument in the tower *that he had not seen* [my emphasis], so, too, these perfect people with us . . ."[85]

Perhaps the language used to describe Abraham "who heard the falling water" conveys the import of the missing sentence of the parable and the precise meaning of the shepherd's invention. Yagel reminds us that "our fathers were always shepherds" who "knew the wisdom of nature" and who, like Abraham, heard the falling water, which enabled them to unlock the divine mysteries.[86] Was Yagel not arguing that although Abraham's wisdom was cut off from his descendants, there remained the possibility that "shepherds" could arise in every generation among his people, and that the highest magic remained the exclusive preserve of these Jewish practitioners?

120 On Stretching the Permissible

Moreover, when performed by individuals with proper credentials and adequate preparation like himself, was this occult activity not only permissible but also praiseworthy? For whom else might he have meant by his unfinished sentence: "So, too, these perfect people with us . . ."?[87]

Yagel's ambitious effort to promote his prodigious craft and his manifold skills raises finally the most obvious question: To what extent was his enthusiastic endorsement of magic a self-indulgent exercise in rationalizing his own peculiar proclivities, or rather a commitment shared by a significant number of Jewish contemporaries? Moshe Idel has already provided a partial answer in his discussion of the magical interests of Yohanan Alemanno and some of his contemporaries.[88] Yagel was clearly part of a circle of Jewish practitioners of magic, beginning with Alemanno at the end of the fifteenth century and extending at least into the seventeenth century. How large a circle and how significant a role it played in shaping Jewish culture are questions that still require further investigation. The precise relationship between the kind of magic practiced by naturalists such as Yagel and that of the mystics of Safad requires clarification. What Yagel's testimony does suggest is that for some Jews the practice of magic was sanctioned and informed by appeal to traditional texts as well as by passionate medical and scientific commitments. For Yagel, magic was an essential part of his medical activity. In this context, it would be useful to examine more closely the practice of magic by the prominent university-trained physicians and its impact on Jewish culture in the sixteenth and seventeenth centuries.[89] Without sufficient data, there can be no definitive conclusion about the significance of such a group and their occult concerns. Nevertheless, it might be safe to assume that, like Alemanno's, Yagel's preoccupations with magic were more conventional than eccentric within the intellectual world of their Jewish community, especially when recast in the intellectually respectable molds so persuasively presented in their respective writings.

8. On Divine Justice, Metempsychosis, and Purgatory

You must establish in your heart as a truthful tradition the belief in transmigration of souls, as it is revealed and known to anyone who calls himself by the name of Israel.

—*Gei Ḥizzayon*, pt. 1, p. 18b

Anything that does not harm religious faith need not be denied as an assumption for the person who believes it or accepts it, either literally or figuratively.

—*Beit Ya'ar ha-Levanon*, pt. 3, chap. 12, fol. 131b

ON A SABBATH DAY in 1585 the rabbi of Modena, Barukh Abraham da Spoleto, startled his congregation by delivering a sermon on the subject of metempsychosis (*gilgul*), in which he argued that sinful souls migrate after death into the bodies of animals, acquire these bodies until the time of the animal's death, and then depart.[1] News of the unusual sermon quickly reached Abraham Yagel, who felt obliged to challenge the legitimacy of the rabbi's argument, despite Spoleto's stature as a legal scholar.[2]

Yagel denied emphatically that it was possible for a human soul to transmigrate into a beastly body, "for it is inappropriate according to the nature of form and matter." God intervenes miraculously in nature only out of extreme need or through the agency of a prophet, and transmigration into animals would fit neither of those cases. But although Yagel denied the possibility of an actual migration of a human soul into an animal body "whereby it [the soul] would give vitality and form to that animal or beast as it does to a human body," he conceded that a soul could be imprisoned "in the body of a beast or animal, fowl or snake, tree or grass or mineral," for a period of "twelve months more or less, and this verdict is called in their [the Christians'] language purgatory."[3]

Upon learning of Yagel's reaction to his sermon, Spoleto immediately wrote angrily to his critic, thus initiating a heated exchange in which other noted authorities (namely Judah Sommo Portaleone and Mordecai Dato) later joined.[4] The rabbi appeared most agitated by the fact that Yagel had challenged his authority: "I heard it said that a divine spirit rested in you to decide before wise men and determine the law of negating gilgul into animals." In addition to Spoleto's own authority, Yagel had challenged that of "books and authors, recent and ancient, from whose mouths we live, who unanimously substantiate the truth of transmigration and not its negation." How was it possible for so many authors to be mistaken regarding "this legal enactment"? The authorities mentioned by Spoleto in support of his view were known primarily as kabbalists and not as legal scholars.[5] Having defined a theological issue as a matter of Jewish law, he undoubtedly felt confident in enlisting kabbalistic authorities to validate his position.[6]

Before answering the rabbi with his own list of notable authorities, Yagel traveled to Mantua, where he visited his dear friend, the distinguished Jewish playwright and stage director Judah Sommo, already well advanced in years.[7] Sommo proudly showed Yagel a scale-model of the Temple in Jerusalem that he had constructed in exacting detail. They conversed throughout the evening on a variety of subjects; eventually Yagel brought up the subject of Spoleto's sermon. He explained to Sommo that the rabbi was mistaken since the author of the kabbalistic work *Tikkunei ha-Zohar* (Later appendices to the *Zohar*) *tikkun* 70, alleged to be the ancient rabbi Simon Bar Yoḥai, was unquestionably the final authority on the matter and he understood *gilgul* quite differently. Yagel even showed Sommo his proof text; his agreeable host seemed pleased with Yagel's reading, although he admitted his own difficulty in understanding transmigration into animals. Later in their conversation, Sommo related the following anecdote, which Yagel transcribed:

"When he [Sommo] was about twenty years old, he had occasion to travel to Rome with a group of friends. When he arrived in the city of Viterbo—a place he had never visited—and when he observed the gate of the city, he looked at the place as if he recognized it and as if he had dwelt there for some time. He was an expert on its pathways and alleys and he found his way in any direction he wished to go. Upon approaching a certain street, he said to his companions: "Let us go this crooked way, which turns to the right." They took that path, and he knew every place they passed until they found one particular house. He asked the owner if he would be kind enough to allow him to enter the house. The man agreed, and he entered. Here too, he recognized every internal and external room in the house without exception. He then asked the owner if he could ascend to a most remote room. The man answered: "Do as you please." He went into the room accompanied by the owner and proceeded to speak to him: "Please, master, examine the wall beyond the window." He did so, striking it with a hammer, and they discovered a cache of old Hebrew books.[8]

Sommo went on to say that the books were so old that the letters had been blurred and the bindings had been eaten by worms. The astonished owner asked Sommo how he had known of the whereabouts of these books. Sommo had no recollection of how he had acquired his knowledge, since neither he nor his ancestors had ever set foot in the city. Sommo asked the owner in return if he knew whether the house had ever been owned by Jews. The owner replied that the property had been in his family for the last eighty years and there was no record of Jewish ownership. Sommo could explain the bizarre experience only by recourse to the concept of transmigration: his soul must have displayed a faint memory of a previous life.[9]

Fortified by this personal testimony, Yagel composed an elaborate reply to Spoleto. Citing the unassailable authority of *tikkun* 70 of the *Tikkunei ha-Zohar*, Yagel argued that animal faces are clearly visible in certain human beings according to their natural and astrological disposition. This phenomenon is also a secret available to those professional readers of the lines of the forehead, the practitioners of the art of metoposcopy. Historians had often pointed out that Cyrus and Attila had canine faces; the latter even needed a dog in his presence before making any decision. Nebuchadnezzar also was reported to look like a lion. But such a phenomenon is not to be equated with the actual transmigration of human souls into animal bodies. Unfortunately, the later kabbalists, who held to a literal view of transmigration into animals, misconstrued the intention of their acknowledged teacher, the author of the *Zohar*. Their authority cannot outweigh that of their master, whose position remains the correct one. Yagel especially discredits the view of Isaac Abrabanel, of whom he mockingly exclaims: "Who is he . . . to deal with] matters of *gilgul,* which is the special province of masters of the kabbalah?" Nevertheless, he admits, even Abrabanel deserves some faint praise for trying to defend the general concept of *gilgul* "with mistakes taken from the investigation of the sciences to justify this belief." [10] Abrabanel was at a disadvantage, since the published *Tikkunim* were unavailable in his day. Meir ibn Gabbai's understanding was limited in a similar manner. Yagel defiantly concludes: "Just as one should not trust the authority of any physician who contradicts the words of Galen and Hippocrates, the fathers of the physicians, nor of any philosopher who contradicts what Aristotle said regarding the knowledge of the material world, nor of any astronomer or astrologer who negates Ptolemy, similarly one should not believe in any kabbalist who contradicts the words of Rabbi Simon Bar Yoḥai." [11]

Before concluding, Yagel offers an alternative hypothesis to which he has alluded earlier. In the name of a tradition he attributes to Moses Cordovero, [12] he acknowledges the possibility of the temporary imprisonment of the soul in an animal body, though not of its actual transmigration. He revealingly adds: "Thus several Christian scholars declared who deny transmigration unequivocally; they uphold only this imprisonment [*ma'asar*], which might be a purgatory in any place that the Holy One, blessed be He, desires." He carefully distinguishes between *ma'asar* and *gilgul,* underscoring that the former is temporary and, unlike the latter, does not allow the soul to intermingle at all with its host body. [13] To his tour de force against the rabbi of Modena Yagel appends a short letter of warm support from no less a kabbalistic authority than Mordecai Dato. [14] To all appearances, Abraham Yagel has won his argument.

So FORCEFUL a response to a single sermon indicates that the issue of *gilgul,* especially *gilgul* into animal bodies, held special significance for Yagel. Moreover, he discusses transmigration at length in two striking passages in *Gei Ḥizzayon* and again in the third part of *Beit Ya'ar ha-Levanon.* Each of these passages reveals a thoroughly coherent stance as well as a major area of concern in the large corpus of Yagel's writing.

In *Gei Ḥizzayon,* in his discourse on the order of divine justice in the world, Yagel's father has this to say about metempsychosis:

> You must establish in your heart as a truthful tradition the belief in transmigration of souls, as it is revealed and known to

anyone who calls himself by the name of Israel. Only a root that bears gall and wormwood shall deviate from this belief; one who drinks as water the words of the philosophers and desires to establish together the words of the Torah with philosophic speculation so that miracles are understood as natural processes and similarly confused beliefs will never know nor understand that our holy Torah, its words . . . are superior to nature and [physical] reality.[15]

Although he has discounted the need for philosophic support for this belief, the father adds: "Also many great philosophers believed in the transmigration of souls, such as the sects of the Pythagoreans and Platonists and many of the philosophers among our people." In the last category he includes Isaac Arama and Isaac Abrabanel, who is depicted here in a positive light. After citing scriptural proof passages he concludes: "Thus when we accept graciously this holy and true belief, all doubts regarding the good and righteous who suffer will be removed . . . thus the law is a law of truth."[16]

Thus Yagel emphatically declares that *gilgul* is a cardinal principle of Judaism. By placing the doctrine squarely in an exoteric homiletic discourse, he underscores its necessity in the scheme of divine justice and in sustaining the belief that the Torah is "a law of truth." But what of the more obnoxious belief regarding *gilgul* into animals?

Elsewhere in *Gei Ḥizzayon*, the son and father listen to the story of a sinful woman who received the divine punishment of entering the body of a mad dog until she had paid for all her sins. This horrific retribution prompts Yagel to ask his father how a human soul can enter the body of an animal by metempsychosis and whether this belief is firmly implanted in rabbinic Judaism. His father's answer is equivocal. He mentions the tradition of Menahem Recanati and the later kabbalists in favor of such a belief but admits that "this view is not considered correct by all kabbalists." He again identifies the belief with the Pythagoreans, "who used to say that the soul of a murderer will enter a dog."[17] Finally, he relates a story told to a Rabbi Lappidot, "a great wise man and kabbalist who predicted the future":

There was a man in his time who owned an ass that brayed all night. Once it brayed more than it usually did. Also, in the morning the ass would not carry on its back the load to which it was accustomed. The owner of the mule treated it harshly, hitting it and wounding it to restore it to its original state of doing his work.

One day, however, the ass opened its mouth because of the pain of the beating and said to the man hitting it: "Was I ever wont to do this to you?" And he said: "No." "But now know that it is in vain since I am the soul of your father, your begettor, who, because of his sins, was decreed by heaven to dwell in the body of this unclean animal until a specified time had passed. But now be kind to me. Don't make this mule work and carry until the time has passed when I will leave it."

The man was astonished, so he went and related the incident to the wise Rabbi Lappidot. The wise man answered him: ". . . Don't work him as he commanded you, because it is possible that his iniquities trapped this evil man. Since he committed an animalistic act, it was decreed that he should enter an animal."[18]

The rabbi is uncertain that the soul is that of the owner's father, but because it could be "an evil spirit capable of harming you when [you] violate his command," he advises the man to comply with the request. The man obeys the rabbi. When the soul leaves the mule, the animal suddenly dies. Yagel's father evaluates the credibility of this story in a cautious manner: "These are the words which the elder told me. If they are true, accept the truth from whoever tells it, and if it is false, let the truth follow its course."[19]

The story of Rabbi Lappidot bears a clear resemblance to Xenophanes' sarcastic anecdote about Pythagoras, who forbade the beating of a dog because he recognized in its howls the voice of a friend.[20] If the stories are indeed related, Yagel ostensibly had linked the anecdote with his previous statement identifying the belief in animal transmigration as Pythagorean. However, his statement about *gilgul* into animals is still tentative. He only identifies the view as that of the Pythagoreans and later kabbalists; he suggests an alternative viewpoint, but he remains uncommitted to either opinion.

By the time he considered the question years later in *Beit Ya'ar ha-Levanon*, Yagel's position on *gilgul* was well developed. He states flatly: "all the children of Israel acknowledge that metempsychosis and migration of the soul [exist] in the order of divine justice."[21] Unlike the philosophers, who uphold this idea as a chance occurrence in nature, a Jew must believe it to be a sign of divine retribution, since this belief is embedded "in the secrets of reward and punishment according to divine providence."[22]

Initially Yagel appears to accept the possibility of transmigration into animals: "this belief is not heresy [*apikorsut*] or a false opinion, for no wisehearted person will dispute this even if he does not believe it or affirm it according to his investigations and [rational] assumptions. Anything that does not harm religious faith need not be denied as an assumption for the person who believes it or accepts it, either literally or figuratively."[23] But he immediately qualifies his statement: transmigration into animals occurs only in the sense that certain human beings seem to display animal characteristics; actual metempsychosis never takes place. Alternatively, others conceive of this process as a temporary incarceration by which the soul is purgated. In either case, the concept is useful in "distancing human beings from sin": "For they are moved more by these things [the visions of metempsychosis into animals] than by hearing about the pangs of hell, which they do not see with their own eyes."[24]

In sum, Yagel arrives at the same position he had articulated earlier in his letter to Spoleto. He is prepared to elevate transmigration to a principal doctrine of Judaism. He is even willing to allow for transmigration into animals as long as it is conceived of only as the acquisition of animal characteristics observable in the visage of human beings or as a temporary purgation in which there is no contamination of the sinful soul by the animal body. Here, more than in any other passage, his motivation is highly transparent: such a concept fortifies one's belief in divine justice, inhibits unvirtuous behavior, and functions as a formidable vehicle of social control.

IN THE LARGER CONTEXT of late sixteenth-century Italian Jewish thought and society, Yagel's reflections on metempsychosis appear at first to differ little from those of his coreligionists. Many historians have already located an explosion of popular interest in *gilgul* precisely in sixteenth-century Jewish culture—specifically, in the spiritual awakening of Safad; in the imaginative myths of Luria, Vital, and others; and even earlier, in the elaborate speculations of the author of the *Gallei Razayya*.[25] According to Gershom Scholem, any Jewish interest in metempsychosis can be understood as a theological solution to the flagrant contradictions of the moral universe—the suffering of the righteous and the contentedness of the wicked—in which Jews lived. The renewed interest in *gilgul* arose specifically after the expulsion of 1492 and quickly became "an integral part of Jewish popular belief and Jewish folklore" as a result of specific historical circumstances, namely the Spanish expulsion and its aftermath. *Gilgul* poignantly expressed the universal predicament of exile experienced by all Jews and by the entire universe. It was part of the process of *tikkun* (restoration of the divine sparks); its function was "to lift the experience of the Jew in Galuth, the exile and migration of the body, to a higher plane of a symbol for the exile of the soul." It became a universal law of the universe whereby "all transmigrations of souls in the last resort are only migrations of the one soul whose exile atones for its fall." In Scholem's view, it thus "explained, transformed, and glorified the deepest and most tragic experience of the Jews in Galuth; Galuth was not only a punishment and test but also a mission."[26]

In striking contrast to the popularization of this concept among sixteenth-century Jews was its utter lack of acceptance in the larger Christian culture in which they lived.[27] Accordingly, Scholem views the Jewish emphasis on metempsychosis in this period as an internal development arising out of the particular communal tragedy of Jewish life.

Yagel's preoccupation with *gilgul*, however, does not entirely fit this explanation. Although Yagel lived in the era of Safad's resurgence and maintained a close association with such Lurianic enthusiasts in Italy as Menahem Azariah da Fano, the main body of Lurianic ideas affected him only peripherally and partially. To the extent that Yagel can be labeled a kabbalist, he belonged to a different school of kabbalistic-philosophic speculation whose spiritual mentor was Yohanan Alemanno.[28] Nor was the problem of exile and redemption at the very center of his intellectual enterprise and emotional psyche. Even without the Lurianic influence, Yagel had undoubtedly exposed himself to the rich tradition of Jewish speculations on *gilgul*.[29] He was especially attuned to the heated deliberations about metempsychosis into animals that had originated in Spain in the fourteenth century.[30] But his response is more than a mere echo of previous or contemporary discussions. In the many nuanced formulations in which Yagel shapes his understanding of *gilgul*—in the record of his fantastic heavenly odyssey, in his heated exchange with Spoleto, and in his systematic dissertation on the soul; in the strains and tensions reflected in his apparent need to rethink and redefine the problem; and in his clear reservations about a concept he perceives to be no less than a cardinal principle of Judaism—the strategies he adopts are patently symptomatic of the larger thought processes in his literary work and in Italian Jewish culture. His struggle to frame an argument supporting the notion of *gilgul* without offending his own rational and scientific sensibilities reflects a larger cultural tension. It underscores from a totally different vantage point his compelling need to harmonize the apparent contradictions between received religious traditions and contemporary thought, to create an integrated world view out of seemingly irreconcilable religious and cultural concepts.

YAGEL'S COMMITMENT to the concept of metempsychosis was based primarily on his belief in the sanctity of Jewish texts affirming its validity. Yet he was also aware of parallel traditions, which likewise affirmed the possibility of transmigration, even into animals— the traditions of Plato and Pythagoras. For Yagel, both philosophers were more than intellectual props used to bolster a divine truth available exclusively from Judaic sources. Both also spoke the truth, a deeply spiritual and religious truth. If their assumptions seemed to conflict with the indisputable tenets of Judaism, they were not to blame. Like Lady Philosophy, the majestic hero of Boethius' classic, whose dress was ripped by her vile and arrogant scoffers, those Greek sages were misrepresented by their students, who distorted their truths and misconstrued their real intentions.[31]

References to metempsychosis, including transmigration into animal bodies, occur in several of Plato's writings.[32] For Plato, the transportation of human souls into various bodies constituted part of the very order of nature based on universal moral justice. In the *Phaedo* he discussed the concept in the context of righteous behavior and the need to punish sinful behavior. Evil souls "are compelled to wander about such places in payment of the penalty of their former evil way of life; and they continue to wander until through the craving after their constant associate, the corporeal, they are finally imprisoned in another body. And they may be supposed to find their prisons in natures of the same character as they have cultivated in their former lives."[33] Most prominent in Plato's conception was the idea that transmigration into brutes was a kind of prison for the soul that is morally purgated. Clearly, this formulation was a potential source for Yagel's similar understanding of metempsychosis.

Pythagoras' view appears to be identical with Plato's. Aside from the testimony of Xenophanes, mentioned earlier, numerous other ancient sources made it clear that Pythagoras believed in metempsychosis into animals and emphasized its moral function of purgation for the sinner.[34]

Plato's views on metempsychosis remained prevalent among the second- and third-century A.D. Middle Platonists and Neoplatonists, particularly Albinus, Numenius, and, later, Plotinus.[35] According to Augustine, Porphyry was the first to reject the concept of transmigration into animals, despite the fact that his teacher, Plotinus, supported it:

> Plato said in writing that after death the souls of men return to earth in a cycle and pass even into bodies of animals. This theory was held by Plotinus also, the teacher of Porphyry, but Porphyry was right to reject it. He held that human souls return to earth and enter human bodies, not indeed those they had discarded, but new and different ones. He was ashamed, apparently, to adopt the Platonic theory, for fear that a mother, returning to earth in the form of a mule, might perhaps carry her son on her back.[36]

The later Neoplatonists likewise found Plato's concept of transmigration into animals distasteful. From the third through the fifth century, Iamblichus, Sallustius, and Proclus either interpreted Plato to mean that the evil man acquires a beastlike character, or at most they allowed that his soul, while remaining human, may be temporarily associated with an animal body.[37] It is not surprising that Yagel's interpretation of metempsychosis into animals essentially followed the same lines. He certainly knew the works of these earlier interpreters of Plato; he was particularly familiar with the *Liber de Causis*, based on Proclus.[38]

Understandably, Augustine was even less sympathetic to Plato's position. After speculating on Porphyry's reasons for rejecting Plato's theory about transmigration into beasts, he continued:

> Yet he was not ashamed to believe in a doctrine by which a mother, referring to the form of a girl, might perhaps marry her son. How much more respectable is the belief, in accord with what holy and truthful angels have taught men, with what the prophets, moved by the spirit of God, announced, with the words of the Saviour himself, whose coming was foretold by messengers sent in advance, and with the preaching of the apostles whom he sent forth and who covered the whole earth with the Gospel—how much more respectable it is, I say, to

believe that souls return once to their own bodies than to believe that they return so many times to all sorts of bodies!"[39]

This same abhorrence to Plato's (or Pythagoras') view was shared by Christian Neoplatonists of the fifteenth and sixteenth centuries. With the exception of Guillaume Postel and Giordano Bruno, none of them could tolerate the notion that human souls could be imprisoned in the bodies of animals.[40] Marsilio Ficino interpreted Plato's statements on transmigration allegorically; thus transmigration into other species represented the emergence of different forms and habits of human life, and metempsychosis into beastly bodies represented the soul's reversion to the body during its passion, when it generates a gaseous body capable of assuming the shape of different beasts, according to the attitude of the soul.[41] Similarly, for Pico della Mirandola, metempsychosis represented the mutability of man's essence, his potential to become a plant, animal, or angel.[42]

Agrippa discussed metempsychosis into animals by referring to the views of Plotinus, Pythagoras, and Hermes, who, he claimed, held that "wicked souls do oftentimes go into creeping things and into brutes . . . but as an inmate dwell there as in prison."[43] He took no personal stand on the issue but observed incorrectly that the kabbalists did not accept this position. Johann Reuchlin was more outspoken in repudiating this view and lamented the resulting defamation of Pythagoras' character. "How could he associate the human essence, his own form, with animals? . . . Thus it is not possible to cross into the life of other living things of a different kind, whatever they may be. Species can't be confused with species."[44]

Another typical reaction by a contemporary Christian writer was that of the Jesuit missionary Matteo Ricci. Ricci saw Pythagoras' idea as a mere allegorical teaching device that came into being in a period when European morality was particularly lax. The doctrine was absurd because it denied the lordship of man over the beast, made marriage impossible, and would destroy the structure of domestic service.[45]

Yagel read many of the Christian Neoplatonists of his day. There was much in the writings of Agrippa, Ficino, Pico, and Reuchlin to which he could have subscribed. He may also have known the pious opinions of Ricci. Yagel had once written about China and may have heard of Ricci's reports on that country.[46] He easily could have followed their example and dismissed the concept altogether. Instead, he constructed an elaborate interpretation resembling that of the

Neoplatonists of late antiquity. He also knew, unlike Agrippa and Reuchlin, that at least some kabbalists believed that wicked souls entered "creeping things and brutes." Unlike his Christian contemporaries, he was not offended by the notion as long as it was understood properly.

YAGEL'S NONLITERAL UNDERSTANDING of metempsychosis into animal bodies was based on the ancient art of physiognomy, the art of determining people's character—and frequently their fate and fortune—from their outward appearances, especially that of the face and hands.[47] By the sixteenth century there existed an extensive literature in the field in Latin and other Western languages, in Arabic, and in Hebrew and Aramaic.[48] In the early sixteenth century Bartolommeo Cocles had written his *Chyromantie ac Physionomie Anastasis*, proposing a renewal of interest in this form of prognostication and divination. The work was translated into several languages and was read widely throughout the century; by the middle of the next century, over twenty-one editions had appeared.[49]

One reason for the popularity of this ancient art in the early modern period was its status as a kind of scientific discipline, an intellectually respectable procedure reputably practiced by physician-scientists. Giambattista della Porta, whose *De Humana Physiognomia* (1586) superseded Cocles' work in popularity at the end of the sixteenth century, defined physiognomy as "a science that learns from signs that are fixed in the body, and [from] accidents that transmit the signs to reveal the natural attributes of the soul."[50] Elsewhere he defined physiognomy as "the laws and rules of nature," which, when known from the form of the body, "allow one to know the passions of the heart".[51] The physiognomist's search for signs, for "the laws and rules of nature," was intimately related to the larger intellectual agenda of physician-naturalists of the sixteenth and seventeenth centuries: to search for external signatures in nature that offered clues to internal essences or occult properties and ultimately to reveal the profundity and harmony of the divine creation. Whether in the physical landscape of the expanding material world, in the chemist's laboratory, or in the physician's examination room, the scientist's ultimate objective was to identify signatures, to compare data from all corners of the universe, to correlate, organize, and construct a system based on resemblance or opposition, sympathy or antipathy.

As a physician and diagnostician, Yagel based his understanding of physiognomy on the authority of the *Zohar*, and especially on *tikkun* 70 of the *Tikkunei ha-Zohar*, which provided direct correlation between two sources of higher knowledge, that of Judaism and that of European scientific culture. Here the Jewish physician could find special gratification in the unique intellectual achievements of his own religious tradition. As a prominent offshoot of Jewish mystical lore, the two major areas of physiognomy, *hokhmat ha-parzuf* (metoposcopy) and *hokhmat ha-yad* (chiromancy), had long been held in esteem in both the intellectual and popular cultures of medieval Judaism. In the sixteenth century these fields were still firmly rooted in Jewish esoteric pursuits.[52] In fact, with the rise of Lurianic kabbalah in Safad by the second half of the century, Luria's pupils spread a tradition that he was the acknowledged master of physiognomy.[53] This affiliation, however, in no way undermined the intellectual credibility of the discipline in the eyes of its practitioners. No less a Jewish authority on science than Tobias Cohen devoted an entire section to the subject in his medical encyclopedia, *Ma'aseh Tuviyyah*.[54]

For Yagel, too, the subject warranted extensive treatment in his *Beit Ya'ar ha-Levanon*. There he used the format of a lengthy commentary on *tikkun* 70 to explicate the various dimensions of what he considered the "science" of physiognomy. This discussion provides the context for his particular explanation of metempsychosis into animals.[55]

Yagel first defines the three areas of metoposcopy. The first is the diagnosis of the various temperaments and humors of the body "in order to recognize the nature of man and his temperament on the basis of the appearance of the face and the bodily organs, the appearance of the hair, its abundance or scarcity. From this part, they [physicians] acquire knowledge about [a person's] qualities from the [external] functions either by understanding the accidents related to the quality of temperaments or . . . by comparing his quality and disposition with those of one of the animals that display these same functions."[56] The second is the examination of the lines of the forehead; the third is an approach to which Nahmanides referred in his Torah commentary in relation to the fifty gates of wisdom: "one who reflects on the secret of the soul, understands its essence and its strength in its sanctuary, will attain [that degree of understanding] to which the sages allude: If a person steals, he knows and recognizes it on him . . . greater than all, he recognizes all masters [that is, kinds] of witchcraft."[57] Yagel then elaborates: "This knowledge was passed down to the kabbalists, who recognized the secret of the soul in its sanctuary." Furthermore, he adds:

> Our forefathers told us that in our days and in their days there lived in Israel soldiers, learned in warfare, the war of Torah, who recognized souls whether they were recent ones or whether they had transmigrated two or three times. And in their seeing human faces, they would know if a person [literally, his head] sinned and which sin or iniquity he had committed. [Yagel mentions here Luria's prominent role in the art] . . . It is worth knowing that R. Simon Bar Yoḥai in the portion of Jethro and in the *tikkun* 70 revealed a little and concealed twice as much regarding these signs and *followed all three approaches that we have described* [my emphasis].[58]

Yagel's description of the three aspects of metoposcopy unambiguously assigns a special role to the Jewish kabbalist-practitioner. The first two approaches—studying the external bodily signs and the lines on the forehead—can be used by the physician and natural scientist. The third approach, however, is available only to one "with divine assistance" to fathom "the science of the signs of the soul . . . that which is hidden and concealed from the eyes of all naturalists."[59]

Ultimately, the true scientist requires a higher authority to perfect his discipline. A naturalist, using only the first two approaches, is confined to reading "the external face" and its purely external signs. But one who has perfected the divine science penetrates "the hidden and covered face."[60] Science alone, in the absence of Jewish esoteric wisdom, proves wanting. When combined with this divine wisdom, it is perfected. Thus when "secret faces" are decoded by means of the kabbalah that approximate the features of animals, the kabbalist-diagnostician can detect the moral depravities or strengths of an individual and can also ascertain the relationship between facial changes and moral inclinations. His function is precisely like that of "the wise physician who recognizes the appearance of the face of a sick person, its variations, the effects of the disease and its character."[61]

When Yagel earlier had contrasted the authority of Simon Bar Yoḥai with that of the "fathers" of philosophy, medicine, and astronomy—Aristotle, Hippocrates, and Ptolemy[62]—it was not only to argue in typically Renaissance fashion in favor of the superiority of all ancient wisdom. Perhaps he was also aligning, consciously or unconsciously, his kabbalist hero with the still dominant scientific figures of Western civilization. As the acknowledged master of this divine science, Bar Yoḥai's word was as authoritative as the others, and the science he represented was as significant as, indeed more significant than, those they represented. Was it not Bar Yoḥai who had established the real nexus between metempsychosis into animal bodies and the metoposcopy of animal faces? Was he not the only authority who had provided Yagel with a legitimate strategy for upholding a kabbalist-Platonic-Pythagorean idea without offending his scientific-medical sensibilities?[63] Here was a remarkable example of how a Jewish concept of seeming irrationality and primitive fantasy could be made intellectually credible and scientifically palatable by appeal to a supreme authority located in the Jewish tradition itself. In one majestic sweep, Yagel had both salvaged the concept of *gilgul* into animals and demonstrated the supremacy and centrality of kabbalistic knowledge in the scientific world of his day.

IN HIS DISCUSSION Yagel offered an alternative explanation of the notion of metempsychosis into animals, namely, the possibility of a temporary imprisonment of the soul in a beast's body if not an actual transmigration. He added that although Christian scholars rejected metempsychosis, they accepted the idea of this temporary imprisonment, which they called purgatory. As we saw earlier, the Jewish view of transmigration in the sixteenth century, though remarkably prevalent in the Jewish community itself, existed in a larger culture that was hostile to such an idea. The notion of transmigration as a kind of incarceration, which originated with Plato, was one that even enthusiastic Christian admirers of Plato and Pythagoras could not tolerate. Living in Catholic Italy in an era of sweeping religious changes, Abraham Yagel was by no means oblivious either to official church doctrine or to popular Christian culture. His choice of the word *purgatory* constituted a conscious strategy to make plausible a doctrine morally significant to him but theologically abhorrent to the majority among whom he lived. Just as he had sought to legitimate *gilgul* into animals by appealing to contemporary "science" and medicine, he sought to validate its inviolability by appeal to post-Tridentine Roman Catholic doctrine.

The concept of purgatory had become prominent in Catholic theology by the second half of the twelfth century. Reflecting the spiritual needs of a burgeoning urban society, it provided the individual believer with a more personal sense of divine justice, one that supplemented the Last Judgment, modified the Christian attitude to death by dramatizing the last phase of terrestrial existence and charging it with renewed hope and fear.[64] By the fifteenth and sixteenth centuries, the concept of purgatory was well established as church dogma by a variety of church councils and by papal authority.[65] It was defined as "that place or state of temporal punishment where those who have died in the grace of God expiate their unforgiven venial sins and undergo such punishment as is still due to forgiven sins, before being admitted to the Beatific vision."[66]

In the early sixteenth century, however, Luther and his disciples argued that it was "clearly false and foreign to the Holy Scriptures as well as to the Church fathers" to promise that "by the power of the keys, through indulgences, souls are delivered from purgatory."[67] The Protestants found purgatory objectionable primarily because of its conspicuous link with the excessive system of indulgences, which they had bitterly repudiated. The Protestant challenge unleashed a rigorous and voluminous Catholic defense of church doctrine beginning in the wake of the Council of Trent and lasting throughout the sixteenth century. Especially significant were the eloquent treatises on behalf of purgatory by the theologians Roberto Bellarmino and Francisco Suarez.[68]

By the end of the sixteenth century purgatory had become more than an official Church doctrine; it had also become a popular religious belief. Indeed, in this age characterized by a morbid fascination with death, purgatory, as an intermediary period between death and the Last Judgment, where the promise of salvation was still available to the sinner, became the object of a new form of devotion. From the seventeenth century on, special prayers, special altars, iconographic images, and specialized fraternities further promoted the concept of purgatory, stressing particularly the obligation of the living to intervene in behalf of the souls of the dead. It eventually became the most widespread and popular devotion in the Roman Catholic church.[69] And of course Dante and numerous other Christian writers created a special place for purgatory in the literary imagination of Western Christendom.[70] Thus by Yagel's day purgatory, in both the elite and popular cultures of Catholic society, was very much a household word.

But what might seem perfectly acceptable to a Christian—enlisting the doctrine of purgatory in support of a questionable theological statement—need not have resonated in the same way for a Jew.

Did Yagel believe that by favorably comparing *gilgul* with purgatory he would win greater credibility among his Jewish readers? On the contrary, by establishing so close and conspicuous a link between *gilgul* and the Christian doctrine, he might have undermined further the Jewish orthodoxy of his concept, which was already on shaky theological ground in certain Jewish circles.

The attractiveness of such logic obviously failed to impress Yagel. He could refute the charge that purgatory was a Christian concept utterly alien to Jews by arguing that rabbinic Judaism had long upheld such a concept. What was the rabbinic *gehinom*, an intermediate state of twelve months for those sinners neither thoroughly righteous nor thoroughly wicked, if not the state referred to by Christians as purgatory?[71] Indeed, Yagel had elsewhere expounded upon purgatory in an elaborate excursus in Hebrew on the ten circles of hell. After the first rung of hell, which he called limbo, he described the second circle: "The second place is a place where those with secret sins dwell. It is worse than the first place because this place is lower and more distant from the boundaries of heaven. This place is called in the language of Christian sages *purgatory* and in the language of our sages *gehinom*. They declared regarding the place: the judgment of the wicked in *gehinom* is twelve months in Tractate *Eduyyot* chap. 2 . . . meaning not actually wicked people because of the small amount of pain they experience . . . of only twelve months' duration."[72]

By defining purgatory as *gehinom*, he Judaized the Christian concept. For an author who had innocently adapted Canisius' Catholic catechism for Jewish readers, the appropriation of Christian theological terms into Jewish thought seemed perfectly legitimate.[73] In the case of purgatory, a concept that may have entered Christianity via Judaism in the first place,[74] Yagel could easily afford to be ecumenical. It was a notion well supported by Christian and Jewish authority alike; it needed only to be translated into terms familiar to Jewish faith. By thus formulating metempsychosis into animals as a temporary incarceration of twelve months called purgatory, Yagel established yet another strand in his intricate web of cultural and religious correlations.[75] For Yagel, there could never be multiple truths; there was only one. On the surface, Pythagoreans, Platonists, and kabbalists, physicians and scientists, Christian theologians and rabbinic sages seemed to speak in different languages; but ultimately they spoke in only one tongue.

YAGEL'S SPECIAL SENSITIVITY to the issue of metempsychosis appears to have derived from still more than the knowledge he had gained from his substantial reading in ancient theology, kabbalah, natural philosophy, and Catholic theology. It is often hazardous to attribute intellectual postures to specific life experiences in the world of a writer. But in this case Yagel's personal situation appears to reveal as much about his response as do his intellectual influences. We need only recall Yagel's failures in his business ventures and his incarcerations during the 1570s in Mantua and Luzzara. In fact, the image of prison appears to be the most prominent motif of his *Gei Ḥizzayon*. There he describes both his physical captivity and the imprisonment of his soul in the fetters of the material world.[76]

Furthermore, Yagel, like all physicians, whether Jewish or Christian, knew firsthand the intense miseries of human existence, of disease and physical pain. His preoccupation with death and suffering in much of his writing is no doubt attributable to this constant struggle to maintain life. Yet as his correspondence to his patients poignantly testifies, his medical care proved insufficient on more than one occasion. His best efforts to heal the sick often seemed futile against the severe limitations of sanitary conditions and medical knowledge in which he labored. And Yagel the physician and unsuccessful banker was himself a victim of political unrest, economic instability, religious discrimination, and physical hardship. For so sensitive a soul and for so thoughtful a religious man, the subjects of God's justice, the meaning of human existence, and the profound need of human beings to transcend suffering claimed his diligent attention. Since life is not futile, Yagel surmised, it must represent a form of purgation; and since divine justice permeates the universe, there must be a life beyond earthly existence. Thus the notion of transmigration of human souls into animals seemed neither distasteful nor inappropriate in a dark physical and moral universe that desperately required reassurance about God's supreme justice.

9. Ancient Theology, the Kabbalah, and the Status of Judaism in Western Civilization

These are the words of the great Hermes and his prayer to God . . . [which] is close to what is found in the Torah of Moses, if one understands all the details of its statements precisely, without the intrusion of any false thought, doubt, or suspicion.

—*Beit Ya'ar ha-Levanon*, pt. 2, chap. 2, fol. 47b

Many casual readers encountered a difficulty regarding the name . . . kabbalah, for its name denotes that all its teachings were received from one man to the next without disagreement. Yet we have found in . . . the books and investigations of the kabbalists that they discourse . . . in a forensic and rational mode of inquiry . . . it is not right to call it kabbalah but rather a science.

—*Beit Ya'ar ha-Levanon*, pt. 2, chap. 3, fol. 49a

WE HAVE ALREADY SEEN how consistently Yagel tried to integrate his medical-scientific concerns with Judaic sources and values, especially those in its mystical tradition. For Yagel, the ultimate medical therapy was kabbalistic; the highest and most powerful magic was based on kabbalistic knowledge and praxis; and the hidden mysteries of nature were detectable by appeal to Jewish esoteric wisdom. Kabbalistic sources could even provide the "scientific" key to enigmatic Jewish beliefs such as metempsychosis into animal bodies. In each instance, Yagel deferred to the kabbalah in his quest to comprehend the ultimate harmony of the universe.

What remains to be clarified is Yagel's precise relationship to the kabbalah. Was he a kabbalist in the sense that his contemporaries Menahem Azariah da Fano or Mordecai Dato were kabbalists? How did he respond to the dramatic transformations in kabbalistic thought and activity emanating in his own lifetime, from the school of Isaac Luria and Ḥayyim Vital in Safad?[1] And exactly how did he react to the reformulations of Jewish kabbalah by contemporary Christians who discovered in Jewish mysticism an invigorating source for Christian reform and renewal? To what extent did Yagel, like them, view the kabbalah as a vital part of an ancient theology, a universal core of philosophic and religious truth common to all peoples and cultures—pagans, Jews, and Christians? At least a generation before Yagel's time, kabbalah had become a kind of cultural and religious bridge between some Jewish and Christian scholars, opening up new avenues of intellectual exchange.[2] Could a Jew as conversant as Yagel in Jewish and non-Jewish sources feel comfortable with this relatively recent Christian fascination with Judaism? Would he ultimately recoil from the new Christian embrace of kabbalah fused with pagan thought, considering it a distortion and denudation of a uniquely Jewish inheritance?[3] A more positive Christian perception of Judaism was sure to cause a Jew such as Yagel to reevaluate the comparative study of religions and cultures in general, and the appropriate place Judaism might assume for itself within the larger community of Western civilization.

Yagel himself provides explicit answers to many of these questions. In several highly revealing chapters in *Beit Ya'ar ha-Levanon*, he reflects quite intensely on the relative value of non-Jewish philosophies and beliefs.[4] He also defines his own attitude toward the kabbalah and its role in Jewish and Western culture. These ruminations illuminate Yagel's own sense of Jewish identity and, indirectly, that of some of his contemporaries.

THE TERM *prisca theologia*, or ancient theology, has usually been associated with Marsilio Ficino and Giovanni Pico della Mirandola, the leading Neoplatonists in Florence in the second half of the fifteenth century.[5] Ficino was the first to argue that a single truth pervades all historical periods. He maintained that a direct line of thinking could be traced back to Plato through such pagan writers as Zoroaster, Hermes, Orpheus, Aglaophemus, and Pythagoras. By discovering, translating, and innocently misdating the primary writings of these authors, Ficino came to argue that all of them believed in God, that underlying the external differences between each of them and Christian teaching was a unity of harmonious religious insight, a basic core of universal truth. The history of culture was nothing more than the accretions and predilections of particular cultures and traditions that had surrounded the common nucleus with disparate customs, ideas, and artistic expressions. In this new version of the universal history of mankind, every philosophy and every religion had some value. Moreover, there was no longer any clear demarcation between philosophy and religion. The aim of philosophy was piety and the contemplation of God, and thus the subject of philosophy could be located simultaneously in an Aristotelian demonstration, an Orphic chant, or an esoteric Hebrew commentary. Moreover, the search for truth constituted a search for the earliest expressions of wisdom from ages supposedly more profound and more spiritually inclined than the present one. Ficino's and Pico's genealogy of knowledge through pagan sources to Plato eventually led them to an even earlier era, that of the Hebrew Bible and the Mosaic tradition. By universalizing all religious knowledge, Ficino and Pico fashioned an open and more tolerant theology of Christianity; in searching for the source of universal truth in ancient cultural and religious settings, they came to appreciate the centrality and priority of Hebraic culture in Western civilization.[6]

Related to the concept of ancient theology was the idea of poetic theology, prominent in the writings of Pico.[7] According to Pico, the ancient pagan religions had concealed their sacred truths by creating a kind of "hieroglyphic" imagery of myths and fables designed to attract the attention of their following while safeguarding their esoteric character.[8] Thus, in commenting on the Orphic hymns Pico wrote: "In this manner, Orpheus interwove the mysteries of his doctrines with the texture of fables and covered them with a poetic veil, in order that anyone reading his hymns would think them to contain nothing but the sheerest tales and trifles."[9] But so, too, Moses had addressed the Hebrews with his face veiled and had revealed to the many only what they were capable of understanding. Spiritual understanding of the Mosaic law was available only to an elite in the Jewish community, the kabbalists. The wisdom of their writings had not been conceived in the Middle Ages—so thought Pico along with most other contemporary Jews—but instead reflected the real intentions of Moses himself as conveyed to him by divine revelation. The kabbalah therefore constituted that part of the Jewish tradition in which the essential divine truths could be located. The kabbalah corresponded both to the divine secrets extrapolated from the Orphic hymns by the Neoplatonists and to the mysteries of Christ revealed to St. Paul, understood through the mystical writings of the sixth-century Dionysius the Areopagite. Outwardly, pagan, Jewish, and Christian theologies appeared to have little in common; but an unraveling of their inner cores revealed an unsuspected affinity.[10]

For Pico and a small but notable group of "Christian kabbalists" of the sixteenth and seventeenth centuries, the kabbalah was the key to laying bare the secrets of Judaism, to reconciling them with the mysteries of other religions and cultures, and thus to universalizing them. Through the kabbalah, the essential differences between Judaism and Christianity could be eradicated: "Taken together, there is absolutely no controversy between ourselves and the Hebrews on any matter, with regard to which they cannot be refuted and gainsaid out of the cabalistic books, so there will not even be a corner left in which they may hide themselves."[11] What Pico transparently had in mind was a Judaism reconstituted so as to embrace openly a universal Christianity. If the vibrant and indispensable sparks of divine consciousness as manifest in the kabbalah were extracted from Jewish culture, he thought, Judaism would become lifeless and ghostly; it would have no rationale to exist in and of itself. It would have meaning only in its merger with the esoteric, ageless, and catholic divine truths which were common to all humanity, and which ultimately were to be incorporated into the newly reformulated Christian theology of Pico and his followers. Clearly, such a blurring of religious boundaries through Christian use of the kabbalah and pagan philosophies presented a formidable theological problem to contemporary Jews.

Recently, some scholars have begun to assess the impact of the Christian idea of ancient theology on contemporaneous Jewish thought. In an essay on Isaac and Judah Abrabanel (Leone Ebreo) Moshe Idel has argued that both Isaac and Judah polemicized against the Christian view of ancient theology.[12] Unlike their Christian counterparts, who (according to Idel) acknowledged two independent paths to universal truth, the pagan and the Christian, they claimed that there was only one path, which came exclusively from the revelation on Sinai.[13] They had little interest in ancient pagan writers, with the exception of Plato, who, they claimed, became a student of Jeremiah and was thus "Judaized." By subordinating Plato to Jewish revelation, Judah and Isaac allowed ancient theology to infiltrate Judaism only to the extent that it promoted their notion of Jewish superiority.

Abraham Yagel's attitude to ancient theology provides a good test for Idel's hypothesis with respect to other Jewish thinkers of the sixteenth century. Let us begin by examining Yagel's attitude toward Plato, the ancient philosopher to whom Yagel most often appealed. Idel has already noted two passages in which Yagel comments favorably on Plato, emphasizes his connection with Jeremiah, and even quotes Augustine in support of this "Jewish connection."[14] In yet another passage he does the same things:

> A righteous person could utter [the words] of his [Plato's] mouth [cf. Psalms 37:30] most of the time, because the Torah of Moses was available to him and he listened to its teachings interpreted by the priest and prophet Jeremiah, may his memory be blessed. He drank his words thirstily, as Augustine mentioned in the seventh chapter of the *Confessions*.[15] Although many vilified him, saying that he claimed that the world had no beginning, that it has no purpose, and that it is coeternal with its creator, their efforts were in vain, for they did not really penetrate his true intention.[16]

Yagel also outspokenly praises the wisdom of other pagan writers, especially Zoroaster, whether he can demonstrate their Jewish lineage or not. In one long passage he makes a feeble effort to underscore Zoroaster's biblical origins: "Ancient Zoroaster was the father of all the magicians, the first of them all to write and compose books in this craft. He was Ham, the son of Noah[17] . . . in his wisdom, he discovered the seven disciplines, wrote them down, and inscribed them on seven pillars of metal and on seven pillars of charred stone so that it would be a memorial of his great wisdom and understanding for the generations to come. He was the first to laugh immediately at his birth."[18]

There follows a detailed description of the evil spirits and the angels who fell to earth, including their names and Zoroaster's procedures for calling them up. Only at the end of this passage does Yagel add perfunctorily a word of caution about the possible misuse of such instructions.[19] Yagel not only fails to "Judaize" Zoroaster; he fully identifies this sage's pivotal role in black magic and unhesitantly divulges the nature of his craft.

Yagel also mentions the magical curative powers of Asclepius, especially his famous association with serpents.[20] He refers to the writings of Hermes and Homer and compares a rabbinic homily with the myth of Prometheus.[21] He quotes Apuleius on demons and Pythagoras on the nature of the soul, the elements of fire and earth, the force of light, and his calculation of epicycles in studying the heavenly movements.[22] According to Yagel, Pythagoras deserves the same spiritual status as Plato. In discussing a rabbinic homily that, Yagel claims, refers to the relationship between the ancient philosophers and their students, he concludes; "This clearly alludes to those philosophers who truly deserved that distinction [of being true philosophers] such as Plato, Pythagoras, and the ancients who were believers."[23] Whether "believers" or not, Yagel has no qualms about quoting the ancients, praising their exceptional wisdom, comparing them with expositors of Jewish knowledge, and even pointing out their idolatrous practice of magic. Yagel leaves little doubt about his fascination with ancient pagans and their esoteric wisdom, even those who did not avail themselves of Jeremiah's instruction.

YAGEL'S MOST SUSTAINED and systematic explication of ancient theology and its relationship to Jewish belief and the kabbalah is found in his introduction to the second part of *Beit Ya'ar ha-Levanon*. He begins by stressing the need for caution in revealing religious secrets to the untutored masses.[24] After citing conventional Jewish sources—the Talmud, Maimonides, and the Aramaic translation of Jonathan ben Uziel—he offers similar testimony from pagan sources—Hermes, Plato, and Pythagoras—whose concern for concealing secrets appears to have been as great as that of their Jewish counterparts.

Yagel's primary source for these and later references was Cornelius Agrippa's *De Occulta Philosophia*.[25] In his chapter "Of concealing those things which are secret in religion," Agrippa offered the same witnesses in precisely the same order.[26] Yagel's mention of the practice of the ancient Egyptians, who protected their mysteries by writing in a cryptic language, is also based on Agrippa.[27] However, instead of repeating Agrippa's numerous additional references, Yagel succinctly concludes that the strategy of concealment is confirmed "by Hebrew, Persian and Greek sages." And although Yagel openly quotes Augustine (by way of Agrippa) on the same point, he modifies Agrippa's explicit citation of the New Testament: he copies the line from Matthew 7:6, "that holy things should not be given to dogs, nor pearls cast to swine," but attributes it only to "Christian sages."[28]

Agrippa's chapter was concerned with the responsibility of the magician who performed ceremonial magic to conceal his magical experiments. Yagel, on the other hand, refers only to secrets of a religious nature. In fact, his enlistment of authorities cautioning restraint is only a strategy to assure his reader that he would not commit any impropriety in revealing further secrets in his own composition and to plead his own piety and humility. Nevertheless, he could easily have achieved the same goal without any reference to pagan philosophers. Why, then, his need to copy from Agrippa? He openly discloses his intention: "to search in the pouches of the ancients, either from our blessed sages or from the rest of the sages of the nations, so that we can bind them in a cluster in order to penetrate the deeper meaning of the inquiry and investigation. For many words written in the name of one scholar are impenetrable, but with the words of another scholar they can be interpreted and clarified."[29]

Here is the approach of a scholar who recognizes that any writer and any text are potentially potent sources of truth. Like the poetic theologians, he is aware of the need to decode all texts in order to extract their hidden meanings. His method of decoding is comparative—to evaluate one text in juxtaposition with another, to illuminate an insight by holding it up to the light of another insight, literary usage, or context. Yagel's approach boldly implies the equivalent value of any text, any author, or any idea. A pagan or Christian source can be used to untangle an unintelligible Jewish one, and vice versa, and all literatures, all writers, share common features. The uniqueness and sanctity of Jewish texts appear to be undermined dramatically by such a formulation; moreover, Yagel seems to imply that in the pursuit of truth, no writing is devoid of some value, no matter what its source.[30]

Yagel is intent on illustrating how his "cluster" of disparate texts and witnesses can confirm one single truth. In the next chapter he turns to the most fundamental belief of Judaism, the belief in one God, defining it philosophically in accordance with Maimonides' definition in the opening chapter of his *Sefer ha-Madda*.[31] Yagel emphasizes the unity, indivisibility, incorporeality, and immutability of the Jewish conception of God. His innovation, however, is in demonstrating that fundamental religious principles regarding God can be substantiated by the testimony of external witnesses from the most unexpected source. The miracle of the parting of the Red Sea illustrates convincingly the notion of God's providence and ability to intervene in nature. Quoting a recent account of the discovery of Peru, Yagel is thrilled to find precise confirmation of the biblical miracle.[32] He is convinced that the discovery of new lands and new worlds offers new possibilities to reaffirm old beliefs.

In the following chapter Yagel expands his "cluster" of witnesses even further, turning from contemporary observers to the weighty authority of ancient philosophers.[33] In *Gei Ḥizzayon* he had already labeled Plato, Pythagoras, and other ancients "believers."[34] In this chapter, one of the most remarkable in all his writings, Yagel attempts to demonstrate that all of these pagans actually believed in the God of "the holy seed of the children of Abraham," despite the fact that they "never saw the light of the Torah nor of worship, prophecy, wonders, and miracles."[35] Yagel explicitly points out that these "believers" discovered their faith independently of Jewish revelation, for despite never having seen "the light of the Torah" they worshiped the one God. I know of no more outspoken acknowledgment of the notion of ancient theology in premodern Jewish literature than this chapter.

In the final version of this chapter, Yagel appears perfectly comfortable with utilizing such pagan witnesses. An earlier draft, however, indicates that he may initially have felt a need to justify the use of such external testimony, as if it might imply that the arguments of Jewish witnesses were insufficient: "Although our tradition is correct, not only as an investigative science but also as the true tradition, and one does not require a more correct and faithful testimony than this, nevertheless, listen to what these scholars have to say about the Creator."[36] His list of authorities includes the major representatives of the ancient philosophy delineated by Ficino: Orpheus, Zoroaster, Apuleius, Hermes, and Plato. Again, his principal source is Agrippa, specifically the chapter "That the knowledge of the true God is necessary for a magician and what the old magicians and philosophers have thought concerning God."[37]

Although Yagel copies extensively from Agrippa's chapter, he does so discriminately, avoiding especially the anthropomorphic descriptions of the Deity that Agrippa was fond of quoting. For example, Agrippa included large sections of the Latin translation of Orpheus' *Palinode*, describing God's neck, "his glorious head," "his golden locks," and, later, his eyes, wings, and breast. Here is the first part of Agrippa's quotation:

> The Heaven's Joves Royall Palace, he's king,
> Fountain vertue and God of everything.
> He is Omnipotent, and in his breast
> Earth, water, fire, and aire do take their rest.
> Both night and day, true wisdom with sweet love,
> Are all contain'd in this vast bulk of Jove

His neck and glorious head if you would see,
Behold the heavens high, and majesty;
The glorious rayes of stares do represent
His golden locks, and head's adornment.[38]

Yagel offers the following paraphrase:

The angels and the heavenly forces attribute their origin, their
existence, and their beginning to the singular master and king
and creator, whose ability is above all forces and whose power
is infinite. From this unique being, everything comes into existence, according to his desire, one by one, according to their
degrees; earth, air, water, fire, day and night. He created them
out of his love and compassion and gave them power. With this
love of his, He created everything that will remain forever.[39]

Instead of continuing with the long quotation that followed in
Agrippa's version, Yagel simply adds: "At this point he [Orpheus]
continued to relate the initial creation of the higher and lower
beings and the love common to them all and sworn among them."[40]
When he encounters another quotation of Orpheus soon afterward,
Yagel invents a new witness, "another sage," and places in his
mouth a line of Orpheus with his own embellishment, emphasizing
that mere mortals can comprehend only God's activities, not his
character.[41] Finally, Yagel copies an enigmatic line of Orpheus referring to God's teaching being delivered in two tablets. Whereas
Agrippa quickly passed over the line, Yagel interprets it as a reference to the tablets that Josephus said were erected by the ancients
as a memorial to their civilization before the Flood.[42]

Yagel's paraphrases of Zoroaster and Apuleius closely approximate
Agrippa's citation.[43] At this point Agrippa closed his chapter, turning to his next subject, "What the ancient philosophers have
thought concerning the Divine Trinity."[44] Yagel, who no doubt had
no interest in following Agrippa any further, instead includes two
additional witnesses, Hermes and Plato. The testimony of Hermes
was inserted after the close of the first draft of this chapter.[45] In the
final version Yagel gives it a more prominent place, after the citation
of Apuleius. He not only cites the pagan magician but includes an
entire prayer attributed to him. Apparently somewhat uneasy about
quoting a pagan prayer, Yagel offers some words of explanation:

These are the words of the great Hermes and his prayer to God
as he wrote it at the end of the first chapter of the *Pimander*,

after he related the manner of creation and existence of the world. This [prayer] is close to what is found in the Torah of Moses, if one understands all the details of its statements precisely, without the intrusion of any false thoughts, doubt, or suspicion. He said that with all the strength of his soul, upon seeing [God's] acts, he praises and extols God and says: "God is holy, the father and creator of everything. God is holy whose will is more perfect than its essential powers."[46]

Like other good students of ancient theology, in citing the pagan philosophers Yagel ends with "the divine Plato." He takes his quotations from a work entitled *Ha-Azamim ha-Elyonim*,[47] which is another name for the *Sefer ha-Sibbot (Liber de Causis)*, a well-known medieval European source of Neoplatonic thought based on Proclus' *Elements of Theology*. Yagel probably copied the passage describing the ineffability of the Creator from the work of Yohanan Alemanno, who had seen this passage in the writing of Abraham Abulafia.[48] Yagel's list of ancient philosophers was now complete. From Orpheus to Plato, there existed an unbroken tradition of pagan belief in monotheism, a chain of transmission parallel to but independent of that of "the holy seed of Abraham" who "saw the light of the Torah." No doubt Yagel could have easily located in rabbinic and medieval Jewish texts a fully developed attitude of tolerance and respect for "the righteous of the nations of the world."[49] However, he appears to have extended that attitude beyond the usual understanding of tolerance within Jewish tradition. In recognizing an autonomous tradition of pagan belief in one God; in comparing pagan attitudes favorably with those of the rabbis; and in openly quoting, albeit in a carefully edited manner, the pagans themselves, even an entire prayer of Hermes, he implied that Judaism, despite its unadulterated tradition originating at Sinai, could not claim that its truths were either unique or exclusive.

Yet if the pagan philosophers were truly "believers," was it not possible to rely totally on their teachings and utterances rather than on those of the rabbis? To this question, Yagel responds unequivocally. Although the ancient philosophers were unanimous in their monotheism, their students twisted and distorted their original intentions until the originally pure formulations were no longer recognizable.[50] Yagel had made the same point even more emphatically in the second part of *Gei Hizzayon*. There, following Boethius and the long tradition of his interpreters, he had interpreted the image of the torn garment on the figure of Lady Philosophy to refer to these unworthy students. Her clothes

> were torn by scoffing men, groups of common people who arose after the death of Plato and Socrates his teacher . . . They became arrogant, thinking that they are like the ancients and even better than they. But only the ancients understood and knew; they [the disciples] are like donkeys. Moreover, they conceived false ideas regarding the secrets of nature and creation and wrote down their fantasies and misconstrued the few ideas . . . they had taken from the ancients . . . Thus came the misconceptions of the sects of the Stoics and Epicureans, the philosopher's sect that Maimonides mentioned in the *Guide*[51] as well as the students of the Manicheans . . . Therefore, the students of the ancient philosophers were mistaken in [understanding] the words [of their teachers] and from them [these misunderstandings], they learned to lie.[52]

In *Beit Ya'ar ha-Levanon* Yagel concludes his reflections on ancient theology with a long discourse on the various names of God.[53] Having consulted earlier chapters of Agrippa's book, he could not have failed to notice one titled "Of Divine Emanations, which the Hebrews call Numerations, others attributes; the gentiles gods and Dieties; and of the ten Sephiroths and ten most sacred names of God which rule them, and the interpretation of them."[54] Although the announced topic of this chapter may have inspired his own remarks, he does not use Agrippa's examples. For Apollo, Jupiter, and Minerva Yagel substitutes "creator," "deus", and the tetragrammaton; instead of the pagan authorities quoted by Agrippa, Yagel cites rabbinic sources, Maimonides and Meir ibn Gabbai. And from Agrippa's relatively brief comments, Yagel expands the discussion to the subject of negative theology, especially the incapacity of mere mortals to know God and to define his ineffable nature. Having established this context, Yagel introduces the kabbalistic notion of the *ein sof,* the unknowable aspect of the Deity. Finally, having led his reader to the treasure chest of kabbalistic theosophy, he invites him to examine the entire subject of the kabbalah more closely in the next chapter.[55] Perhaps Yagel had noticed Agrippa's provocative conclusion to his own analysis of the names of God: "Whosoever understandeth truly the Hymnes of Orpheus and the Old Magicians, shall find that they differ not from the Cabalisticall secrets and Orthodox traditions."[56] Agrippa had provided him with much of substance on magic and ancient theology, but regarding his own mystical tradition, Yagel would have the last word.

YAGEL BEGINS his excursus on the kabbalah with a general statement about mastering any new discipline. An investigation of a field should include the following five categories: the name of the field, which identifies the subject matter; the purpose of the subject; its benefit to one who masters it; its advantage over other fields; and the order or organization of the discipline. Yagel proposes to explicate the field of kabbalah by examining these five categories.[57] The implication of this approach is that kabbalah is no more and no less than a scientific discipline, subject to the same rules and categories appropriate to the study of other fields of learning. Through this formulation Yagel reduces the kabbalah to a science, one that can be explained by rational categories and is translatable into the language of academic discourse.

In his initial discussion of the name of this discipline, Yagel shows that he is aware of the problem of reducing the kabbalah to only a scientific field of investigation.

> Many casual readers encountered a difficulty regarding the name of this divine science called kabbalah, for its name denotes that all its teachings were received [*mekubalim*] from one man to the next without disagreement. Yet we have found in looking at the books and investigations of the kabbalists that they discourse in their homilies in a forensic and rational mode of inquiry and seek reasons and explanations for their teachings. Because of the differing interpretations of their sages, they possess divergent views regarding their principles and basic ideas. As a result of this situation, it is not right to call it kabbalah [a revealed tradition] but rather a science.[58]

Yagel's statement of the problem of defining the essence of kabbalah undoubtedly reflects his own ambivalent stance on the subject. On the one hand, he is aware of the divine origin and higher spiritual authority embedded in kabbalistic theosophy; on the other hand, he approaches this wisdom as he does any other body of knowledge. It is meaningful to him as long as he can explain its doctrines in rational terms. Moreover, it is meaningful to him precisely because it constitutes a body of esoteric knowledge. He is fascinated by its speculative nature, not by its praxis, theurgy, or myths.

In response to the dilemma he has presented, he attempts to refine further his characterization of kabbalah. He identifies two modes of investigation—from a known cause to an unknown effect (a priori) and from a known effect to an unknown cause (a posteriori)—and points out that most sciences proceed in the first manner, establishing their causes and from them inferring their effects.[59] In the case of the divine science, however, where God is the primary cause, one begins by investigating the visible effects of God's creation in order to fathom the creator: "Out of the perfect and permanent order found among all reality, they [the investigators] recognized the organizer and the director, for from their true rational proofs they were obliged [to comprehend] the reality of God, His ability and wisdom."[60] Yagel adds that Abraham as a young boy came to know God in this manner. These remarks at first appear rather bizarre. Is Yagel suggesting that rational proofs based on the design of creation are sufficient for determining the divine reality? Moreover, what does this have to do with the divine mysteries of kabbalah?

A clarification immediately follows: this is the path of the philosophers whose investigations can reach only a certain level of understanding and who can never penetrate the reality of God himself. The secrets of the universe, the sublime mysteries of the divine world, are available only to one who has been enlightened through prophetic inspiration. This, then, is kabbalah—a prophetic revelation passed down from generation to generation whose source of knowledge surpasses that of all rational inquiry.[61] This esoteric wisdom was first recorded in the *Sefer Raziel ha-Malakh*, which was seen by Enoch, who was inspired to write his own book of divine secrets. He in turn instructed Abraham in this superior wisdom, and the latter composed the *Sefer Yezirah*.[62]

All these early visionaries were instructed by angels. Later, God did not automatically send these supernal mentors to enlighten his initiates in the wisdom of the divine mysteries. Thus the later kabbalists were obliged to use particular prayers and divine names to call down the angels. Repeating a well-known tradition, Yagel claims that Elijah himself appeared in a vision to a number of medieval kabbalists, including Rabbi Abraham ben David, Isaac Sagi Nahor, Ezra and Azriel, and Nahmanides. He adds parenthetically that at the time of his death Menahem Recanati was also visited by Elijah.[63]

Yagel's brief survey of the history of kabbalistic revelation quickly reaches the kabbalistic masters of his day. He is effusive in his praise of Moses Cordovero, whom he considers to be the leading kabbalist of his generation and the major exponent of the *Zohar*. He mentions that he had heard that Cordovero was also visited by a celestial teacher [*maggid*] but later corrects this impression on the basis of information acquired from his associate Menahem Azariah da Fano.[64] According to Fano, Cordovero had no *maggid* because he did not desire one; instead he was given a pure soul, like Simon Bar Yoḥai, the alleged author of the *Sefer ha-Zohar*. Furthermore, Cordovero was considered to be a reincarnation of Bar Yoḥai.

Yagel also acknowledges the importance of Isaac Luria and Ḥayyim Vital, but his knowledge of both these luminaries is far less intimate. He adds only that Luria's teaching was based on prophetic inspiration. He describes Vital as "the wondrous teacher R. Ḥayyim Vitalo, his [Luria's] student, about whom I heard said that he is the father of all the kabbalists in that region and wrote righteously words of truth, and that his knowledge of talmudic *pilpul* [penetrating analysis of legal arguments] is sharp and masterful."[65] "I heard said" indicates that Yagel had no firsthand knowledge of Vital or his writings. Moreover, the phrase "in that region" might indicate that Yagel considered Vital important as a master in Safad but not necessarily in Italy or the rest of the diaspora.[66] It is interesting that Yagel knew nothing of Vital's kabbalistic works but only of his reputation as a Talmudist. Certainly Yagel's writing as a whole confirms this impression: he often refers to the writings of Cordovero but rarely mentions Luria and never refers to any of his kabbalist teachings. Although he alludes once to a text of Israel Sarug, the Lurianic kabbalist, it had no significant influence upon him.[67] And Vital's name appears only here in his writings. The impression Lurianic kabbalah made on Yagel was almost nil.

Having shown to his satisfaction the development of kabbalah among the Jewish people, and having explained why it was called kabbalah, since it derived ultimately from angelic instruction, Yagel returns to the troublesome matter of controversies among the various kabbalistic schools. He proposes two explanations for these disagreements. First, he mentions the natural tendency among kabbalists to correlate their kabbalistic visions with their intellect, attempting to explain a mystical insight by reducing it to a rational explanation. As a result, a wide array of kabbalistic interpretations had emerged.[67] Rather than lamenting the intrusion of philosophy into the realm of pure kabbalah, Yagel is not troubled in the least: "For these [interpretations] and those [other interpretations] are both the words of the living God; so investigate and receive a re-ward."[68] Although he may also have noticed a parallel between the corruption of ancient philosophy by later generations of students and the distortion of the kabbalistic tradition by its later interpret-ers, he passes over this striking similarity in silence. Although he had vented his hostility against the former group, he remains un-critical of the latter. The reason for this inconsistency is not difficult to imagine: he must have realized that he, too, would be counted among those rational exegetes of the kabbalah.

Yagel's second explanation for the disagreements among kabbal-ists is related to the limitations of language. When these oral teach-ings were put into writing, the mode of expressing kabbalistic no-tions often obscured or contradicted their original meaning. Students learned kabbalah from books instead of from teachers, and thus they often misconceived an idea inadequately presented in writing.[69] Yagel's comment seems to reflect especially the way in which the kabbalah was learned in Italy, in contrast to the more traditional forms of oral instruction from masters in the academies of Safad.[70] In any case, Yagel's only advice is to consult the earlier kabbalist writings, which contain considerably fewer mistakes and misinterpretations, especially the *Zohar* itself.

Following carefully the outline presented at the beginning of his discussion, Yagel next considers the purpose of kabbalah. Its goals are to impart a higher intelligence to human beings; to inform them of the processes of the higher celestial realm; to reveal the concate-nation of the four worlds; and to explain how the divine effluvia from above are received below, and how man is a microcosm, an exemplar of the larger universe, with a capacity to enjoy divine blessing and approbation.[71] These objectives are virtually identical with those of Yagel's medical-magical-naturalistic pursuits. Yagel's quest to comprehend the natural world involved a search for identi-fying signs of the mystery of creation, a fascination with controlling the supernal forces through the practice of natural and celestial magic, and especially a passion to connect and to correlate the man-ifestations of God's creation throughout every level of reality. In short, from Yagel's perspective, the scientist pursues the same goals as the kabbalist. Only the kabbalist, however, can fully realize these objectives, since he is armed with the divine sapience of angels. Only he can fathom the mysteries of creation in a manner unavail-able to even the most gifted and erudite physician and naturalist. Here, in an excursus meant to clarify the objectives of the Jewish mystical tradition, Yagel underscores what attracts him most about the kabbalah and how easily and naturally he could assimilate it to his own world view and his own professional self-image as a physician and naturalist. He had defined the object of his scientific pursuits independently, and here he defines his kabbalistic ones; and they are interchangeable!

Yagel cannot ignore completely the more spiritual and religious aspirations of the kabbalist. He waxes eloquent on the spiritual ecstasy "in this world and in the next." He quotes the *Zohar* on the goal of clinging [*devekut*] to God through the spiritual acts associated with kabbalah.[72] But his true inclination is again transparent. Kabbalah is ultimately the pursuit of knowledge; the central concern of Judaism is not merely believing but also understanding that there is one God. Having flirted momentarily with the more spiritual kabbalah, he returns to the primary commandment of Maimonides to know God, upon which he had previously discoursed and upon which he has still more to descant. In an eloquent oration on the significance of this commandment in Judaism, he maintains that every other commandment, every prayer with the right intention, and the ultimate religious aim of fearing and loving God are all dependent on the fulfillment of this one injunction.[73]

Having demonstrated that Jewish identity rests on knowledge, Yagel needs only to reiterate that this kind of knowledge, made accessible to Jews through the resources of their kabbalistic legacy, is superior to any other form of knowledge. "There is no rational investigation greater than seeing the eyes of true intelligence,"[74] he writes, by which he means the sublime insights of the kabbalah. Having made his major point, he relies on Moses Cordovero's *Or Ne'erav,* "small in quantity but great in quality," to expand upon the virtues of the kabbalah, the moral and educational requirements of study, and the preferred texts a student should master. He concludes with an invitation to his reader to enter this earthly paradise of kabbalistic learning.[75]

THERE ARE FEW extended and systematic discussions of kabbalistic theosophy in Yagel's writings. Instead, as we have seen, he uses kabbalistic ideas and texts to supplement and buttress his conclusions regarding a variety of other subjects. However, he does consider more thoroughly the *sefirot,* those ten manifestations of the Deity knowable to man and central to kabbalistic theosophy and mythology.[76] Although most of his remarks are unoriginal and merit no special attention, several aspects of his discussions of the *sefirot* illustrate vividly Yagel's particular formulation of kabbalistic ideas and their place in his general thought.

Yagel was fully aware of a major, centuries-long controversy among kabbalists regarding the nature of the *sefirot*, which had flared up again in the late fifteenth century. Kabbalists had conceived of the *sefirot* in various ways: as an intimate part of the divine essence itself; as nondivine in essence, functioning as instruments in creating or governing the world or as vessels containing the divine influx; or as divine emanations immanent in nature itself. The controversy centered mainly on the divine or extradivine status of the *sefirot*, and thus was reminiscent of the philosophical debates about the existence of ideas within or outside the divine mind.[77] The issue had been heatedly discussed in the fifteenth and sixteenth centuries by Isaac Mar Ḥayyim, Yohanan Alemanno, David Messer Leon, Moses Cordovero, Meir ibn Gabbai, and others.[78]

It is not difficult to establish the relation between Yagel's views and those of his predecessors. Like David Messer Leon, he reinterpreted the *sefirot* to fit into a philosophic framework. Like him, he drew an analogy between the divine attributes and the *sefirot:* in both cases, their apparent multiplicity did not signify their true mode of existence but only the manner in which their diverse activities appeared to human beings.[79] Yagel was especially dependent on Cordovero's elaborate discussions of the subject. Cordovero had tried to reconcile the two opposing views regarding the *sefirot* by maintaining that they were simultaneously part of the divine essence and also instruments perceived by humans as external to God. Yagel generally adopted this position and even borrowed some of Cordovero's analogies, including one comparing the relationship between the Deity and the *sefirot* to that between the sun and its rays. The rays exist as part of the one sun; however, they are perceived by the recipients as having an independent and plural existence.[80] In *Gei Ḥizzayon* Yagel had borrowed another analogy, one equally relevant to his own naturalistic tastes and interests. In this case Cordovero had compared the character of the *sefirot* to the flowing of water through different-colored vessels; although the water is always the same, it is perceived differently as it flows through the containers.[81] Here is Yagel's embellishment of the same analogy:

The matter that is called *sefirot* is like ten changeable vessels different in kind from each other; however, the emanation and the light that passes through them from the *ein sof* is one, and from its perspective there is no plurality . . . It is like ten glass vessels different in coloring. A well of fresh, clear, and pure water passing through them makes the ten different-colored vessels appear to change so that they look like ten wells. This is the case because the water passing through each vessel will appear different from the outside according to the coloring of the vessel. In actuality, the water passing through all of them is one.[82]

An even better example of Yagel's reduction of kabbalistic theosophy to philosophical categories has already been noticed by Moshe Idel.[83] In an earlier chapter of *Beit Ya'ar ha-Levanon* in which Yagel compares the notion of the four kabbalistic worlds to a Neoplatonic passage found in Agrippa's *De Occulta Philosophia*, he also considers the essence of the *sefirot*. He explicitly identifies the *sefirot* as Platonic ideas:

For all issues from the Lord of Hosts. He spoke and it was. He commanded and it stood [Psalms 33:9], but the creatures and formations above and below exist by the spirit of his mouth . . . And the power that is in the lower beings is to be found in the upper worlds in a more subtle, exalted, and sublime manner. It is to be found [also] in great purity and clarity in the holy, pure *sefirot* which are in truth the *ideii* for all things. They are the beginning of God's way, and all His acts course through the four degrees which are the mystery of the four worlds of emanation, creation, formation, and construction.[84]

As Idel has pointed out, Yagel eschewed the dynamic and theurgic aspects of the *sefirot*, one of the major preoccupations of kabbalistic speculation. Instead, he integrated them with Neoplatonic philosophy, thus reducing them to objects of the mind, to ideas in his intellectual construction of the cosmos.

Yagel's tour de force of speculation on the *sefirot* is at the end of his heavenly odyssey in *Gei Ḥizzayon*.[85] Here, too, he expands upon the notion that every process in the highest level of creation has its analogue in the lower levels. In *Beit Ya'ar ha-Levanon* he had shown that the four elements existed simultaneously in every one of the kabbalistic four worlds in conformity with the essence of that world.[86] In describing the ultimate knowledge the narrator gains from his spiritual ascent in *Gei Ḥizzayon*, Yagel similarly elaborates upon the ten *sefirot* and their analogous existence in all of the worlds of reality. He first describes each *sefirah*, then points to its analogue in the celestial world as one of the ten celestial spheres.

Attempts to relate the ten *sefirot* with each of the spheres of the medieval cosmos—the seven spheres of the planets, the firmament of the fixed stars, the empyrean, and the *primum mobile*—were not uncommon among both Jewish and Christian interpreters of the kabbalah.[87] What is distinctive about Yagel's version is its meticulous elaboration of analogies and correlations between the various levels of reality, extending far beyond the celestial spheres to the lowly parts of the human body: "Observe well that all the reality of the lower world, whose foundation is dust, corresponds to the ten spheres and to the ten *sefirot*." These ten parts include "nature, which binds and bestows strength to processes in potentia to actualize them"; primal matter; the elements of fire, water, air, and earth; minerals; vegetables; animals; and, finally, human beings.[88]

But Yagel has not yet exhausted the possible additional correlations of ten. This time he turns to a subject well known to him: the human body. He states that the body offers a "hint" of all four worlds, and within each of these four, ten distinct categories are present. He begins with the head:

> first, one finds ten special things in the head, three of them hidden, which divide into three parts: the picture, in the front part of the head; the thought, in the middle part; and the memory, in the end part. From them an energy and special property flow to the seven revolving forces, which are the two eyes, the two ears, the two nostrils of the nose, and the mouth, which equal seven, corresponding to the last seven *sefirot*, which also receive influx and light from the first three secret worlds. Thus the head is the shape of a ball without a top or bottom, which is the most praiseworthy shape of all, as the engineers explain. For this part corresponds to the highest world of emanation, the most important of all.[89]

In the second of the four worlds of the body, Yagel includes the heart, liver, lungs, esophagus, trachea, stomach, abdomen, intestines, spleen, and sexual organs. To the third world he assigns the ten fingers of the hands, and to the fourth, the ten toes of the feet.[90] From the lowly toes of the feet to the divine realm, a reflection of the ten *sefirot* is present in everything. The *sefirot* are no longer mere objects of Jewish mystical speculation; in Yagel's elaborate construction they have become the keys to unlocking the divine mysteries, the universal principles of nature that bind all of creation, and the primary concepts by which humans are capable of grasping the essential harmony of being. Here is the most colorful example of the fusion of Yagel's medical and naturalistic interests with his kabbalistic ones, and of his obsession to discover a unity embedded in the multiformity of all life experience.

If ABRAHAM YAGEL had been asked his opinion on the status of Judaism in Western civilization, his response would have been unambiguous. Like most other Jewish savants of his day, he would have underscored the superiority of Judaism over philosophy and all other religions and cultures, its unique legacy based on divine revelation, and especially its singular tradition of theosophic speculation, one well appreciated by contemporary Christians and Jews alike.[91] The following passage from *Gei Ḥizzayon* is typical of his response and that of many of his coreligionists:

> What the philosophers know in their investigations and disputations regarding the creation of the world, its nature and character . . . even after their toil and effort, will amount to nothing; for which one of them has grasped the secret of God? The Jewish schoolchild is taught by his father: "In the beginning God created and in six days he made His world; on the seventh day He rested. He also knows God's purpose and capacity and His providence [extending] over buffalo's horns to gnats. . . . From these accounts [of the superiority of the Torah in rabbinic literature . . . you may understand the great wisdom, either natural, mathematical, or divine, which was in the hearts of our fathers, the sages. They learned everything in a manner different from that of the philosophers. The latter spend their lives finding evidence and proofs for one fact that afterward is taken as a premise or an assumption to understand something else . . . Such a premise . . .[is] unnecessary for our sages in order for them to grow accustomed to intelligence and to acquire wisdom. They can understand and learn much from the order [of the *Mishnah*] *Seeds*, of the laws of forbidden mixtures in the orchard . . . of measurements that contain geometry and mathematics . . . things that train their minds in wisdom and establish the truth.[92]

If we were to take this statement at face value, we might assume that, according to Yagel, the Jewish sage has no need to consult the wisdom of the philosophers or sages of other religions and cultures, since he already possesses the superior truth of the Torah. Yet it is clear that Yagel was deeply committed to the study of authors and texts outside the Jewish tradition, that he recognized their independent value and even their capacity to discover the divine truth, and that he was passionately concerned with "binding a cluster" of Jewish and non-Jewish testimonies, correlating the two, and confirming Jewish truths with those found in other traditions. His intellectual agenda can be seen as an attempt to reduce or eliminate the sense of cultural isolation and alienation afflicting Jewish culture. Integrating Judaic wisdom with that of the nations of the world would enhance and ennoble Judaism's image. When translated into the language and cultural context of Western civilization, the Judaic legacy would become even more prominent and praiseworthy in the estimation of Jews and non-Jews alike. Thus it was important to demonstrate that the rabbis knew mathematics as well as and even better than the philosophers, and that the kabbalists were in the possession of a science surpassing that of the best naturalists and astrologers. Yet undoubtedly such an agenda carried risks. There was always the possibility that a comparison of Judaism with other cultures might show Judaism to disadvantage, or that a correlation of Jewish concepts with those of other religions might show that Jewish culture was not unique.

The tension inherent in simultaneously demarcating the boundaries and promoting dialogue and integration between Judaism and other cultures constitutes the central dilemma of Jewish thought, especially in the modern era. Several Italian Jews living in his own period shared many of Yagel's cultural interests and wrestled with similar tensions. Moshe Idel has correctly identified the following as the major features of Italian Jewish kabbalah in the sixteenth and early seventeenth centuries: the kabbalah was increasingly viewed as an ancient Jewish lore and interpreted philosophically; since it was now open to speculative interpretation, it became more accessible to both Jews and Christians; and it was considered to be a form of higher magic providing the practitioner with a most efficacious means of drawing down the divine effluvia of the *sefirot* and using them for his own benefit. Under the influence of Renaissance culture, particularly the stimulus of Pico and his followers, Italian kabbalists tended to shape the kabbalah differently from some of their predecessors in Spain and from most of their contemporaries in Israel. Both Idel and Reuven Bonfil have also emphasized the function of kabbalah in this era as a bridge between Jews and Christians.[93] Idel demonstrates the parallel function of Italian kabbalah to that of Jewish philosophy in Spain centuries earlier; Bonfil describes the kabbalah in Italy as a kind of *concordantia oppositorum*, bringing together Jews and Christians, mystics and philosophers, this-worldliness and other-worldliness.

It is not surprising that Abraham Yagel figures prominently in Idel's overview of the period: he clearly embodied all the trends Idel mentions. Occasionally he appears even to have surpassed most of his contemporaries in his enthusiastic endorsement of them. We have noted Yagel's admiration of pagan thought and his recognition of the originality and independence of ancient philosophers in arriving at the truth of one God. His tolerance of non-Judaic sources is especially apparent in his conspicuous usage of magical works. As Idel has observed: "More than any of his intellectual predecessors, Yagel was ready to quote approvingly from the most notorious magical writings of Christian tradition."[94] Like some of his contemporaries, he interpreted the kabbalah in rational terms; but he surpassed them in integrating its theosophy with his medical, magical, and astrological interests.

Did Yagel's passionate pursuit of wisdom outside the traditional categories of Jewish learning attenuate his own loyalty to Judaism? Did his quest for integration of knowledge blur in his own mind the distinctions between Judaism, Christianity, and paganism? Here was a Jew who not only mixed Judaism with Zoroaster and Plato; he was even capable of "presenting Augustinian maxims on human salvation and Jesuit definitions of religious faith as authentically Jewish."[95] After extolling the singularity of Judaism, he devoted his intellectual energies to reducing it to the vanishing point. We need only recall the aspirations of Pico and the devotees of the ancient philosophy in reconciling Judaism and Christianity to appreciate the precarious position in which Yagel's syncretism placed him. In the appendix I examine and dismiss the evidence regarding Yagel's possible conversion to Christianity. Nevertheless, Yagel's multiple loyalties posed an undeniable intellectual, spiritual, and social challenge to his Jewish identity. Taking into account both his intellectual eccentricity and his economic instability, we should view Yagel as a Jew who stood perilously on a spiritual precipice, notwithstanding his ambitious attempts to achieve a religious and intellectual concord in his own life.[96]

Afterword

HAVING DEFINED Yagel's notion of the kabbalah and having explored his conception of magic, we are left with the task of conceptualizing his understanding of science. Throughout the preceding chapters I have deliberately avoided an abstract definition of the term so as not to prejudge Yagel's usage or to distinguish arbitrarily and anachronistically his "occult" mentality from a "scientific" one. It is clear that in the mind of this sixteenth-century Jewish physician, the three disciplines—kabbalah, magic, and science—were inextricably linked. Through this interlocking cluster, Yagel believed a Jew could achieve his highest aspiration: the penetration of the sublime mystery of creation and its underlying divine unity.

Yagel's idea of science was clearly distant from the modern usage of the term. By *science*, Yagel meant the drive to explore nature in all its multifarious dimensions.[1] He passionately desired to disclose and to comprehend every tiny speck of creation, from medical cures, to unusual beasts, to Siamese twins, to wonder children, to comets and faraway stars. His sense of wonder at and admiration for nature stemmed from his profound faith in a creator who had fashioned all creatures in a perfect harmony. It was the task of human beings to attempt to relate each created thing to another, to classify and organize all available data, and to fathom the regularity of creation, so as to extol the handiwork of the Deity. Yagel also believed that God, as the omnipotent creator, had imposed upon his contingent world a series of natural laws. In fact Yagel once defines nature as "the divine will and judgment"; every natural creature is stamped with a divine seal, signifying that it is the work of God's hands.[2]

This quest to comprehend the divine seals of nature rested on the assumption that every source, every author, and every book was a potential storehouse of information and should be combed for whatever truth it might disclose. For Yagel, there were no limits to learning; there were potential value and meaning in every reference and utterance, whether Jewish, Christian, or pagan, and no opportunity to learn something new should be ignored, for "the truth follows its own course."[3] This genuine openness to all knowledge was accom-

panied by a commitment to empirical observation. Yagel was prepared to trust his own sensory perception even when it appeared to
contradict standard philosophical presuppositions about nature.
Thus he considered demons real because he trusted foremost
the testimony of eyewitnesses, although the existence of demons
seemed to conflict with reason. Yagel recognized that humans generally observe order in nature. Yet when he encountered a reality
that seemed to him irrational or inexplicable, he still felt obliged to
accept its existence. He would attempt to find a rational explanation
for every seeming irregularity, from demons to monstrous children,
but he would not deny what his senses told him. Reality could be
perceived only by observation of the laboratory of nature, not pre-
conceived according to the theories of a venerated ancient philosopher.[4]

Most of all, Yagel accepted the premise that human beings must
try to gain dominion over nature. It was a duty, a divine commandment, to understand nature in order to master it. Like the shepherd
who learned to replicate the intricate clock in the city square, it was
incumbent upon humans to create, because they were created to
imitate God's ways. Even the creation of human beings through
magic was sanctioned by rabbinic authority. Thus, for Yagel, it was
legitimate to compete with nature, to imitate her wondrous acts,
and even to try to surpass her.

Yagel, then, was a kabbalist who believed that the highest knowledge came only through divine revelation and angelic intervention.
He was a practicing *magus* who assumed that the universe contained a network of correspondences and who placed great credence
in the power of magical words and formulas to transform reality. But
he was also an empiricist who sought to understand nature by ob-
serving it, by constructing it, and by mastering it.[5] And above all, he
was a masterful architect of an integrated view of reality that fused
his religious identity with his medical-magical and scientific aspirations. In constructing this view he creatively highlighted those
aspects of Judaism that promoted his own professional and intellectual concerns. He stretched the meaning of Jewish culture so as to
incorporate new ideas and sources, shaping a novel configuration
of Judaism while boldly asserting the unique vocation of the Jewish people within the emerging scientific culture of early modern
Europe.

The last chapter closed with a picture of Yagel as a Jew standing
perilously on a spiritual precipice as a result of his syncretistic proclivities and his personal economic and social hardships. But the

towering intellectual edifice he had labored to erect was also totter-
ing on the brink of disaster through no fault of his own. The marriage between kabbalah and science was soon to break asunder as a
result of historical forces unforeseeable by Yagel. By the end of his
life the Lurianic kabbalah had helped to inject a new spiritual mood
of prayer, ritual, and piety, especially in Italy's proliferating Jewish
confraternities. The focus of this kabbalah was ritualistic activism
rather than theosophic speculation. Its primary concern was to en-
rich the religious and spiritual needs of the Jewish community
rather than its purely intellectual ones. And it emphasized the singularity of Judaism at the expense of speculative syncretism with
other religions and cultures. The kind of intellectual construct Yagel had fashioned from kabbalistic materials was quickly proving
irrelevant and alien to the tastes of a Jewish reading public nurtured
by homilies, moral treatises, and liturgical innovations. Almost simultaneously, the mechanical and mathematical sciences of the
seventeenth century were slowly discarding their occultist character and gradually moving in a direction that increased the distance
between kabbalistic theosophy and scientific explanation. Yagel's
elaborate harmonization of Judaism and science was soon to become
hopelessly obsolete.

Thus the influence of this erudite but eccentric Jewish savant was
restricted to a small coterie of Jewish intellectuals in his own lifetime and was almost nonexistent by the next generation. If there
was any recognizable group within the Jewish community of the
seventeenth and eighteenth centuries who generally followed in his
footsteps, it was the small but conspicuous society of physicians and
scientific enthusiasts in the Jewish communities of both eastern
and western Europe—Marrano physicians who had fled the Iberian
peninsula and were dispersed throughout the Continent; Jewish
graduates of the medical schools of Padua, Leiden, and other European cities; and general devotees of astronomy and natural science
in Prague, Krakow, and elsewhere. But even this group would no
longer have viewed Yagel's kabbalistic or scientific views as either
good kabbalah or good science. Abraham Yagel undoubtedly had expected instant recognition and a well-earned place of honor among
later generations of Jews for the ambitious intellectual plan that had
taken him almost a lifetime to conceive and explicate. Instead, he
is remembered by modern historians only as a curious footnote in
the long history of creative encounters between Judaism and Western civilization.

Appendix: Did Abraham Yagel Convert to Christianity?

As early as the end of the seventeenth century, a number of scholars hypothesized that Abraham Yagel had converted to Christianity and was identical with Camillo Jaghel, the well-known censor of Hebrew books.[1] This assumption was proven untenable by a number of nineteenth-century historians who noticed that Camillo was already working for the Roman Inquisition in the same years that Abraham Yagel was unmistakably a practicing Jew.[2] Anyone who remains in doubt about this misidentification should recall Raphael Modena's explicit statement about Abraham and himself when captured by kidnappers: "They never caused us to transgress the Jewish religion."[3] This statement was written some time after 1614, years after the beginning of Camillo's employment as censor.[4] As late as 1623, Yagel's letters to the Rieti family in Luzzara unambiguously reveal his Jewish loyalty. The Rietis even contended that he was responsible for the upkeep of a Jewish synagogue and cemetery in his former home—hardly a claim to be made about an apostate.[5] Camillo and Abraham could never have been the same person.

More recently, Meir Benayahu of Jerusalem has revived the hypothesis of Yagel's apostasy at least once in print and more rigorously in conversations with me.[6] Disregarding, for the moment, Benayahu's mistaken assumption that Abraham became the censor, can we still entertain the possibility that Yagel simply converted at the end of his life? Benayahu has graciously shown me the following "evidence" to support his hypothesis, to which I respond point by point.

1. At the end of a volume of Isaac Abrabanel's *Naḥalat Avot* (Venice, 1545) in Benayahu's personal library, Camillo Jaghel had signed his name as censor in 1603. Below the censor's signature, a later hand added the following remark in Hebrew: "You should know, my brother, that this censor called Camillo Jaghel was a Hebrew man whose name in Israel was called Abraham Yagel from the Gallico family. He composed *Lekaḥ Tov* and his other compositions and afterward converted and changed his name to Camillo, and soon

after was appointed to the Inquisition." This person signed his name with two letters that are unidentifiable.

The comment identifying Abraham with Camillo is clearly in a nineteenth-century hand. This was confirmed for me by Professor Malachi Beit-Arié, the expert Hebrew paleographer and head of the National and University Library, Jerusalem, who examined the comment with me. This person obviously was familiar with the mis-identification of Bartolocci and others and repeated it here. The comment offers no proof of Yagel's conversion.

2. On the opening page of Yagel's *Bat Rabim,* there is a note in the corner that Benayahu claims is in the hand of Abraham Graziano.[7] The Hebrew note reads: "Writings and legal decisions and various pamphlets from kabbalah, philosophy, and other novelties that were composed *when he was called by the name of Israel* [my emphasis] Abraham Yagel, who collected them, etc." Benayahu infers from the italicized words that Abraham had once been a Jew but later relinquished that status.

The comment allegedly written by Graziano may have implied Yagel's conversion; alternatively, Yagel may have been emphasizing his Hebrew name, in contrast to the name he may have been called in Italian non-Jewish society.

3. In *Beit Ya'ar ha-Levanon,* part 4, chapter 114, folio 256a, there is a comment written in square Hebrew letters in the side margin that Benayahu considers to be further proof of Yagel's apostasy. According to Benayahu, this line was written by a younger contemporary, Samuel Portaleone.[8] The comment reads: "Regarding this author who made a statement in the name of the person who said it, *his name was* [once] [my emphasis] R. Abraham Yagel of Monselice."

This comment is even less convincing than the one attributed to Graziano. It refers to Yagel in the past tense, implying that he has already died, not necessarily that he has converted.

4. In addition to these comments, Benayahu contends that Yagel's son refers to himself without mentioning his father's name, a sure indication that the father had converted and the son had totally dissociated himself from him. Benayahu further identifies Abraham's son as Hananiah of Monselice, whose commentary on *Pirke Shira* was printed posthumously by his children in Mantua in 1661.

The only lingering doubt centers on Yagel's progeny. We have seen that Yagel was married, that he had at least one brother, a son, and a grandson. At the age of seventy Yagel still maintained contact with his son, who defended his father's interest in the conflict over the synagogue and cemetery in Luzzara. He clearly was not alienated from his father at that late date, and there is no indication whatever that his father was Christian when this entanglement took place. Is it reasonable to assume that Abraham suddenly converted after the age of seventy? It is possible but highly unlikely.

Abraham never mentioned his son (or sons) by name. Was he Hananiah of Monselice, as Benayahu assumes? Hananiah was known primarily for his commentary on *Pirke Shira*, an anonymous collection of hymns put in the mouths of various creatures, personifying nature.[9] By Hananiah's time the kabbalists of Safad, especially Cordovero and Luria, were drawn to the work because of its emphasis on the mystical relationships of all creatures to one another, and recommended its daily recitation.[10]

Hananiah's commentary on the book is eclectic, drawing upon a number of earlier commentaries by Joseph Albo and others. He reveals little about himself except that he was a student of Menahem Azariah da Fano and had been in Mantua.[11] In one instance he mentions a Solomon Terracini, of a Jewish family from Mantua with whom Abraham had had some contact.[12]

Several rabbinical *responsa* in manuscript are also attributed to Hananiah. In one he signs his name as the "young Hananiah of Monselice" in the town of Soliera (in Reggio nell'Emilia) in 1610.[13] In another *responsum*, regarding the wearing of phylacteries on Sabbaths and holidays, he refers to the opinion of his teacher, Menahem Azariah da Fano, "singular in his generation, excelling in wisdom and in saintliness." This time he signs his name "Hananiah b. Hananiah of Monselice."[14] His praise of Fano is reminiscent of that in his commentary on *Pirke Shira*. If this is the same Hananiah, then perhaps he was not Abraham's son at all, but rather a younger brother, who came under the influence of Fano and lived part of his life in the area of Mantua.[15]

Although Abraham never divulges the name of his son, he does mention Hananiah of Monselice. *Bat Rabim* contains a copy of a certificate of rabbinic ordination (*tofes ḥavrut*) granted to Hananiah of Monselice, *marbiẓ Torah* in Portomaggiore (in the Ferrara region), by Nathaniel Trabotto, the rabbi of Modena, in 1616, and an accompanying letter from Trabotto to an Israel Foa of Soragna.[16] Abraham obviously valued this document because it recognized someone close to him. Was this his brother who wrote the works mentioned above? If so, Hananiah's name cannot be used as proof that Abraham had converted, since his father's name was Hananiah and not Abraham. The only problem with this explanation is the late date (1616) for the ordination. Yagel was then sixty-three, and even if he had a much younger brother (Yagel's father had died in the early 1570s), it would seem inappropriate that a man at least forty-five years old in 1616 was only then receiving his ordination. Yagel's first son, born in Luzzara, was not much younger. If he did become a rabbi, 1616 seems also to be very late for his ordination. Could this Hananiah perhaps be a younger, still-unidentified son or nephew of Yagel? Despite the evidence pointing to a liaison between the two, there is not yet any way to establish the precise relationship between Abraham Yagel and Hananiah of Monselice.

The evidence that Abraham Yagel converted to Christianity is at best inconclusive. What seems more relevant is the general direction and consistency of Yagel's thought from at least 1578 to 1623, the years when he was writing. Although he was interested in a wide array of esoteric and bizarre subjects and in Christian and pagan ideas, books, and authors, he remained firmly implanted in the soil of Judaism; indeed, he continually declared his belief in the superiority and uniqueness of Judaism. That his intellectual influence was restricted to one generation does not imply that he became an apostate. Until more conclusive evidence regarding his conversion can be offered, we should assume that Abraham Yagel lived and died as a Jew.

Notes

Introduction

1. For a sampling of the scholarly literature on the general subject of religion, magic, and science, see the essays by P. Corsi and M. MacDonald in *Information Sources in the History of Science and Medicine*, ed. P. Corsi and O. Weindling (London, 1983).

2. See R. Bonfil, "The Historian's Perceptions of the Jews in the Italian Renaissance: Towards a Reappraisal," *Revue des études juives*, 143 (1984), 59–82.

3. See, for example, W. E. H. Lecky, *History of the Rise and Influence of the Spirit of Rationalism in Europe*, 2 vols. (London, 1865); J. W. Draper, *History of the Conflict between Religion and Science* (New York, 1875); and A. D. White, *A History of the Warfare of Science with Theology in Christendom*, 2 vols. (New York, 1896).

4. See, for example, M. B. Foster, "The Christian Doctrine of Creation and the Rise of Modern Natural Science," *Mind*, 43 (1934), 446–468; reprinted in D. O'Connor and F. Oakley, eds., *Creation: The Impact of an Idea* (New York, 1969); idem, "Christian Theology and the Modern Science of Nature," *Mind*, 44 (1935), 439–466, and 45 (1936), 1–28. More recent proponents of this view include F. Oakley, "Christian Theology and the Newtonian Science: The Rise of the Concept of the Laws of Nature," in O'Connor and Oakley, *Creation*, pp. 54–83; R. Hooykaas, *Religion and the Rise of Modern Science* (London and Edinburgh, 1972); S. L. Jaki, *Science and Creation: From Eternal Cycles to an Oscillating Universe* (New York, 1974); and E. M. Klaaren, *Religious Origins of Modern Science: Belief in Creation in Seventeenth-Century Thought* (Lanham, Md., 1985).

5. See the recent collection in D. C. Lindberg and R. L. Numbers, eds., *God and Nature: Historical Essays on the Encounter between Christianity and Science* (Berkeley and Los Angeles, 1986), and its bibliography. On the debate over the so-called Merton thesis (presented in Robert K. Merton's classic study, *Science, Technology, and Society in Seventeenth-Century England* [New York, 1970]), see especially the essays by Gary B. Deason and Charles Webster, in Lindberg and Numbers, *God and Nature*, pp. 167–191, 192–217, and their bibliographic references.

6. See A. Funkenstein, *Theology and the Scientific Imagination from the Middle Ages to the Seventeenth Century* (Princeton, 1986).

7. See, for example, H. Butterfield's classic account, *The Origins of Modern Science: 1300–1800*, rev. ed. (New York, 1965).

8. See especially F. A. Yates's *Giordano Bruno and the Hermetic Tradition* (London, 1964) and "The Hermetic Tradition in Renaissance Science," in *Art, Science, and History in the Renaissance*, ed. C. S. Singleton (Baltimore, 1967), pp. 255–274. The extensive literature for and against the so-called Yates thesis is cited by B. Vickers in his introductory essay to *Occult and Scientific Mentalities in the Renaissance* (Cambridge, 1984) and by P. Curry in "Revisions of Science and Magic," *History of Science*, 23 (1985), 291–325.

9. For a full discussion of the debate regarding "the Yates thesis," see Curry, "Revisions of Science and Magic." See also P. Rossi, "Hermeticism, Rationality, and the Scientific Revolution," in *Reason, Experiment, and Mysticism in the Scientific Revolution*, ed. M. L. Righini Bonelli and W. E. Shea (New York, 1975), pp. 247–273; and J. E. McGuire and R. S. Westman, *Hermeticism and the Scientific Revolution* (Berkeley and Los Angeles, 1977).

10. On this problem see C. B. Schmitt, "Recent Trends in the Study of Medieval and Renaissance Science," in Corsi and Weindling, *Information Sources*, pp. 221–240.

11. For the time being, see D. B. Ruderman, "The Impact of Science on Jewish Culture and Society in Venice," in *Gli ebrei e Venezia*, ed. G. Cozzi (Milan, 1987), pp. 417–448. See also the works cited below in Chapter 6, note 4.

12. For references to ancient and medieval Jewish magic and rabbinic attitudes toward magic, see below, Chapter 7, note 33. On a Jewish tradition of Hermeticism before the Renaissance, see M. Idel, "Hermeticism and Judaism," in *Hermeticism*, ed. A. Debus and I. Merkel (Washington, D.C., 1987).

13. On biblical and rabbinic medicine, see the standard work of Julius Preuss recently translated into English by F. Rosner, ed., *Julius Preuss' Biblical and Talmudic Medicine* (New York, 1978). On later Jewish medical involvement, see H. Friedenwald, *The Jews and Medicine*, 2 vols. (1944; reprint, New York, 1967); D. Margalit, *Ḥokhme Yisra'el ke-Rofim* (Jerusalem, 1962); M. Steinschneider, "Judische Aerzte," *Zeitschrift für hebräische Bibliographie*, 17 (1914), 63–96, 121–168; 18 (1918), 25–57; E. Carmoly, *Histoire des médecins juifs anciens et modernes* (Brussels, 1944); and S. R. Kagan, *Jewish Medicine* (Boston, 1952). See also *Encyclopedia Judaica*, 16 vols. (Jerusalem, 1972), XI, 1178–1205 (hereafter cited as *EJ*).

14. See, for example, M. Steinschneider, *Die Hebräischen Übersetzungen des Mittelalters und die Juden als Dolmetcher*, 2 vols (Berlin, 1893); S. Gandz, *Studies in Hebrew Mathematics and Astronomy* (New York, 1970); W. H. Feldman, *Rabbinical Mathematics and Astronomy* (London, 1931). For additional material see the indexes of G. Sarton, *Introduction to the History of Science*, 5 vols. in 3 (Baltimore, 1927–48); and L. Thorndike, *A*

History of Magic and Experimental Science, 8 vols. (New York, 1923–58). For other references see below, Chapter 4, note 74, and Chapter 6, note 6.

15. I elaborate upon this theme later, especially in Chapter 4.

16. See Curry, "Revisions of Science and Magic," pp. 304–308.

17. Ibid., p. 304.

1. The Ordeals and Rewards of Living

1. On the decline of Jewish life in the second half of the sixteenth century, see, for example, K. Stow, *Catholic Thought and Papal Jewry Policy 1555–1593* (New York, 1977); idem, "The Burning of the Talmud in 1553, in the Light of Sixteenth Century Catholic Attitudes toward the Talmud," *Bibliothèque d'humanisme et Renaissance*, 34 (1972), 435–459; D. Carpi, "The Expulsion of the Jews from the Papal States during the Time of Pope Pius V and the Inquisitional Trials against the Jews of Bologna" (in Hebrew), in *Scritti in memoria di Enzo Sereni*, ed. D. Carpi and R. Spiegel (Jerusalem, 1970), pp. 145–65; R. Bonfil, "Some Reflections on the Place of Azariah de Rossi's *Me'or Enayim* in the Cultural Milieu of Italian Renaissance Jewry," in *Jewish Thought in the Sixteenth Century*, ed. B. Cooperman (Cambridge, Mass., 1983), pp. 23–48; and their bibliographic references.

2. On Jewish life in Renaissance Italy, see the standard surveys by C. Roth, *The Jews in the Renaissance* (Philadelphia, 1959); M. A. Shulvass, *Jews in the World of the Renaissance* (Leiden and Chicago, 1973); A. Milano, *Storia degli ebrei in Italia* (Turin, 1963); R. Bonfil, *Ha-Rabbanut be-Italyah bi-Tekufat ha-Renesance* (Jerusalem, 1979); and D. B. Ruderman, *The World of a Renaissance Jew* (Cincinnati, 1981). On Jewish intellectual life in the period, see idem, "The Italian Renaissance and Jewish Thought," in *Renaissance Humanism: Foundations and Forms*, 3 vols., ed. A. Rabil, Jr. (Philadelphia, 1988), I, 382–433.

3. For an overview of Jewish loan banking in Italy, see the surveys mentioned in the previous note and L. Poliakov, *Jewish Bankers and the Holy See*, trans. M. L. Kochan (London, Henley, and Boston, 1977). For the Mantuan region, the location of Yagel's bank, see S. Simonsohn, *History of the Jews in the Duchy of Mantua* (Jerusalem, 1977).

4. I expand on this theme in the introduction to my English translation and critical edition of *Gei Ḥizzayon* (Univ. of Pa. Press, forthcoming).

5. *Beit Ya'ar ha-Levanon*, pt. 1, Bodleian Ms. Reggio 9, introduction, fol. 2a. The passage is crossed out but still legible. I also consulted an earlier draft of this composition, in the opening pages of Bodleian Ms. Reggio 8, where it is not crossed out. Unless otherwise indicated, all citations of parts 1–3 of *Beit Ya'ar ha-Levanon* are from Bodleian Ms. Reggio 9, all citations of part 4 are from Bodleian Ms. Reggio 10, and all translations are my own. Bodleian Mss. Reggio 8–10 are listed as nos. 1303–1305 in A. Neubauer, *Catalogue of the Hebrew Manuscripts in the Bodleian Library*, 2 vols. (Oxford, 1886, 1906).

6. On this region's Jewish population, see C. Roth, *History of the Jews of Venice* (Philadelphia, 1930), chap. 8. Yagel reveals his birthdate on two occasions, the first in a letter written in 1613 on his sixtieth birthday, and the second in a 1623 letter to Hananiah Rieti; *Bat Rabim*, Ms. Moscow Günzburg 129, no. 67, fols. 106b–108b, and fol. 174a (Hebrew University and National Library, Jerusalem Microfilm 6809; hereafter cited as Jerusalem microfilm). All citations of *Bat Rabim* are to this manuscript.

7. On the Gallico family in Italy, see the interesting testimony of Solomon Graziano, who cites Mordecai Dato that this family was one of the famous four families to be exiled from Jerusalem when the Second Temple was destroyed. See E. Zimmer, "Biographical Details concerning Italian Jewry, from Abraham Graziano's Handwritten Notes" (in Hebrew), *Kiryat Sefer*, 49 (1974), 442.

8. *Bat Rabim*, fol. 195b.

9. See Simonsohn, *Jews in Mantua*, p. 28; Roth, *Jews in the Renaissance*, pp. 88–92; and B. Ravid, "The Socioeconomic Background of the Expulsion and Readmission of Venetian Jews 1571–1573," in *Essays in Modern Jewish History: A Tribute to Ben Halpern*, ed. F. Malino and P. C. Alpert (Rutherford, N.J. 1981).

10. See *Gei Ḥizzayon*, pt. 1, ed. A. B. Mani (Alexandria, Egypt, 1880), p. 20a. All references to part 1 of *Gei Ḥizzayon* are to Mani's edition.

11. See my forthcoming edition of *Gei Ḥizzayon* for a fuller treatment of this narrative.

12. *Gei Ḥizzayon*, pt. 1, p. 6a.

13. Simonsohn briefly summarizes almost all of Yagel's experience in Luzzara (*Jews in Mantua*, pp. 252–253). He could not find in the Mantuan archives any record of a bank in either Abraham's or his father's name; nor could he identify Rina's husband, whose name he omits altogether.

14. *Gei Ḥizzayon*, pt. 1, pp. 9a–10a. He was warned by Adam Forti (Ḥazak). Forti signed a letter along with other Mantuan Jewish officials offering assistance to the Jewish community of Ancona in 1569. See I. Sonne, *Mi-Pa'olo ha-Revi'i ad Pi'us ha-Ḥamishi* (Jerusalem, 1954), p. 211.

15. *Gei Ḥizzayon*, pt. 1, pp. 9b–10a.

16. On the Almagiati family see Simonsohn, *Jews in Mantua*, pp. 224, 228, 252–253; Simonsohn records (p. 224) that on May 11, 1577, the brothers Graziadio (Hananel) and Vitale (Jehiel) Rieti, as well as Lazzaro (Eleazar) Almagiati and his brother, were granted licenses to open banks in Luzzara. Since Almagiati battled Yagel for his bank in the period just before this and the Rieti family eventually gained the right to collect the rents from Yagel's property, it appears that this official license sealed the outcome of the miserable events Yagel describes in his autobiography: his bank was wrested from his control and handed over to the Almagiatis; eventually he was forced to leave and depended on the Rietis to supervise his remaining property.

17. *Gei Ḥizzayon*, pt. 1, pp. 19b–20a.

18. Ibid., pp. 20a–21a. On the plague in Mantua, see Simonsohn. *Jews in Mantua*, p. 30, and the sources he cites. Leon Modena discusses the impact of the plague on Cremona in his collection of *responsa*, *Zikne Yehudah*, ed. S. Simonsohn (Jerusalem, 1956), no. 78. See also M. Benayahu and G. Laras, "The Appointment of Health Inspectors in Cremona in 1575" (in Hebrew), *Michael*, 1 (1973), 78–143. On the plague in Venice, see P. Preto, *Peste e società a Venezia, 1576* (Vicenza, 1978).

19. *Gei Ḥizzayon*, pp. 28a–29a.

20. On Azariah (Bonaiuto) b. Solomon Finzi, see Simonsohn, *Jews in Mantua*, pp. 226–228, 236. He was the brother and banking partner of Yagel's closest friend, Hananiah Finzi. Together they opened banks in San Martino and Gazzuolo.

21. On Barukh b. Joseph Senigo, see Simonsohn, *Jews in Mantua*, p. 30. He was one of three community health supervisors for Mantua during the plague of 1576.

22. Also known as Reuben Yare, he served as a teacher in the home of Solomon Segal Ostiglia of Mantua and reported to Yagel about a supposed case of demons in the house. See Chapter 3 and Simonsohn, *Jews in Mantua*, p. 716.

23. On this family in Mantua, see Simonsohn, *Jews in Mantua*, index.

24. On Barukh (Benedetto) b. Abraham Finzi, see ibid., pp. 348–350, 407. Finzi was a banker in Gazzuolo who was granted the patent to run the inn of the Jewish community—a tavern, restaurant, and hostelry serving visitors and the poor.

25. *Gei Ḥizzayon*, pt. 1, pp. 34a–b.

26. On Gershon (Grassino) b. Abraham Porto, see Simonsohn, *Jews in Mantua*, pp. 221–222, 423–424, 511. He was a banker in Mantua in 1577.

27. On Isaac b. David Cohen Porto, see ibid., pp. 30, 218, 253, 415, 622, 727; D. Kaufmann, "Meir b. Ephraim of Padua, Scroll-writer and Printer in Mantua," *Jewish Quarterly Review*, 11 (1899), 218; E. Kupfer, "New Documents regarding the Polemic over the Publication of the *Zohar*" (in Hebrew), *Michael*, 1 (1982), 313. Isaac had served as an arbitrator in other communal disputes.

28. Simonsohn, *Jews in Mantua*, p. 226, identifies him with Judah Sinai of Colonia, but perhaps he was the banker Judah b. Solomon mentioned in transactions with the family of Yagel's father-in-law (ibid., p. 224). Judah also interceded on behalf of his friend Azariah Finzi regarding the tragic murder of his daughter by his son (discussed later in this chapter).

29. *Gei Ḥizzayon*, pt. 1, p. 41b.

30. Judah Moscato was the famous preacher and rabbi; on his relationship with Yagel see the discussion later in this chapter. Simonsohn, *Jews in Mantua*, p. 253, seems to identify Katz Porto as someone other than Gershon b. Abraham Porto.

31. *Gei Ḥizzayon*, pp. 43b–44a.

32. *Gei Ḥizzayon*, pt. 2, Ms. Cincinnati Hebrew Union College 743, fols.

71b–73a. All citations of part 2 of *Gei Ḥizzayon* are to the Cincinnati Ms.

33. Yagel probably referred to the proclamation of Duke Gugielmo of March 1, 1576, intended to distance Jews from Christians. Among other provisions, Jews were forbidden to purchase property or to visit each other's houses for festivities and celebrations. The punishment was usually a fine of twenty-five scudi. See Simonsohn, *Jews in Mantua*, pp. 113–14.

34. See Y. Dan, *Ha-Sippur ha-Ivri bimai ha-Beinayim* (Jerusalem, 1974), p. 217; and Y. Yuval, "A German Jewish Autobiography from the Fourteenth Century (in Hebrew), *Tarbiẓ*, 55 (1986), 541–566.

35. On this new awareness see N. Davis, "Fame and Secrecy: Leon Modena's Life as an Early Modern Autobiography" (Paper presented at the conference Jewish Societies in Transformation in the Sixteenth and Seventeenth Centuries, Van Leer Institute, Jerusalem, January 1986, to be published by Princeton University Press as part of the new edition and English translation of Leon Modena's autobiography).

36. Ms. London British Museum 6469, add. 22094 (Jerusalem microfilm 5043), fol. 62a; M. Margoliouth, *Catalogue of the Hebrew and Samaritan Manuscripts in the British Museum*, II (London, 1965), 261.

37. On Hosea see Simonsohn, *Jews in Mantua*, pp. 224–226. His father was the banker Abraham b. Angelo da Colonia, who had also been a banker in Viadana and other cities.

38. Some of the notices in Simonsohn already refer to Batsheva as widow and guardian of Dina.

39. *Bat Rabim*, no. 6, fols. 9a–10a. The document is signed by three rabbis: Barukh Uziel Ḥasachetto, of Ferrara; Raphael b. Yohanan Treves; and Aaron b. Israel Finzi.

40. The sick woman is recorded in *Beit Ya'ar ha-Levanon*, pt. 1, chap. 15 (and see Chapter 2). He mentions the traveler in *Be'er Sheva*, Bodleian Ms. Reggio 11 (listed as no. 1306 in Neubauer, *Hebrew Manuscripts in Bodleian*), pt. 2, chap. 21, fol. 72b. All citations of *Be'er Sheva* are to this manuscript.

41. In a letter of January 1582 asking the leaders of the yeshiva of Pesaro to assist the wife of Judah Moscato because her husband has been called away and cannot provide for her, Yagel mentions that he was in their city some years earlier; *Bat Rabim*, fol. 177a (the later folios contain no item numbers). As late as 1619 he inspected a manuscript by Yohanan Alemanno in Pesaro (fol. 118b).

42. In *Be'er Sheva*, pt. 2, chap. 22, fol. 78a, he mentions spending a summer evening in the home of Judah da Revere in Revere, where he saw a copy of Abraham Farissol's geographic work. On the latter see Ruderman, *World of a Renaissance Jew*, chap. 11. In *Beit Ya'ar ha-Levanon*, pt. 1, chap. 7, fol. 13a, he refers to Judah's medical skills in curing infections on women's breasts. There he places him in Zittone, near Ferrara. See also Chapter 2, note 19, below.

43. In June 1587 Yagel served as a tutor in the home of Joseph Fano out-

side Ferrara; Ms. Montefiore 462, no. 73, fol. 43b. My thanks to Professors Reuven Bonfil and Jacob Boksenboim for this information. See now J. Boksenboim, *Iggrot Melamdim* (Tel Aviv, 1985), p. 89.

44. In 1590–91 in Carpi Yagel copied some selections from the work of Joseph ibn Shraga, the Spanish kabbalist; *Bat Rabim*, fol. 153a.

45. In January 1605 Yagel was in the home of "the nobleman da Revere" (Judah?) in Correggio, where he inspected a letter of Israel Sarug, the disciple of Isaac Luria and teacher of Menahem Azariah da Fano; *Bat Rabim*, no. 61, fols. 94a–95b.

46. In *Beit Ya'ar ha-Lavanon*, pt. 4, chap. 31, fol. 75b, he mentions having seen a ferocious wild animal in Reggio in 1601. He probably frequented Reggio on account of his relationship with Menahem Azariah da Fano, who lived there.

47. He was in Modena in August 1613, in 1617, and in 1620; *Bat Rabim*, fols. 184b–185a; no. 64, fols. 102b–105a; no. 68, fols. 108b–112a.

48. From Rubeira in 1585 Yagel criticized a sermon of the rabbi of Modena; Mordecai Dato wrote to Yagel later in that year, supporting his position on metempsychosis; see *Bat Rabim*, no. 72, fols. 114b–116a, and Chapter 8. On the document of 1593, see Chapter 2. He also corresponded with a number of people from Rubeira in 1600; *Bat Rabim*, nos. 47, 52, fols. 81b, 86b.

49. On Fano see C. Roth, "Josef Da Fano, il primo ebreo italiano nobile," *La rassegna mensile di Israel*, 14 (1948), 190–194. Cf. Simonsohn, *Jews in Mantua*, p. 32, nn. 114 and 115. He is referred to in some contemporary chronicles; see Giovanni Battista Spaccini, *Cronaca modenese*, ed. G. Bertoni, T. Sandonini, and P. Vicini, Monumenti de storia patria delle provincie modenesi, XVI and XVII (Modena, 1911), XVI, 332, where the duke attempts to pressure Fano to convert. See also Lodovico Vedriani, *Historia dell'antichissimi città di Modena* (Modena, 1667), p. 609, where he recounts that Fano was wounded while playing cards.

50. On this work see S. Maybaum, *Abraham Jagel's Katechismus Lekah-tob* (Berlin, 1892).

51. His correspondence with Daniel is in *Bat Rabim*, fols. 118a–b, 183b, and is discussed in Chapter 2.

52. Genealogical information on the Modena family is found in the beginning of Ms. Bologna University 2206 (Jerusalem microfilm 27795) and Ms. Cambridge 40/32 (Jerusalem microfilm 15877).

53. The latest and most complete account of Menahem's life is R. Bonfil, "New Information on R. Menahem Azariah da Fano and His Age" (in Hebrew), in *Perakim be-Toledot ha-Ḥevra ha-Yehudit . . . le-Professor Ya'akov Katz* (Jerusalem, 1980), pp. 98–135.

54. See *Bat Rabim*, no. 47, fol. 81b.

55. On Hezekiah Foa see Simonsohn, *Jews in Mantua*, p. 510; M. Ghirondi and H. Neppi *Toledot Gedolei Yisrael ve-Geonei Italyah* (Trieste, 1853), p. 110; Bonfil, "New Information," pp. 105–106.

56. *Bat Rabim*, fols. 184b–185a. I could find no reference to this incident in A. Balletti, *Gli Ebrei e gli Estensi*, 2d ed. (Reggio nell' Emilia, 1930).

57. See note 52 above.

58. The event is preserved in three manuscripts: Ms. Budapest Kaufmann A557/14 (Jerusalem microfilm 12688), Bodleian Ms. Mich. 186 (listed as no. 2061/2 in Neubauer, *Hebrew Manuscripts in Bodleian*), and Ms. Warsaw 680. I have consulted the Budapest manuscript, which was also published by M. Stern, "Zur Berichte des Raphael aus Sassuolo" (Hebrew title "Megillat Nes"), in *Festschrift . . . D. Hoffman* (Berlin, 1914), Hebrew section, pp. 267–280; German, pp. 460–462.

59. Ms. Budapest Kaufmann A557/14, fol. 310.

60. See Simonsohn, *Jews in Mantua*, p. 712: "It is doubtful whether a scholar like Gallico would spend his last days as a servant, even if we give a wide interpretation to the term."

61. *Bat Rabim*, no. 64, fols. 102a–105b. The accused were a Michael Sanguinetti, Joseph Pontasso, and Solomon Katz. The Sanguinetti bank is mentioned by Spaccini, *Cronaca modenese*, XVI, 8, 11, 216; XVII, 57. On Pontasso see Balletti, *Gli Ebrei*, p. 149. There are additional documents on this incident in the Archivio de Stato in Modena.

62. *Bat Rabim*, fols. 171a–172a, 174a–175a.

63. Ibid., no. 44, fols. 78a–79b.

64. On Hananiah Rieti and his son, Elḥanan Yedidiah, see Simonsohn, *Jews in Mantua*, p. 731, and the sources he gives there.

65. *Bat Rabim*, fol. 174a.

66. Ibid., fol. 171a.

67. This correspondence reveals the existence of a synagogue in Yagel's former house, a fact also mentioned in passing in *Gei Ḥizzayon*. On this synagogue, see the interesting 1640 document cited by Balletti, *Gli Ebrei*, p. 100, pointing out that the synagogue had been used continuously for seventy years, at about the same time Yagel first acquired the property in Luzzara.

68. See Maybaum, *Abraham Jagel's Katechismus Lekahtob*; also J. H. Greenstone, "Some Early Jewish Catechisms" (Address delivered at the Jewish Theological Seminary of New York, March 25, 1909; published in the Philadelphia *Jewish Exponent*, 1909), *EJ*, IX, 1268–69.

69. See my forthcoming edition and English translation of *Gei Ḥizzayon*.

70. Compare G. Sermoneta, "Encyclopedias in the Medieval Hebrew World," and A. Melamed, "Hebrew Italian Renaissance and Early Modern Encyclopedias," both in *Rivista di storia della filosofia*, 40 (1985), 7–50 and 91–112.

71. *Bat Rabim*, no. 37, fols. 70a–b.

72. On Finzi see Simonsohn, *Jews in Mantua*, pp. 30, 50, 226–228, 236, 357, 622, 708–709, 724. Finzi also had close contacts with Menahem Azariah da Fano. He was one of the publishers of Fano's edition of the Roman

high holy day prayer book, and he served with Fano in 1601 in Viadana in distributing the monies owed Jewish refugees from Milan.

73. *Beit Ya'ar ha-Levanon*, pt. 1, introduction, fol. 2b.

74. *Be'er Sheva*, pt. 2, chap. 11, fol. 38b.

75. *Beit Ya'ar ha-Levanon*, pt. 4, chap. 100, fol. 230a.

76. *Bat Rabim*, no. 44, fol. 78a.

77. Ibid., no. 77, fol. 199a.

78. Ibid., no. 27, fol. 57b. The rabbis were Ishmael Hananiah of Vallemonte and Hillel Modena of Viadana.

79. Ibid., nos. 39, 40, fols. 72b–74a. Yagel also copied a number of Fano's rabbinic *responsa;* ibid., nos. 16, 43, fols. 29a–b, 77a–b (discussed in Chapter 5).

80. Ibid., nos. 41, 45, fols. 74b–75b, 80a (discussed in Chapter 2).

81. Ibid., no. 59, fol. 93a.

82. Menahem Azariah da Fano, *Asarah Ma'amarot*, Ms. Strasbourg 3973 (Jerusalem microfilm 2867) (J. Landauer, *Katalog der hebräishen, arabischen Mss.* [Strasbourg, 1881], p. 67, n. 47), chap. 29, fol. 125b.

83. *Beit Ya'ar ha-Levanon*, pt. 2, chaps. 25, 26, and 29.

84. Ibid., chap. 25, fol. 103a.

85. Ibid., chap. 29; cf. chap. 28.

86. In ibid., chap. 26, fol. 104b, Yagel quotes Fano's *Rimmon ha-Pelaḥ.* In fol. 50b he mentions that Fano taught him that Cordovero did not have a *maggid* (a heavenly mentor).

87. This is the view of M. Idel, "Major Currents in Italian Kabbalah (1550–1650)," in *Italia Judaica*, II, ed. S. Simonsohn and G. Sermoneta (Rome, 1987). See also A. Altmann, "Notes on the Development of Rabbi Menahem Azariah Fano's Kabbalist Doctrine" (in Hebrew), in *Studies in Jewish Mysticism Presented to Isaiah Tishby* (Jerusalem, 1984), pp. 241–267.

88. On Dato see Y. Jacobson, "The Messianic Doctrine of Mordecai Dato" (in Hebrew) (Ph.D. diss., Hebrew University, 1982); R. Bonfil, "One of the Italian Sermons of R. Mordecai Dato" (in Hebrew), *Italia*, 1 (1976), 1–32; I. Tishby, "The Image of R. Moses Cordovero in a Composition of R. Mordecai Dato" (in Hebrew), *Sefunot*, 7 (1962–63), 121–161; reprinted in *Studies in Kabbalah and Its Branches* (in Hebrew) (Jerusalem, 1982), pp. 131–86. All three authors provide a useful bibliography.

89. Ms. London British Museum 6469, add. 22094, fol. 60b.

90. *Bat Rabim*, fol. 255a. On Meir see Kaufmann, "Meir of Padua."

91. *Bat Rabim*, no. 73, fol. 116b; see also Chapter 8. Yagel also quotes Dato in nos. 54 and 55, fol. 183a, and in *Eshet Ḥayil* (Venice, 1605), p. 5b.

92. See Jacobson, "Messianic Doctrine of Dato," pp. 11, 43, 50, 66, 85, 95.

93. Both composed autobiographical stories that ultimately lead to the spiritual ascent of the author; both were fascinated with shepherdlike figures such as Moses and with child prodigies.

94. See *Be'er Sheva*, chap. 22, published by A. Neubauer (with the wrong title) in *Kovez al Yad*, 4 (1888), 37–44.

95. R. Bonfil discusses this correspondence from Ms. Parma 130 in "Italian Sermons of Dato," p. 6, and more fully in his *Rabbanut*, pp. 189–90.

96. In Bonfil, *Rabbanut*, p. 189.

97. Ibid, p. 190.

98. See Chapter 8 for a discussion of their meeting.

99. See, for example, *Moshi'ah Hosim* (Venice, 1587), p. 18a; *Be'er Sheva*, pt. 2, chap. 4, fol. 21b. Moscato acted as arbitrator in Yagel's feud with the Almagiatis.

100. *Bat Rabim*, fol. 177a.

101. Yagel used Azariah's chapter on the history of the Hebrew language when composing his own in *Gei Hizzayon*; he probably also consulted Azariah's discussion of the suitability of reading Ben Sira (see Chapter 7); and he clearly copied a section of his discussion of the crimes of Herod in *Bat Rabim*, fol. 144b.

102. This fact has already been noted by M. Idel in "The Magical and Neoplatonic Interpretations of the Kabbalah in the Renaissance," in *Jewish Thought in the Sixteenth Century*, ed. B. Cooperman (Cambridge, Mass., 1983), pp. 224–227, and in "Major Currents in Italian Kabbalah," p. 247. In the latter work he mentions some fifteen references to Alemanno's works in Yagel's writing. There are clearly more. See, for example, *Beit Ya'ar ha-Levanon*, pt. 4, chaps. 45, 53, 57, 67, 73, 74, 83–86, 88–91; *Bat Rabim*, fols. 126a, 126b, 181b; *Eshet Hayil*, p. 7a.

2. The Art of Healing

1. *Bat Rabim*, Ms. Moscow Günzburg (Jerusalem microfilm 6809), no. 49, fol. 82b. The line is based in part on Ps. 36:10.

2. Ibid., no. 51, fol. 85b.

3. Ibid., no. 75, fol. 118a.

4. Ibid., no. 77, fol. 119a. For the first expression, see B.T. Babba Batra 12a; J.T. Berakhot 1, 4; and elsewhere.

5. *Bat Rabim*, no. 77, fol. 119a.

6. *Beit Ya'ar ha-Levanon*, pt. 4, Bodleian Ms. Reggio 10, chap. 96, fol. 214b.

7. Padua's medical school is the only such institution in Italy with relatively complete records of Jewish medical graduates, although most are for the sixteenth century. See A. Modena and E. Morpurgo, *Medici e chirurgi ebrei dottorati e licenziati nell'Universita di Padova dal 1617 al 1816*, ed. A. Luzzato, L. Münster, and V. Colorni (Bologna, 1967); E. Veronese Ceseracciu, "Ebrei laureati a Padova nell Cinquecento," *Quaderni per la storia dell'Universita di Padova*, 13 (1980), 151–168; D. Carpi, "Jews Holding the Doctoral Degree from the University of Padua in the Sixteenth Century and the Beginning of the Seventeenth Century" (in Hebrew), in *Scritti in me-*

moria di Nathan Cassuto, ed. D. Cassuto et. al. (Jerusalem, 1986), pp. 62–91.

8. Archivio di Stato, Rome, Fondo camerali I: Diversorum del Camerlengo, filza 407, fol. 158b. I am indebted to Professor Bernard Cooperman for this reference.

9. K. Thomas, *Religion and the Decline of Magic* (New York, 1971), pp. 5–14; C. Webster, ed., *Health, Medicine, and Mortality in the Sixteenth Century* (Cambridge and New York, 1979); C. M. Cipolla, *Fighting the Plague in Seventeenth-Century Italy* (Madison, Wis., 1981).

10. C. M. Cipolla, *Public Health and the Medical Profession in the Renaissance* (Cambridge, 1976), esp. p. 83.

11. Cipolla discusses these problems in *Fighting the Plague* and *Public Health*. See also idem, *Faith, Reason, and the Plague in Seventeenth Century Tuscany* (Ithaca, N.Y., 1979); R. J. Palmer, "The Control of Plague in Venice and Northern Italy" (Ph.D. diss., University of Kent, England, 1978).

For a succinct evaluation of the medical field in the sixteenth century, its generally conservative bent, and its relatively modest and unspectacular advances in diagnosis and treatment of illness over those of previous centuries, see the introduction in A. Wear, R. K. French, and I. M. Lowie, eds., *The Medical Renaissance of the Sixteenth Century* (Cambridge, 1985). For a similar evaluation of sixteenth-century science in general, see C. B. Schmitt, "Recent Trends in the Study of Medieval and Renaissance Science," in *Information Sources in the History of Science and Medicine*, ed. P. Corsi and O. Weindling (London, 1983), pp. 221–240. Schmitt accordingly treats the twelfth to seventeenth centuries as a single historical unit.

12. On the Galenic system see V. Nutten, ed., *Galenism: Rise and Decline of a Medical Philosophy* (Ithaca, N.Y., 1973); R. E. Siegel, *Galen's System of Psychology and Medicine* (Basel and New York, 1965). A good summary of Galen's diagnosis and treatment of melancholy, as practiced in the sixteenth century, is found in L. Babb, *The Elizabethan Malady: A Study of Melancholia in English Literature from 1580 to 1644* (East Lansing, Mich., 1951). See also G. Zilboorg, *A History of Medical Psychology* (New York, 1969); M. Heyd, "Robert Burton's Sources on Enthusiasm and Melancholy: From a Medical Tradition to Religious Controversy," *History of European Ideas*, 5 (1984), 17–44. On the inadequacy of Galenic treatments, see Thomas, *Religion and Decline of Magic*, p. 8; Cipolla, *Public Health*, p. 5.

13. This subject is admirably developed by M. MacDonald in *Mystical Bedlam: Madness, Anxiety, and Healing in Seventeenth Century England* (Cambridge, 1981). See also Webster, *Health, Medicine, and Mortality*, esp. the chapters by A. Chapman; "Astrological Medicine," M. Pelling and Webster, "Medical Practitioners," and Webster, "Alchemical and Paracelsian Medicine"; Thomas, *Religion and Decline of Magic*, esp. pp. 151–158; P. J. French, *John Dee: The World of an Elizabethan Magus* (London, 1972); G. Zanier, *La medicina astrologia e la sua teoria: Marsilio Ficino e i suoi critici contemporanei* (Rome, 1977).

14. On the theme of correlations and analogies in the mental universe of the sixteenth century, see Chapter 4.

15. On Cardano see A. Ingegno, *Saggio sulla filosofia di Cardano* (Florence, 1980); I. Maclean, "The Interpretation of Natural Signs: Cardano's *De subtilitate* versus Scaliger's *Exercitationes*," in *Occult and Scientific Mentalities in the Renaissance*, ed. B. Vickers (Cambridge, 1984). On Cardano's medical practice see H. Morley, *The Life of Jerome Cardan of Milan, Physician*, 2 vols. (London, 1854). On Levinus Lemnius, see his *De Miraculis Occultis Naturae* (Antwerp, 1581). Both Cardano and Lemnius were well known to Yagel; see Chapters 4–6. On Napier see MacDonald, *Mystical Bedlam*; on Forman see A. L. Rowse, *Simon Forman: Sex and Society in Shakespeare's Age* (London, 1974).

16. *Beit Ya'ar ha-Levanon*, pt. 4, chap. 7, fol. 12b.

17. Ibid., fol. 13b.

18. Ibid., fols. 12b–13a.

19. Yagel quotes from Peter of Abano's *Conciliator Differentiarum Philosophorum et Praecipue Medicorum* (Venice, 1496, and many other editions). On the importance of Abano's *Conciliator* in the sixteenth century, see C. B. Schmitt, "Aristotle among the Physicians," in Wear, French, and Lowie, *Medical Renaissance*, p. 3.; N. G. Siraisi, *Arts and Sciences at Padua: The Studium of Padua before 1350* (Toronto, 1973). Yagel also quotes from Francesco Giuntini, *Speculum Astrologiae* (Lyons, 1575), here and elsewhere. He refers to Pseudo-Albertus' . . . *de Mirabilibus Mundi (Sefer Nifla'ot ha-Olam)*, printed in Italy after 1478; on this work see R. Klein, *Form and Meaning* (New York, 1979), p. 51. Among his Jewish sources, he is especially fond of mentioning the various examples of magical healing through incantations in B.T. Shabbat 66b–67b, and the "spiritual healing" described in the *Sefer ha-Zohar*, 3, 56a–57a. Members of the families of Ḥazak (Forti) and Revere are mentioned in S. Simonsohn, *History of the Jews in the Duchy of Mantua* (Jerusalem, 1977); M. Ghirondi and H. Neppi, *Toledot Gedolei Yisrael be'Italia* (Trieste, 1853), p. 215.

20. *Beit Ya'ar ha-Levanon*, pt. 4, chap. 7, fol. 14a. Cf. the parallel approach of Jean Fernel (1497–1558), discussed by L. D. Richardson, "The Generation of Disease: Occult Causes and Diseases of the Total Substance," in Wear, French, and Lowie, *Medical Renaissance*, pp. 175–94.

21. *Beit Ya'ar ha-Levanon*, pt. 4, chap. 10, fols. 18b–21a, in which he explicates expecially the *Sefer ha-Zohar*, 3, 299a–b.

22. Ibid., fol. 19a.

23. Ibid., fol 19b.

24. Ibid. This is based primarily on Rashi's comments on bad doctors in B.T. Kedushin 82a and *Sefer ha-Zohar*, 3, 299b.

25. Ibid., fol. 20a. Cf. *Sefer ha-Zohar*, 3, 299b, where a merchant describes the book to Rabbi Eleazer. On the use of holy names in healing, see M. Idel, "Psalms, Kabbalah" (in Hebrew), in *Ha-Enciclopedia ha-Ivrit*, XXXII (Jerusalem, 1980–81), 536.

26. *Beit Ya'ar ha-Levanon,* pt. 4, chap. 10, fol. 20a.

27. Ibid., fol. 20b.

28. See Chapter 7 for a discussion of Yagel's indebtedness to Agrippa's work and Pico della Mirandola's school. Cf. M. Idel, "The Magical and Neoplatonic Interpretations of the Kabbalah in the Renaissance," in *Jewish Thought in the Sixteenth Century,* ed. B. Cooperman (Cambridge, Mass., 1983), pp. 224–226. See also idem, "Differing Conceptions of Kabbalah in the Early Seventeenth Century," in *Jewish Thought in the Seventeenth Century,* ed. I. Twersky and B. Septimus (Cambridge, Mass., 1987), pp. 168–169, n. 155. On Agrippa see P. Zambelli, "Cornelio Agrippa nelle fonti e negli studi recenti," *Rinascimento,* 8 (1968), 169–199; idem, "Agrippa of Nettesheim," *Journal of the Warburg and Courtauld Institute,* 39 (1976), 69–103. On Yagel's use of the triadic schematization in the context of magic, see Chapters 4, 5, and 7 and the introduction to my forthcoming edition of Yagel's *Gei Ḥizzayon.*

29. *Beit Ya'ar ha-Levanon,* pt. 1, Bodleian Ms. Reggio 9. Unless otherwise indicated, all citations of parts 1–3 are to this manuscript.

30. Bodleian Ms. Reggio 8 is apparently a first draft of several chapters of *Beit Ya'ar ha-Levanon,* including long sections from pt. 1.

31. *Beit Ya'ar ha-Levanon,* pt. 1, chap. 15, fols. 29a–31a.

32. Ibid., fol. 28b.

33. *Gei Ḥizzayon,* ed. A. B. Mani (Alexandria, Egypt, 1880), pp. 24–25.

34. This dialogue is considered more fully in Chapter 5.

35. *Bereshit Rabbah,* 20, 7; *Moshi'ah Ḥosim,* p. 3a.

36. *Moshi'ah Ḥosim,* pp. 3b–4b.

37. Ibid., pp. 5a–7b.

38. Ibid., pp. 7b–10a.

39. Ibid., p. 10b.

40. Ibid., pp. 12b–16a and 21a–27a.

41. Ibid., pp. 16a–18b (quotation pp. 17a–b).

42. Ibid., p. 16b.

43. Ibid., pp. 30a–31b.

44. Yagel refers especially to *Sefer ha-Zohar,* 2, 218b–219b.

45. *Moshiah Ḥosim,* p. 32a. On Joseph ibn Shraga see G. Scholem in *EJ,* X, 243. For other Jewish examples of the use of the incense ceremony in fighting plague in the fifteenth century, see M. Idel, "Investigations in the Methodology of the Author of 'Sefer ha-Meshiv,'" *Sefunot,* n.s., 2 (1983), 262–266. On the origin of the ceremony see Num. 17:11–12; B.T. Keritot 6a (mentioned by Yagel, *Moshi'ah Ḥosim,* p. 18a); Yoma 44a; J.T. Yoma 4, 5.

46. P. Preto, *Peste e società a Venezia, 1576* (Vicenza, 1978). I was unable to consult the plague tract by the Jewish physician David de Pomis, *Breve discorsi et efficacissimi ricordi per liberare ogni citta oppressa dal mal contagioso* (Venice, 1577). The fact that Yagel composed his treatise in Hebrew, unlike his Jewish colleague, suggests that it was written exclusively as a manual for Jews.

47. See esp. Preto, *Peste e società*, pp. 51–74.

48. Ibid., pp. 62, 180–183.

49. Ibid., pp. 70–71, 178–179, 195–203.

50. Ibid., p. 65.

51. See N. Siraisi, *Taddeo Alderotti and His Pupils: Two Generations of Italian Medical Learning* (Princeton, 1981), chap. 9, on *consilia* in the thirteenth and fourteenth centuries; MacDonald, *Mystical Bedlam*, on Richard Napier's *consilia* and on the genre in general. On the parallel relationship between medical and legal *consilia*, see P. Riesenberg, "The Consilia Literature: A Prospectus," *Manuscripta*, 6 (1962), 3–22.

52. On Napier see MacDonald, *Mystical Bedlam*; on Lilly see D. Parker, *Familiar to All: William Lilly and Astrology in the Seventeenth Century* (London, 1975); on Forman see Rowse, *Simon Forman*.

53. To my knowledge, *consilia* of Jewish physicians have never been studied systematically by modern historians. One promising source is the manuscript in the David Kaufmann collection in Budapest titled *Consulti medici de Guglielmo Portaleone Mantovano e di altri Italiani*, discussed briefly by D. Kaufmann, "Abraham Sommo Portaleone's Testament," *Jewish Quarterly Review*, 4 (1892), 333–41. See now S. Kottek and A. Anati, "Benjamin [Guglielmo] Mi-She'ar Aryeh [Portaleone]" (in Hebrew), in *Scritti in memoria di Nathan Cassuto*, pp. 92–109.

54. *Beit Ya'ar ha-Levanon*, pt. 4, chap. 18, fols. 37b–38b.

55. Ibid., pt. 2, chap. 30, fols. 110b–112b. This was printed by I. Reggio in *Iggerot Yashar*, I (Vienna, 1834), 21–29.

56. *Beit Ya'ar ha-Levanon*, pt. 1, chap. 15, fol. 31a.

57. Levinus Lemnius, *The Touchstone of Complexions*, trans. T. Newton (London, 1576), p. 151b.

58. *Beit Ya'ar ha-Levanon*, pt. 1, chap. 15, fol. 30b.

59. Ibid., pt. 4, chap. 75, fols. 173b–174b. Cf. Henry Cornelius Agrippa, *De Occulta Philosophia* (Cologne, 1533), bk. 1, chap. 64; Robert Burton, *The Anatomy of Melancholy*, ed. A. R. Shilleto, 3 vols. (London, 1912–13), I, 291–295.

60. *Beit Ya'ar ha-Levanon*, pt. 4, chap. 75, fol. 173b.

61. Ibid., fols. 173b–174a.

62. In one instance, Yagel offers his readers a recipe for a memory drug and for illnesses "of the head and stomach" that he had tried on several occasions. See *Beit Ya'ar ha-Levanon*, pt. 4, chap. 94, fols. 213b–214b. The most recent work on the new pharmacology of the sixteenth century is R. Palmer, "Pharmacy in the Republic of Venice in the Sixteenth Century," in Wear, French, and Lowie, *Medical Renaissance*, pp. 100–117.

63. *Beit Ya'ar ha-Levanon*, pt. 4, chap. 76, fols. 175a–176a. On the use of the phrase by Abraham ibn Ezra, see his commentary on Prov. 9:1; by Maimonides, *Shemoneh Perakim*, end of chap. 4.

64. *Beit Ya'ar ha-Levanon*, pt. 4, chap. 77, fol. 176b.

65. Ibid., fol. 177a.

66. The case of Dato's wife is discussed in Chapter 3. The case of Moscato's wife is in *Bat Rabim*, fol. 176b.

67. On the treatment of melancholia in Yagel's day, see esp. Robert Bur-
ton's massive *Anatomy of Melancholy;* Babb, *The Elizabethan Malady;*
Heyd, "Robert Burton's Sources"; R. Klibansky, E. Panofsky, and D. Saxl,
Saturn and Melancholy (London, 1964).

68. *Bat Rabim*, no. 41, fols. 74b–75b.

69. Ibid., no. 75, fols. 118a–b.

70. Ibid.

71. Ibid., fol. 183b.

72. Ibid., no. 33, fols. 65a–66b.

73. Ibid., no. 65, fol. 105b.

74. Ibid., fol. 106a.

75. The letters are in ibid., nos. 45, 48–52, fols. 80a, 82a–88a. On the
Portaleone family see *EJ*, XIII, 907–908, and bibliography. On the Forlì and
Terracini families see Simonsohn, *Jews in Mantua.*

76. *Bat Rabim*, no. 48, fol. 82a.

77. Ibid., no. 45, fol. 80a.

78. Ibid.

79. Ibid., no. 50, fols. 83b–84a.

80. Ibid., fol. 84b.

81. Ibid., no. 51, fols. 85b–86a.

82. Ibid., no. 52, fols. 86b–88a.

83. On this book see, most recently, D. Halperin, "The Book of Remedies,
The Canonization of the Solomonic Writing, and the Riddle of Pseudo-
Eusebius," *Jewish Quarterly Review,* n.s., 72 (1982), 269–272, and the earlier works he cites. See also Mishnah Pesaḥim 4, 9; B. T. Berakhot 10b, Pesaḥim 56a; Maimonides on Mishnah Pesaḥim 4, 9; Abrabanel on 1 Kings 3
(Jerusalem, 1955), p. 473; M. Idel, "The Study Program of R. Yohanan Alemanno" (in Hebrew), *Tarbiz,* 48 (1979), 322, n. 117; idem, "The Magical and
Theurgic Interpretations of Music in Jewish Sources from the Renaissance
to Hasidism" (in Hebrew), *Yuval,* 4 (1982), 44. Yagel also mentions Solomon's "Book of Remedies" in *Beit Ya'ar ha-Levanon,* pt. 4, chap. 57, fols.
134a–b, where he refers to the discussions of Abrabanel and Maimonides.

84. *Bat Rabim*, no. 52, fol. 87a.

85. Ibid., fols. 87a–b.

86. Ibid., fol. 88a.

3. Demonology and Disease

1. *Beit Ya'ar ha-Levanon,* pt. 4, Bodleian Ms. Reggio 10, chap. 99, fol.
228a.

2. Ibid. On the definition of *mazzamauriello* see S. Battagli, *Grande dizionario della lingua italiana,* IX (Turin, 1975), 978.

3. *Beit Ya'ar ha-Levanon*, pt. 4, chap. 99, fol. 228b. Cf. *Bereshit Rabbah*, 10, 8; *Pirke de-Rabbi Eliezer*, 49.

4. See the numerous references to him in S. Simonsohn, *History of the Jews in the Duchy of Mantua* (Jerusalem, 1977).

5. His full name was Berakhia Reuben b. David of Perugia. On his life, see Simonsohn, *Jews in Mantua*, p. 716. Yagel mentions him as Reuben of Perugia in *Gei Ḥizzayon*, ed. A. B. Mani (Alexandria, Egypt, 1880), p. 29a.

6. Cf. *Bamidbar Rabbah*, 20, 10.

7. Hillel of Viadana was later a patient of Yagel's.

8. *Beit Ya'ar ha-Levanon*, pt. 4, chap. 99, fols. 228b–230a.

9. Yagel meant those sections of bk. 5, pts. 1 and 2 of Gersonides' *The Wars of the Lord* devoted entirely to astronomical and scientific matters, which were not printed in the first edition of Riva di Trento, 1560. For a brief summary of these sections and a list of manuscripts that contain the missing sections, see Levi ben Gershom (Gersonides), *The Wars of the Lord*, bk. 1, trans. and annot. S. Feldman (Philadelphia, 1984), pp. 21–23, 61–62. See now Levi ben Gerson, *The Astronomy of Levi ben Gerson (1288–1344): A Critical Edition of Chapters 1–20*, ed. B. R. Goldstein (New York and Berlin, 1985).

10. *Beit Ya'ar ha-Levanon*, pt. 4, chap. 100, fol. 231a.

11. Ibid. Cf. Nahmanides on Deut. 18:9 and Gedaliah ibn Yaḥya, *Shalshelet ha-Kabbalah* (Jerusalem, 1962), p. 197.

12. *Beit Ya'ar ha-Levanon*, pt. 4, chap. 100, fols. 231a–b. Yagel quotes *Sefer ha-Aẓamim* (London, 1902), p. 16, allegedly written by Abraham ibn Ezra. He also refers to ibn Ezra's commentary on Job 1:6. Yagel's criticism of Gersonides' position is precisely the same as that of Manasseh ben Israel some years later; *Nishmat Ḥayyim* (Amsterdam, 1651; reprint, Jerusalem, 1968), p. 50b. Manasseh uses "prophetic" knowledge in the same way that Yagel uses "experiential" ("based on the senses"), as distinguished from philosophical reasoning.

13. *Beit Ya'ar ha-Levanon*, pt. 4, chap. 101, fol. 231b. Manasseh ben Israel, *Nishmat Ḥayyim*, p. 54b, argued explicitly that his proof of the reality of demons substantiates a belief in the immortality of individual souls. On Manasseh's work see Y. Dan, "The Doctrine of Evil and Demonology in the Book *Nishmat Ḥayyim* of R. Manasseh ben Israel" (in Hebrew), in *Studies in Aggadah and Jewish Folklore*, ed. J. Dan and I. Ben-Ami (Jerusalem, 1983), pp. 263–274.

14. S. Anglo, "Melancholia and Witchcraft: The Debate between Wier, Bodin, and Scot," in the anthology *Folie et déraison à la Renaissance* (Brussels, 1976), p. 210. See also idem, "Evident Authority and Authoritative Evidence: The *Malleus Maleficarum*," in *The Damned Art: Essays in the Literature of Witchcraft* (London, 1977), pp. 7–8.

15. Cf. David b. Zimra's admission of his belief in demons, translated from his *responsa*, no. 848, in H. Zimmels, *Magicians, Theologians, and Doctors* (London, 1952), p. 81: "Actually, I believe in all the words of the

sages, even in their profane speech; how much more since the Bible . . .
mentions their existence." Biblical passages referring to demons include
Exod. 22:18; Lev. 17:7, 20:27; Deut. 18:10–12, 32:17; and 2 Sam. 28.

16. Anglo, in "Melancholia and Witchcraft" and "Evident Authority," re-
views many of the appropriate bibliographical references. See esp. E.
Schneweis, *Angels and Demons according to Lactantius* (Washington D.C.,
1944); G. Sovry, *La démonologie de Plutarque* (Paris, 1942); W. C. van Dam,
*Damonem und Bessene: Die Damonem in Geschichte und Gegenwart und
ihre Austreibung* (Aschaffenburg, 1970); S. Eitrem, *Some Notes on the Demonology of the New Testament*, 2d ed. (Oslo, 1966); R. H. Robbins, *The
Encyclopedia of Witchcraft and Demonology* (New York, 1970); D. P.
Walker, *Spiritual and Demonic Magic from Ficino to Campanella* (London
and Notre Dame, 1975); H. C. Lea, *Materials towards a History of Witch-
craft*, ed. A. C. Howland, 3 vols. (Philadelphia, 1939); P. Brown, "Sorcery,
Demons, and the Rise of Christianity," in *Witchcraft, Confessions, and Ac-
cusations*, ed. M. Douglas (London, 1970); W. Shumaker, *The Occult Sci-
ences in the Renaissance: A Study of Intellectual Patterns* (Berkeley and
Los Angeles, 1972); the numerous references in L. Thorndike, *A History of
Magic and Experimental Science*, 8 vols. (New York, 1923–58), esp. V and
VI; and C. Webster, *From Paracelsus to Newton: Magic and the Making of
Modern Science* (Cambridge, 1982), chap. 4.

17. On rabbinic and kabbalistic demonologies, see the essay by D. R. Hill-
ers, L. I. Rabinowitz, and G. Scholem in *EJ*, V, 1522–33; J. Trachtenberg,
Jewish Magic and Superstition: A Study in Folk Religion (1939; reprint,
New York, 1970); E. E. Urbach, *Ḥazal: Pirke Emunot* (Jerusalem, 1969), pp.
142–144; I. Tishby and F. Lachower, *Mishnat ha-Zohar*, 2 vols. (Jerusalem,
1957–61), I, 361–377; Zimmels, *Magicians, Theologians, and Doctors*, pp.
80–86; Manasseh ben Israel, *Nishmat Ḥayyim*, which constitutes a virtual
encyclopedia of Jewish and non-Jewish sources on demonology. For some
classical references see B.T. Ḥagigah 16b; B.T. Berakhot 6a; B.T. Ḥullin
105a; *Sifre Devarim*, 318, 321; Nahmanides on Gen. 4:22, Lev. 17:7 and
16:8; Kimḥi on 1 Sam. 28:25; Abrabanel on 1 Sam. 28:8. On the views of
some of Yagel's contemporaries, see C. Roth, *The Jews in the Renaissance*
(Philadelphia, 1959), pp. 59–63; M. A. Shulvass, *Jews in the World of the
Renaissance* (Leiden and Chicago, 1973), pp. 319–323; Yohanan Alemanno
in G. Scholem, "An Unknown Composition of R. Yohanan Alemanno" (in
Hebrew), *Kiryat Sefer*, 5 (1928–29), 273–274; Abraham Menahem Porto,
Minḥah Belulah (Verona, 1594), p. 201b, where he mentions a work of his
proving the reality of demons; Abraham ha-Levi ibn Migash, *Kevod Elohim*
(Constantinople, 1585), pp. 67b, 69a; ibn Yaḥya, *Shalshelet ha-Kabbalah*,
pp. 203–204. For recent scholarship on *dibbukim*, see note 46 below. Modern historical research, however, has not adequately treated the general subject of Jewish demonology in the sixteenth and seventeenth centuries;
much material in manuscript sources remains unstudied.

18. The Platonic and Neoplatonic sources are described in van Dam, *Da-*

monem und Bessene; Walker, *Spiritual and Demonic Magic;* and Sovry, *La démonologie de Plutarque.* See also Webster, *From Paracelsus to Newton,* p. 100, n. 4, for additional bibliography. Robert Burton, *The Anatomy of Melancholy,* ed. A. R. Shilleto, 3 vols. (London, 1912–13), I, 207, quotes the same source in Apuleius. Henry Cornelius Agrippa, *Three Books of the Occult Philosophy Written by Henry Cornelius Agrippa of Nettesheim,* trans. J. F. London (London, 1651), p. 397, refers to the same quotation. See also Augustine, *City of God,* trans. D. S. Wiesen (Cambridge, Mass., 1968), bk. 8, chaps. 14–16, pp. 63–77.

19. *Beit Ya'ar ha-Levanon,* pt. 4, chap. 101, fols. 232a–232b. See Nahmanides on Leviticus 17:7; *Midrash Rut ha-Ne'elam, Zohar Ḥadash,* 31b. See generally Tishby and Lachower, *Mishnat ha-Zohar,* I, 361–377.

20. Cf. Burton, *Anatomy of Melancholy,* I, 206: "Platonists [call] them Devils, for they name all the spirits daemones, be they good or bad angels."

21. *Beit Ya'ar ha-Levanon,* pt. 4, chap. 102, fols. 233a; chap. 103, fols. 235a–235b. Much of the same material on demons is found, with some variations, in Yagel's apparent earlier draft, Bodleian Ms. Reggio 8, fols. 34b–53b.

22. Bodleian Ms. Reggio 8, fol. 39b. Cf. Agrippa, *De Occulta Philosophia,* bk. 3, chap. 18; Burton, *Anatomy of Melancholy,* I, 214.

23. Bodleian Ms. Reggio 8, fol. 40b. In *Beit Ya'ar ha-Levanon,* pt. 4, chap. 36, fol. 86a, Yagel refers to the recent discovery of an eleventh sphere by the astronomer Magini, who published his finding in 1588. On Magini see Thorndike, *History of Magic,* V, 250–251; VI, 56–59.

24. *Beit Ya'ar ha-Levanon,* pt. 4, chap. 103, fols. 234a–235b; Bodleian Ms. Reggio 8, fols. 38a–40b, 51a–51b. On the threefold division, cf. Manasseh ben Israel, *Nishmat Ḥayyim,* p. 50a; *Ra'aya Meheimna,* 3, 253a.

25. Bodleian Ms. Reggio 8, fol. 34b; cf. Agrippa, *De Occulta Philosophia,* bk. 3, chap. 34; and Burton, *Anatomy of Melancholy,* I, 220, who refers to Felix Malleolus and Johan Wier on the demons of this region ("who seem to do drudgery work, to draw water").

26. Bodleian Ms. Reggio 8, fol. 34b. On the tradition of the seven climatic zones in Hebrew sources of the period, see D. B. Ruderman, *The World of a Renaissance Jew* (Cincinnati, 1981), pp. 135–36 and 231–232, n. 26.

27. Bodleian Ms. Reggio 8, fol. 35a. Cf *Beit Ya'ar ha-Levanon,* pt. 4, chap. 102, fols. 233a–233b; Agrippa, *De Occulta Philosophia,* bk. 3, chaps. 32, 35; Burton, *Anatomy of Melancholy,* I, 220–221, who also quotes Girolamo Cardano, *De Rerum Varietate,* chap. 16 (*Opera Omnia,* 10 vols. [Lyons, 1661; reprint, New York and London, 1967] III, chap. 16), a source well known to Yagel. On Cardano's influence on Yagel, see Chapters 4–6.

28. *Beit Ya'ar ha-Levanon,* pt. 4, chap. 103, fol. 237a.

29. Bodleian Ms. Reggio 8, fol. 41b.

30. Ibid., fol. 42a.

31. Ibid.; cf. *Beit Ya'ar ha-Levanon,* pt. 4, chap. 103, fol. 237b.

32. Bodleian Ms. Reggio 8, fol. 42a. Yagel maintains that this is also the

view of Pseudo–ibn Ezra in *Sefer ha-Aẓamim*, and of the rabbis in B.T. Gittin 67b, who describe a spirit called Kordiakos. Yagel again finds in rabbinic sources the most up-to-date "science."

33. On the epistemology of resemblance and its significance to Yagel, see Chapter 4.

34. Wier writes, for example: "Et tout ainsi comme par les humeurs & fumees l'usage de la raison est interessé es yvrongnes, es frenetiques & aussi es mélancholiques passions; ainsi le diable, qui est un esprit, peut aisément, par la permission de Dieu, les esmouvoir les accomoder à ses illusions, & corrompre la raison"; *Histoires disputes et discours des illusions et impostures des diables, des magiciens infames, sorcières et empoisonneurs etc.* (Paris, 1885), p. 313; cf. p. 308, quoted by Anglo in "Melancholia and Witchcraft," p. 212, where Anglo compares Wier's view with those of Bodin and Scot. See also C. Baxter, "Johann Weyer's *De Praestigiis Daemonum:* Unsystematic Psychopathology," in Anglo, *The Damned Art*, pp. 53–75.

35. Besides Anglo's "Melancholia and Witchcraft" see C. Baxter, "Jean Bodin's *De la Démonomanie des Sorciers:* The Logic of Persecution," in Anglo, *The Damned Art*, pp. 76–105; Baxter mentions there his earlier essay (note 34, above) and that of E. W. Monter ("Inflation and Witchcraft: The Case of Jean Bodin," in *Action and Conviction in Early Modern Europe*, ed. K. T. Rabb and J. E. Siegel [Princeton, 1969], pp. 371–389) on Bodin's demonology. On Scot see S. Anglo, "Reginald Scot's *Discoverie of Witchcraft:* Scepticism and Sadduceeism," in *The Damned Art*, pp. 106–39.

36. I have quoted from the English translation of Lemnius, *The Secret Miracles of Nature in Four Books* (London, 1658), bk. 2, pp. 88, 86, 89. Yagel was familiar with the Italian version, *Degli occulti miracoli et varii ammaestramenti delle cose della nature* (Venice, 1563).

37. Besides Wier and Lemnius, other sixteenth-century physicians held analogous views on the relation of demons to disease. They include Jason Pratz, *De Cerebri Morbis* (Basel, 1549), pp. 213–214, 262 (cf. Anglo, "Melancholia and Witchcraft," p. 211); Daniel Sennert, who maintained that devils can cause disease "non sine interventu humoris" (quoted in Burton, *Anatomy of Melancholy*, I, 228); Martin Del Rio, Jourdain Guibelet, and others, discussed by J. Céard, "Folie et démonologie au XVIe siècle," in *Folie et déraison*, pp. 129–47. Also cf. D. P. Walker, *Unclean Spirits: Possession and Exorcism in France and England in the Late Sixteenth and Early Seventeenth Centuries* (Philadelphia, 1981), pp. 11–13.

Among Hebrew writers, Manasseh ben Israel was the most knowledgeable in the sixteenth- and seventeenth-century literature on demonology. In his *Nishmat Hayyim* he frequently refers to the writings of Wier, Bodin, Del Rio, Vairo, and others. A study of his work in the context of this literature and contemporary culture is still a desideratum.

38. Bodleian Ms. Reggio 8, fol. 42a. A slightly different version appears in *Beit Ya'ar ha-Levanon*, pt. 4, chap. 104, fol. 238a.

39. Bodleian Ms. Reggio 8, fol. 51a.

40. Ibid. Yagel calls the work *Ha-Malakha ha-Ketana,* which means the *Ars parva.* Yagel states that Galen discusses androgynous creatures in the first part of this book, in his threefold division of medicine. I could not locate this reference in the editions of Galen that I consulted. However, I later discovered it in Yohanan Alemanno's *Likkutim,* Bodleian Ms. Reggio 23, fol. 63b, a manuscript in Yagel's possession and probably Yagel's source. On Alemanno's profound influence on Yagel, see esp. Chapters 1 and 9. For a list of sixteenth-century editions of this text, see R. J. Durling, "A Chronological Census of Renaissance Editions and Translations of Galen," *Journal of the Warburg and Courtauld Institute,* 24 (1961), 230–305.

41. Bodleian Ms. Reggio 8, fol. 51b.

42. Ibid., fols. 52a–52b.

43. Ibid., fol. 53a.

44. Ibid., fols. 53b, 34b.

45. *Beit Ya'ar ha-Levanon,* pt. 4, chap. 104, fol. 238.

46. G. Nigal, "The Dibbuk in Jewish Mysticism" (in Hebrew), *Da'at,* 4 (1980), 75–100; idem, *Sippur "Dibbuk" Be-Sifrut Yisra'el* (Jerusalem, 1983); S. Zfatman-Biller, "Exorcisms in Prague in the Seventeenth Century: The Question of the Historical Authenticity of a Folk Genre" (in Hebrew), *Jerusalem Studies in Jewish Folklore,* 3 (1981–82), 7–33, esp. pp. 30–32; Y. Bilu, "The Dibbuk in Judaism: Mental Disorder as Cultural Resource" (in Hebrew), *Jerusalem Studies in Jewish Thought,* 2 (1982–83), 529–563. On the general phenomenon of spirit possession, see E. Bourguignon, *Possession* (San Francisco, 1976); V. Crapanzano and V. Garrison, eds., *Case Studies in Spirit Possession* (New York, 1971); G. Obeyesekeue, "The Idiom of Demonic Possession: A Case Study," *Social Science and Medicine,* 4 (1970), 97–111.

Unlike Nigal and Sfatman-Biller, Bilu analyzes the *dibbuk* phenomenon within the context and methodology of psychology. But surprisingly, none of the researchers relates his or her findings to the Christian cultural world in which their Jewish subjects lived, particularly the phenomenon of the witch craze of the sixteenth and seventeenth centuries. Why, for example, is there little inclination in the Jewish community to accuse the victim who is possessed (usually a woman) of a crime, in contrast to the tendency of the Christian community? Now that the Jewish cases have been conveniently collected, such a cross-cultural study would be useful.

The literature on witchcraft and possession in this period is enormous. See, for example, H. C. Erik Midelfort, "Recent Witch-Hunting Research," *Papers of the Bibliographical Society of America,* 62 (1968), 373–420; Lea, *Materials;* K. Thomas, *Religion and the Decline of Magic* (New York, 1971); and Walker, *Unclean Spirits,* who mentions the recent work of Macfarlane, Midelfort, and Monter, p. 91, n. 9.

47. *Beit Ya'ar ha-Levanon,* pt. 4, chap. 104, fol. 238b. The case was described by ibn Yahya, Hayyim Vital, and Manasseh ben Israel. Zfatman-

Biller, "Exorcisms in Prague," p. 31, n. 7, omits Yagel's reference and also that of Eliezer Ashkenazi, *Ma'aseh Adonai* (Venice, 1583), pp. 5a–5b.

Yagel also refers to another case involving Mordecai Dato in the margin of Bodleian Ms. Reggio 8, fol. 43a. This appears to be related to the Ferrara incident.

48. *Beit Ya'ar ha-Levanon*, pt. 4, chap. 104, fol. 238b.

49. See the classic Jewish commentaries on 1 Sam. 28:8, esp. Abrabanel. Ibn Yahya, *Shalshelet ha-Kabbalah*, p. 198, also provides a useful summary of earlier interpretations. See also Trachtenberg, *Jewish Magic and Superstition*, pp. 22–24. On the rabbinic view of the witch of En-dor, see, for example, B.T. Shabbat 152b; *Vayikrah Rabbah*, 26, 7; L. Ginzberg, *Legends of the Jews*, 7 vols. (Philadelphia, 1909–38), VI, 235–238. For Christian interpretations see J. G. Godelmann, *Tractatus de Magis, Veneficiis et Lamiis* (Frankfurt am Main, 1591), pp. 33–36. Johan Wier (following Augustine) regarded the vision of Samuel as a demonic apparition. See Anglo, "Reginald Scot's *Discoverie*," p. 111. Abrabanel, on 1 Sam. 28:8, rejects Augustine's view but still explains the vision as a demonic intervention. However, Joseph Delmedigo, in *Mazref le-Hokhmah* (Odessa, 1864), pp. 47–56, takes Abrabanel to task by equating his view with the Augustinian one. Delmedigo ostensibly preferred a simple, literal understanding of the biblical text.

50. *Beit Ya'ar ha-Levanon*, pt. 4, chap. 105, fol. 239b. I translate *umehalefet bi-keshafeha* as "disappear because of her sorcery."

51. On the rabbinic distinction between conjuration of demons, which is allowed, and sorcery, which is not, see *Tur Yoreh De'ah*, 179, and the halakhic sources collected in Zimmels, *Magicians, Theologians, and Doctors*, pp. 221–222, nn. 90, 91.

52. Bodleian Ms. Reggio 8, fol. 43b. in *Beit Ya'ar ha-Levanon*, pt. 4, chap. 105, fol. 239b, Yagel refers to the same author as *hakham aher mibenai beli shem*. The reference is found in Bartolommeo Cocles, *Chyromantie ac Physionomie Anastasis* (Bologna, 1504), pp. 20a–21a.

53. *Beit Ya'ar ha-Levanon*, pt. 4, chap. 105, fols. 239b–240b.

54. But others did take that step, including Wier (see note 49 above). See also ibn Yahya, *Shalshelet ha-Kabbalah*, p. 198.

55. Yehi'el Nissim emphatically affirms the existence of demons in *Minhat Kena'ot* (Berlin, 1898), p. 50. For other expressions of contemporary Jewish belief in demons, see note 17 above.

56. Ashkenazi, *Ma'aseh Adonai*, p. 5a.

57. Ibid., p. 5b.

58. Manasseh ben Israel, *Nishmat Hayyim*, pp. 51a–b.

59. Phinehas Elijah Hurwitz, *Sefer ha-Berit* (Brno, 1797), pp. 92b–93a.

60. This point is made by M. MacDonald, *Mystical Bedlam: Madness, Anxiety, and Healing in Seventeenth Century England* (Cambridge, 1981), p. 210.

61. Stuart Clark, "The Scientific Status of Demonology," in *Occult and*

Scientific Mentalities in the Renaissance, ed. B. Vickers (Cambridge, 1984), pp. 351–374.

62. Ibid., pp. 359–360.

4. Unicorns, Great Beasts, and the Marvelous Variety of Nature

1. *Beit Ya'ar ha-Levanon,* pt. 4, Bodleian Ms. Reggio 10, chaps. 45 and 46, fols. 106b–112a.

2. This individual is perhaps identical with the Solomon b. Aminadav Fano referred to in S. Simonsohn, *History of the Jews in the Duchy of Mantua* (Jerusalem, 1977), pp. 269, 374, 417, 418.

3. *Beit Ya'ar ha-Levanon,* pt. 4, chap. 45, fol. 107b.

4. Num. 23:22, 24:8; Deut. 33:17; Isa. 34:7; Ps. 22:22, 29:6, 92:11; Job 39:9–10.

5. See the summary of rabbinic references to the *re'em* in C. G. Jung, *Psychology and Alchemy,* trans. R. F. C. Hull (New York, 1953), pp. 438–443. Cf. H. B. Tristram, *A Natural History of the Bible* (London, 1867), pp. 146–150; L. Lewyson, *Die Zoologie des Talmuds* (Frankfurt am Main, 1858), pp. 128–129, 149–151.

6. *Midrash Tehillim* on Ps. 22:21.

7. B.T. Berakhot 54b; Targum Pseudo-Jonathan on Num. 21:35; B.T. Niddah 24b, Zevaḥim 113b, Babba Batra 73b, etc. See also J. Eisenstein, ed., *Oẓar Midrashim* (New York, 1915), p. 468b; B. T. Ḥullin 60a.

8. Surveys of this history of unicorn lore are found in L. Wehrhahn–Stauch, "Einhorn," in *Reallexicon zur deutschen Kunstgeschichte,* IV (Stuttgart, 1958); H. Brandenburg, "Einhorn," in *Reallexicon für Antike und Christentum,* IV (Stuttgart, 1959), 840–862; J. W. Einhorn, *"Spiritalis Unicornis": Das Einhorn als Bedeutungstraeger in Literatur und Kunst des Mittelalters* (Munich, 1976); R. R. Beer, *Unicorn Myth and Reality,* trans. C. M. Stern (New York, 1977); R. Brown, *The Unicorn: A Mythological Interpretation* (London, 1881); and esp. O. Shepard, *The Lore of the Unicorn* (1930; reprint, London, 1967).

9. Shepard, *Lore of the Unicorn,* p. 34; Aelian, *De natura animalium* 3.41, 4.52, 16.20; Pliny, *Historia naturalis* 8.30, 31; 9.45, 106.

10. Cf. A. H. Godbey, "The Unicorn in the Old Testament," *American Journal of Semitic Languages and Literatures,* 56 (1939), 256–296; and see note 4 above.

11. Shepard, *Lore of the Unicorn,* pp. 47–51; G. Miller, "The Unicorn in Medical History," *Transactions and Studies of the College of Physicians of Philadelphia,* 28 (1960), 84–86.

12. *Beit Ya'ar ha-Levanon,* pt. 4, chap. 45, fol. 108a.

13. G. A. Gmelig–Nijboer, *Conrad Gessner's "Historia Animalium": An Inventory of Renaissance Zoology* (Meppel, 1977), p. 80; F. J. Cole, "The History of Albrecht Dürer's Rhinoceros in Zoological Literature," in *Science, Medicine, and History: Essays ... in Honor of Charles Singer,* ed.

E. A. Underwood, I (London, 1953), 337–356; W. George, "Sources and Background to Discoveries of New Animals in the Sixteenth and Seventeenth Centuries," *History of Science*, 18 (1980), 79–104; P. Delaunay, *La zoologie au seizième siècle* (Paris, 1962); Shepard, *Lore of the Unicorn*, pp. 214–216.

14. *Beit Ya'ar ha-Levanon*, pt. 4, chap. 45, fols. 107a–b.

15. Ibid., chaps. 45 and 46, fols. 107b–108a, 108b–112a.

16. Ibid., fol. 107b.

17. Ibid., 108a. The opening phrase is from Job 40:19, where it refers to the behemoth.

18. Ibid., fols. 109a–b. Cf. Shepard, *Lore of the Unicorn*, pp. 47–56.

19. *Beit Ya'ar ha-Levanon*, pt. 4, chap. 46, fols. 109b–110a. Philostratus, *Vita Apollonii* 3.2.

20. *Beit Ya'ar ha-Levanon*, pt. 4, chap. 46, fol. 110a; Aristotle, *Historia animalium* 2; *De partibus animalium* 3.2; Pliny, *Historia naturalis* 8.30, 31; 9.45, 106.

21. *Beit Ya'ar ha-Levanon*, pt. 4, chap. 46, fols. 110a–b.

22. Ibid., fols. 110b–112a.

23. Ibid., chap. 47, fols. 112a–113a. Yagel probably refers to Mercati's *Metallotheca* (Rome, 1717), which I was unable to consult. On this sixteenth-century naturalist, see *Dictionary of Scientific Biography*, 16 vols. (New York, 1970–80), IX, 308–309.

24. *Beit Ya'ar ha-Levanon*, pt. 4, chap. 48, fols. 113a–115b.

25. Ibid., introduction to pt. 4, titled "Petaḥ Tikvah" (Opening of hope), fol. 1b.

26. Ibid., chap. 48, fol. 113b.

27. Ibid., fols. 114a–115b.

28. Shepard surveys this literature in some detail in *Lore of the Unicorn*, chap. 6. See also Miller, "Unicorn in Medical History," pp. 91–93.

29. See George, "Discoveries of New Animals," pp. 79–104.

30. Shepard, *Lore of the Unicorn*, devotes all of chap. 5 to the horn.

31. The title of ibid., chap. 6.

32. Sebastian Münster, *Cosmographiae Universalis* (Basel, 1550), p. 1036.

33. Girolamo Cardano, *Opera Omnia*, 10 vols. (Lyons, 1662; reprint, New York and London, 1967), III, 530–531 (*De Subtilitate*, chap. 10); 341 (*De Rerum Varietate*, bk. 18, chap. 97). Cardano's influence on Yagel is discussed in Chapters 5 and 6.

34. Konrad von Gesner, *Historiae animalium*, 5 vols. (Frankfurt am Main, 1617–21), I, 689–695; Gmelig-Nijboer, *Gessner's "Historia Animalium,"* p. 103; Edward Topsel, *The history of Four-Footed Beasts and Serpents* (London, 1658), pp. 551–558.

35. Gesner, *Historiae Animalium*, I, 842–844; V, 64–68; Topsel, *Four-Footed Beasts*, pp. 460–463, 733–735.

36. Andrea Marini, *Discorso de Andrea Marini . . . alicorno* (Venice, 1566). This book was unavailable to me. See Shepard, *Lore of the Unicorn*, pp. 158–161, for a summary of its contents.

37. Ambroise Paré, *Discours d'Ambroise Paré . . . de la mummie, de la licorne, des venins et de la peste* (Paris, 1582).

38. Andrea Bacci, *L'alicorno: Discorso dell'eccelente medico, et filosofo, nel quale si tratta della natura dell'alicorno, et delle sue virtu eccellentissime* (Venice, 1556). I have used the Florence, 1573, edition. On Bacci see Shepard, *Lore of the Unicorn*, pp. 161–168; M. Crespi in *Dizionario biografico degli Italiani*, 29 vols. to date (Rome, 1960–), V, 29–30; L. Thorndike, *A History of Science and Natural Magic*, 8 vols. (New York, 1941), V, 484–485; VI, 315.

39. Shepard, *Lore of the Unicorn*, pp. 168, 173–185. See esp. Kaspar Bartholin, *De Unicorn Observationes Novae*, 2d ed., ed. Thomas Bartholin (Amsterdam, 1678); and Ulisse Aldrovani, *De Quadrupedibus Solidipedibus* (Bologna, 1639), pp. 384–414.

40. Andrea Bacci, *Le XII pietre pretiose le quali per ordine di dio nella santa legge, adornavano i vestimenti del sommo sacerdote . . . Discorso dell'alicorno e delle sue singolarissime virtu. Et della gran bestia dette alce da gli antichi* (Rome, 1587).

41. Bacci, *Discorso dell'alicorno*, p. 119: "che solo l'huomo et la coturnice patifcano de mal caduco"; *Beit Ya'ar ha-Levanon*, pt. 4, chap. 48, fol. 113b: "Besides the human being and the fowl called tranquil, that is, 'coturnice,' they are susceptible to falling sickness."

42. Bacci quotes Lemnius on p. 116; Yagel uses the same quotation on fol. 113b. Both refer to the Italian edition, *Degli occulti miracoli et varii ammaestramenti delle cose della nature* (Venice, 1563), to which Yagel also refers in *Gei Ḥizzayon*, pt. 1, ed. A. B. Mani (Alexandria, Egypt, 1880), p. 27a.

43. Amatus Lusitanus, *In Dioscorides Anazarbei de Medica Materia Libros Quinque* (Lyons, 1558), p. 281.

44. David de Pomis, *Dittionario Novo Hebraico, molto copioso, dechiarato in tre lingue, Ẓemaḥ David* (Venice, 1587), p. 181b; Shepard, *Lore of the Unicorn*, p. 117.

45. Isaac Cardoso, *Philosophia Libera* (Venice, 1683), p. 378; Y. Yerushalmi, *From Spanish Court to Italian Ghetto* (New York, 1971), p. 248, n. 88.

46. Abraham b. David Portaleone, *Shilte ha-Gibborim* (Mantua, 1612), p. 56a.

47. Ibid., p. 58a.

48. Ibid., pp. 56b–57a.

49. See N. Shapira, "R. Abraham Portaleone, the Doctor, Encyclopedist, and His Book *Shilte ha-Gibborim* (1542–1612)" (in Hebrew), *Ha-Rofe ha-Ivri*, 33 (1960), 111–112.

50. On the diffusion of the unicorn figure in Jewish art of the period, see R. Wischnitzer, "The Unicorn in Christian and Jewish Art," *Historia Judaica*, 13 (1951), 141–156.

51. Bacci, *Discorso dell'alicorno*, pp. 54–56; summarized in Shepard, *Lore of the Unicorn*, pp. 164–165.

52. I have quoted the English translation, Levinus Lemnius, *The Secret Miracles of Nature in Four Books* (London, 1658), pp. 2–5. The quotation from Aristotle is in *De partibus animalium* 1.5.

53. See R. S. Westfall, *Science and Religion in Seventeenth Century England* (Ann Arbor, 1973), p. 26.

54. Paracelsus, *Selected Writing*, ed. and trans. J. Jacobi (New York, 1951), p. 185; cf. H. E. Sigerist, ed., *Four Treatises of Theophrastus von Hohenheim Called Paracelsus* (Baltimore, 1941), p. 247.

55. Quoted in Westfall, *Science and Religion*, p. 31.

56. Cf., however, the sentiments of other seventeenth-century English "virtuosi," discussed in ibid., pp. 27–69, and Jean Bodin's view of nature in P. L. Rose, *Bodin and the Great God of Nature* (Geneva, 1980), p. 26.

57. *Beit Ya'ar ha-Levanon*, pt. 4, introduction, fols. 1a–b.

58. Ibid., fol. 1b.

59. Ibid.

60. For what follows I am indebted substantially to M. Foucault, "The Prose of the World," trans. in *The Order of Things: An Archeology of the Human Sciences*, (New York, 1970; first published as *Les mots et les choses*, Paris, 1966), pp. 17–50. It captures succinctly and coherently some of the basic epistemological assumptions of Yagel and several of his contemporaries. I have attempted to enlarge upon Foucault's chapter to explore its specific implication for Jews such as Yagel. For a negative view of the chapter, see G. Huppert, "Divinatio et Eruditio: Thoughts on Foucault," *History and Theory*, 13 (1974), 191–207; for a positive view see J. C. Margolin, "Tribut d'un anti-humanist aux études d'humanisme et Renaissance," *Bibliothèque de humanisme et Renaissance*, 29 (1967), 701–711.

Other useful sources were W. Pagel, *Paracelsus: An Introduction to Philosophic Medicine in the Era of the Renaissance* (Basel and New York, 1958), esp. pp. 50–64; E. M. W. Tillyard, *The Elizabethan World Picture* (New York, 1961); J. C. Margolin, "Analogie et causalité chez Jérome Cardan," in *Sciences de la Renaissance*, VIIIe Congrès International de Tours (Paris, 1973); J. Céard, *La nature et les prodiges: L'insolite au XVIe siècle en France* (Geneva, 1977); Delaunay, *La zoologie*; Westfall, *Science and Religion*; Thorndike, *History of Science*, VI; B. Willey, *The Seventeenth Century Background* (New York, 1935).

61. Foucault, "The Prose of the World," pp. 17–25; Margolin, "Analogie et causalité"; Pagel, *Paracelsus*, pp. 50–52; Tillyard, *Elizabethan World Picture*, pp. 80–93.

62. Paracelsus, *De Natura Rerum*, in *Sämtliche Werke*, ed. K. Sudhoff, 15 vols. (Munich and Berlin, 1929), IX, 393.

63. Foucault, "The Prose of the World," pp. 32–33. See also Chapter 7.

64. Foucault, "The Prose of the World," pp. 33–37; on deciphering the "secrets" of the Hebrew language in this period, see E. Wind, *Pagan Mysteries in the Renaissance*, 2d ed. (London, 1968), chap. 1; W. J. Bousma, "Postel and the Significance of Renaissance Cabalism," *Journal of the History of*

Ideas, 15 (1954), 218–232. I treat Yagel's extensive remarks on the centrality of the Hebrew language in my forthcoming edition of *Gei Ḥizzayon.*

65. Foucault, "The Prose of the World," pp. 38–42. On the encyclopedia in the sixteenth and seventeenth centuries, see A. H. T. Levi, "Ethics and the Encyclopedia in the Sixteenth Century," and F. Simone, "La notion d'encyclopédie; Elément caractéristique de la Renaissance française," in *French Renaissance Studies 1540–70,* ed. P. Sharratt (Edinburgh, 1976), pp. 170–180, 234–262; and also G. Strauss, "A Sixteenth-Century Encyclopedia: Sebastian Münster's *Cosmography* and Its Editions," in *From the Renaissance to the Counter-Renaissance: Essays in Honor of Garrett Mattingly,* ed. C. H. Carter (London, 1966), pp. 1320–50. On Jewish encyclopedias in the same period, see Chapter 1, note 70.

66. Foucault, "The Prose of the World," p. 40.

67. Ibid., pp. 41–43.

68. Céard, *La nature et les prodiges;* I. B. Cohen, "La découverte du nouveau monde et la transformation de l'idée de la nature," in *La science au seizième siècle* (Paris, 1960), pp. 189–210.

69. See esp. Westfall, *Science and Religion,* pp. 49–69.

70. *Be'er Sheva,* Bodleian Ms. Reggio 11, chap. 1, fol. 6b.

71. Note Yagel's constant use of words such as *le'egod* (to bind), *hitkashrut ha-ḥokhmot* (the interconnectedness of the sciences), *hishtalshelut ha-ḥokhmot* (the concatenation of the sciences), and *likshor* (to connect).

72. See, for example, Bousma, "Postel and Cabalism"; S. W. Baron, *A Social and Religious History of the Jews,* 18 vols. (New York, 1969–83), XIII, 159–205; C. Roth, *The Jews in the Renaissance* (Philadelphia, 1959), pp. 137–164; J. Friedman, *The Most Ancient Testimony: Sixteenth-Century Christian-Hebraica in the Age of Renaissance Nostalgia* (Athens, Ohio, 1983). See also Chapter 9.

73. I am proposing here that the beginnings of a boldly new apologetic literature in the seventeenth century, written by Jews for non-Jewish consumption, composed in Western languages, and motivated by explicit political aspirations (such as the works of David de Pomis, Leone Modena, Simone Luzzato, and Manasseh ben Israel), might be related directly to the kind of integrative intellectual efforts of Yagel and some of his contemporaries. On the new apologetic literature see M. Cohen, "Leone Da Modena's *Riti:* A Seventeenth-Century Plea for Toleration of Jews," *Jewish Social Studies,* 34 (1972), 287–321.

74. Of course, earlier generations of Jewish scholars also were attuned to the "wonders" of nature as reflections of divine majesty and considered naturalistic learning to be an important intellectual pursuit. I only am suggesting here that, in Yagel's generation, this pursuit was especially important and that the rabbi-physician assumed an even more prominent place in the Jewish intellectual world of his day. See D. B. Ruderman, "The Impact of Science on Jewish Culture and Society in Venice," in *Gli ebrei e Venezia,* ed. G. Cozzi (Milan, 1987), pp. 417–448.

A comprehensive study of earlier Jewish attitudes toward nature does not yet exist. For the time being see Lewyson, *Die Zoologie des Talmuds*; I. Low, *Die Flora der Juden*, 4 vols. (Vienna, 1926–34); F. Rosner, ed. and trans., *Julius Preuss' Biblical and Talmudic Medicine* (New York, 1978); S. Lieberman, "The Natural Science of the Rabbis," in *Hellenism in Jewish Palestine* (1950; reprint, New York, 1962), pp. 180–193; L. Ginzberg, *Legends of the Jews*, 7 vols. (Philadelphia, 1909–38), I, 26–42. One might also consider rabbinic exegesis on such biblical verse as Gen. 1:28, Ps. 19:2, Isa. 40:26, Amos 5:8, and Job 38:41; the rabbinic benedictions on witnessing unusual natural events; and cf. an unsympathetic view of nature in Avot 3, 9.

On the significance of the study of nature and its "signs" (physics, *Ma'aseh Bereshit*) in medieval Jewish philosophy, see, for example, Baḥya ibn Pakuda, *Ḥovot ha-Levavot*, I, 7; II, 1–3; D. Kaufmann, *Meḥkarim be-Sifrut ha-Ivrit shel Yemai ha-Beinayim* (Jerusalem, 1965), p. 45; Maimonides, *Guide to the Perplexed*, Introduction to 1; 3, 32 (cf. also *Mishneh Torah*, Sefer ha-Madda, Yesodei ha-Torah, 2, 2; 4, 12); Yehudah ha-Levi, *Sefer ha-Kuzari*, 1, 68, 77; 3, 17; 4, 25; 5, 8, 20 (third principle), 21; but cf. 2, 56; 3, 23, 53; Joseph Albo, *Sefer ha-Ikkarim*, II, 1; and, generally, H. A. Wolfson, "The Classification of the Sciences in Medieval Jewish Philosophy," in *Hebrew Union College Jubilee Volume* (Cincinnati, 1925), pp. 215–263; reprinted in *Studies in the History of Philosophy and Religion*, ed. I. Twersky and G. Williams (Cambridge, Mass., 1973), pp. 473–545.

75. A social and intellectual history of Jewish physicians in this period has yet to be written. For the time being, see Ruderman, "Impact of Science in Venice."

76. Gedaliah ibn Yaḥya, *Shalshelet ha-Kabbalah* (Warsaw, 1877), p. 146.

77. Judah Sommo, *Zaḥut Bediḥuta de-Kiddushin*, ed. J. Schirman (Jerusalem, 1965), p. 36; Leone Modena, *Ari Nohem* (Leipzig, 1840; reprint, Jerusalem, 1971), pp. 18–19.

78. See Ruderman, "Impact of Science in Venice."

79. See, for example, H. A. Davidson, "The Study of Philosophy as a Religious Obligation," in *Religion in a Religious Age*, ed. S. D. Goitein (Cambridge, Mass., 1974), pp. 53–68.

5. Out of the Mouths of Babes and Sucklings

1. The Hebrew sources describing this incident include Y. Boksenboim, *She'elot u-Teshuvot Mattanot ba-Adam* (Tel Aviv, 1983), pp. 28, 95–96; Ms. Jerusalem Jewish National and University Library Heb. 3428, no. 153 (my sincere thanks to Professor Reuven Bonfil, who provided me with a copy of the manuscript); Ms. Strasbourg Heb. 4085, fol. 291 (a *responsum* of R. Samuel Judah Katzenellenbogan), which, on the basis of Boksenboim's quotations (*Mattanot ba-Adam*, p. 28), seems identical with *Zerah Anashim* (Husiatyn, 1902), *responsum* 34, pp. 50–54. The precise date of the birth is

supplied by Yagel himself in *Gei Ḥizzayon*, pt. 1, ed. A. B. Mani (Alexandria, Egypt, 1880), p. 25a.

2. The time of the death is reported by Katzenellenbogan, Ms. Strasbourg Heb. 4085; the twins are reported to have died at slightly different times.

3. As reported in Ms. Jerusalem Heb. 3428 (Boksenboim, *Mattanot ba-Adam*, p. 28).

4. Ms. Jerusalem Heb. 3428 reports that the father handed over the corpse to the confraternity. Katzenellenbogan, Ms. Strasbourg Heb. 4085, appears to suggest that the father may have been unaware of the society's intentions (Boksenboim, *Mattanot ba-Adam*, p. 28.): "and perhaps without the knowledge of their father." For a similar example of displaying a monstrous corpse for profit, see K. Park and L. J. Daston, "Unnatural Conceptions: The Study of Monsters in Sixteenth- and Seventeenth-Century France and England," *Past and Present*, 92 (1981), 20, 34–35.

5. See Katzenellenbogan, Ms. Strasbourg Heb. 4085, and the *responsum* in *Mattanot be-Adam*, written by R. Raphael Joseph Treves, according to Boksenboim.

6. On the study of monsters in the sixteenth and seventeenth centuries, see L. Thorndike, *A History of Magic and Natural Science*, 8 vols. (New York, 1929–41), VI, 286–287, 488–491; J. Céard, *La nature et les prodiges: L'insolite au XVIe siècle en France* (Geneva, 1977); R. Wittkower, "Marvels of the East: A Study in the History of Monsters," *Journal of the Warburg and Courtauld Institute*, 5 (1942), 159–197; Park and Daston, "Unnatural Conceptions," pp. 20–54; A. J. Schutte, "Such Monstrous Births," *Renaissance Quarterly*, 38 (1985), 85–106.

7. Ulisse Aldrovandi, *Monstrorum Historia* (Boulogne, 1642), pp. 647–648; Johann Schenck, *Monstrorum Historia Memorabilis* (Frankfurt am Main, 1609), p. 70.

8. A. Sonderegger, *Missgeburten und Wundergestalten in Einblatten und Handzeichnungen des 16. Jahrhunderts* (Leipzig and Berlin, 1927), pp. 22–23, who draws on a collection by J. J. Wick (1522–1588) for the years 1560–1587 in the Zentralbibliothek of Zürich. I quote from an Italian poem on p. 23:

> Questo e il vero ritratto d'un
> maraviglioso e stupendo mostro
> qu'al ha partorito una Hebrea nel
> Ghetto della inclita citta de
> Venetia a di XXVI. Maggio 1575.
> Il qual Mostro vacua per il bonigolo, que non ha altro esito
> et latta da ame due le teste.

9. On the Venetian plague of 1575–1577, see E. Rodenwalt, *Pest in Venedig 1575–77. Ein Beitrag zur Frage der Infektkette bei dem Pestepidemien West-Europas* (Heidelberg, 1953); P. Prato, *Peste e società a Venezia, 1576* (Vicenza, 1978), esp. p. 60; G. B. Gallicciolli, *Delle memòrie venete antiche profane ed ecclesiastiche*, 3 vols. in 1 (Venice, 1795), II, 214, who describes

the appearance of the twins (some of his details contradict the information available in the sources mentioned above); B. Pullan, *Rich and Poor in Renaissance Venice* (Cambridge, Mass., 1971), pp. 314–326.

10. E. Morpurgo, "Bibliografia della storia degli ebrei nel Veneto," *Rivista israelitica*, 9 (1912), 226–227, lists the work as no. 662 in his bibliography and indicates that it was published first in Venice in 1575. A Sapadin, "On a Monstrous Birth Occurring in the Ghetto of Venice," *Studies in Bibliography and Booklore*, 6 (1964), 153–158, discusses the second edition. I have consulted a copy of this edition in the Hebrew Union College–Jewish Institute of Religion Library in Cincinnati. Morpurgo lists another pamphlet on the same incident (no. 663 in his list), titled *Nova et ridicolosa esposizione del mostro nato in Ghetto con il lamento del suo padre per la morte di quello ecc.* (Venice, 1575), which I was unable to locate. Morpurgo adds that, according to this work, the father castigated himself for having failed to circumcise the twins.

11. See my forthcoming edition and also G. Busi, "Sulla Ge Hizzayon (La Valle della Visione) di Abraham Yagel," *Annali della facoltà di lingue e letterature straniere de ca' Foscari*, 23 (1984), 17–34.

12. *Gei Ḥizzayon*, pt. 1, pp. 21a–28a.

13. Ibid., p. 21a. See B.T. Babba Kama 60b.

14. *Gei Ḥizzayon*, pt. 1, pp. 21a–22b.

15. Ibid., pp. 23a–27a.

16. Ibid., p. 23b.

17. Ibid., p. 24b. On the phrase "out of the mouths," see Ps. 8:3.

18. *Gei Ḥizzayon*, pt. 1, p. 24b; *Discorso* (Bologna, 1576), p. 10 (my pagination).

19. *Gei Ḥizzayon*, pt. 1, pp. 25a–b; *Discorso*, chap. 2.

20. *Gei Ḥizzayon*, pt. 1, pp. 25b–27a; *Discorso*, chap. 1.

21. Yagel refers to the idea that the womb has seven sacs, three at each side and one in the middle. If the sperm enters at the right, the infant will be male; if it enters at the left, it will be female; and in the middle, it will be androgynous. For earlier Jewish sources for this idea, see J. Trachtenberg, *Jewish Magic and Superstition: A Study in Folk Religion* (1939; reprint, New York, 1970), pp. 188, 303, n. 13; and Mani's note in *Gei Ḥizzayon*, p. 276. On Yagel's idea regarding the role of imagination during the act of intercourse, cf. Trachtenberg, *Jewish Magic and Superstition*, p. 187.

22. The Schor letter is undated, but Joseph Solomon Delmedigo, the first to publish it, had arrived in Poland by the beginning of 1620; see I. Barzilay, *Yoseph Shlomo Delmedigo, Yashar of Candia: His Life, Works and Times* (Leiden, 1974), p. 59. Yagel had already received an extensive report on the Grodek child by late 1620. The letter is found in Delmedigo, *Sefer Elim* (Amsterdam, 1629), p. 65. See also I. Zinberg, *History of Jewish Literature*, ed. and trans. B. Martin, 12 vols. (New York, 1972–78), IV, 169. On Schor see J. Caro, *Geschichte der Juden in Lemberg* (Krakow, 1894), p. 139; Z. Horowitz, *Le-Toledot ha-Kehillot be-Polin* (Jerusalem, 1978), p. 399; *Evreis-*

kaîa entsiklopedîa (St. Petersburg, 1912–14), s.v. "Shor, Avraam." On Katz see R. Margaliot, "Rabbis and Heads of Yeshivot" (in Hebrew), in *Ensiklopediyah shel galuyot*, 11 vols. (Jerusalem and Tel Aviv, 1953–73), IV, cols. 395–396; Caro, *Geschichte der Juden in Lemberg*, p. 144; S. Buber, *Anshei Shem* (Krakow, 1895), p. 144.

Much of what follows in this chapter is based on my article "Three Contemporary Perceptions of a Polish Wunderkind of the Seventeenth Century," *Association for Jewish Studies Review*, 4 (1979), 143–163.

23. Delmedigo, *Sefer Elim*, p. 65.

24. Ibid.

25. Ibid., p. 50; see also p. 15.

26. Ibid., p. 50.

27. Ibid., p. 15.

28. Quoted in Barzilay, *Yoseph Shlomo Delmedigo*, p. 259.

29. Ms. New York, Jewish Theological Seminary of America 3541 (ENA 74), fols. 181a–b (Jerusalem microfilm 29346). My thanks to Dr. Abraham David of the Institute, who first told me of this letter, and to the late Dr. Lawrence Marwick, former head of the Hebraic Section of the Library of Congress, Washington D.C., who identified for me the town of Potylicz in the Belzsk region as well as a number of other Polish towns mentioned in this chapter.

30. Ibid., fol. 181b. The latter part of the letter was transcribed by Saul b. David of Kostelec in the name of the *shammash* of the Jewish community of Lvov.

31. *Bat Rabim*, Ms. Moscow Günzburg 129, no. 68, fols. 108b–109b.

32. Ibid., fol. 111b.

33. Ibid., fols. 111b–112a.

34. For a more extensive discussion of this motif in earlier Jewish literature, see Ruderman, "A Polish Wunderkind," pp. 149–153.

35. *Zohar*, 3, 186a–192a, translated into Hebrew in I. Tishby and F. Lachower, *Mishnat ha-Zohar*, 2 vols. (Jerusalem, 1957–61), II, 66–89.

36. *Bat Rabim*, no. 68, fol. 111a.

37. G. Scholem, "The Sources of the Tale of R. Gaddiel the Infant in the Literature of the Kabbalah" (in Hebrew), in *Le-Agnon Shai* (Jerusalem, 1966), pp. 289–305.

38. On the wonder child of Avila, see R. Solomon b. Adret, *She'elot u-Teshuvot*, 3 pts. to date (Bnai Berak, 1958–), pt. 1, pp. 208–209, no. 548; J. L. Teicher, "The Medieval Mind," *Journal of Jewish Studies*, 6 (1955), 1–13; Y. Baer, *A History of the Jews of Christian Spain*, 2 vols. (Philadelphia, 1961–66), I, 277–278.

39. See *Bat Rabim*, no. 68, fol. 110b.

40. Ibid., no. 39, fols. 72b–73b. On the prophecies of Nahman, see G. Scholem, "The Kabbalist R. Abraham ben Eliezer ha-Levi" (in Hebrew), *Kiryat Sefer*, 2 (1925–26), 101–138, 269–273; idem, "New Researches on R. Abraham ben Eliezer ha-Levi" (in Hebrew), *Kiryat Sefer*, 7 (1930–31), 149–165, 440–456; and the recently revised edition of Scholem's essays by Mal-

achi Beit-Arie, *Ha-Mekubbal R. Avraham ben Eliezer ha-Levi Mavo le-Hoẓa'at Taẓlum shel Ḥibburo Ma'amar Meshare Kitrin* (Jerusalem, 1978); also J. Dan, "Notes on the Matter of the Prophecy of the Boy" (in Hebrew), *Shalem*, 1 (1974), 229–234; E. Strauss (Ashtor), *Toledot ha-Yehudim be-Miẓrayim ve-Suryah taḥat Shilton ha-Mamlukim*, 2 vols. (Jerusalem, 1944), I, 129; J. D. Eisenstein, *Oẓar Midrashim*, 2 vols. (New York, 1915), II, 396–397.

41. Scholem, "The Kabbalist," pp. 117–118.

42. Gedaliah ibn Yaḥya, *Shalshelet ha-Kabbalah* (Jerusalem, 1962), p. 105. See also A. David, "Mifalo ha-historiyografi shel Gedaliah ibn Yaḥya, *Ba'al Shalshelet ha-Kabbalah*" (Ph.D. diss., Hebrew University, 1976), pp. 177–178, 365; Jacob b. Ḥayyim Ẓemaḥ, *Sefer Nagid u-Meẓavveh* (Zolkiew, 1793), pp. 75–79.

43. *Gei Ḥizzayon*, pt. 1, p. 24b; *Discorso*, p. 10 (my pagination). In "A Polish Wunderkind," p. 157, n. 48–50, I indicated that I could not locate Yagel's precise reference to either Xenophon or Aben Ragel in his comments on Nahman's prophecies. I now realize that he did not have to quote the original sources, since he had already found them in the *Discorso*. For additional references to Aben Ragel, see ibid., p. 157, n. 49. Yagel also refers to Aben Ragel's works in *Be'er Sheva*, Bodleian Ms. Reggio 11, pt. 2, chaps. 4 and 15. But see now Busi "Sulla Ge Hizzayon," p. 25, who identifies the passage from *Albohazen Haly Filii Abenragel Libri de Judiciis Astrorum* (Basel, 1551), p. 145b.

44. Although Yagel made no explicit reference to messianism in the case of the Siamese children, the year of their birth (1575) was one of considerable messianic expectation. Among the messianic calculations for this year were those of Mordecai Dato, which Yagel may have known. See D. Tamar, "The Anticipation in Italy of the Year of Redemption of 5335 [1575]" (in Hebrew), in *Meḥkarim be-Toledot ha-Yehudim be-Ereẓ Yisra'el u-ve–Itali-yah* (Jerusalem, 1973), pp. 11–38.

45. This point is developed further in Ruderman, "A Polish Wunderkind," pp. 160–163.

46. *Bat Rabim*, no. 68, fols. 109b–110a.

47. Ibid., fol. 110a. This view parallels that of Maimonides in the *Guide to the Perplexed* 2.32, 36. See also A. Reines, *Maimonides and Abravanel on Prophecy* (Cincinnati, 1970), p. xxxv.

48. *Bat Rabim*, no. 68, fol. 110a. On Balaam's exalted position in rabbinic literature, see L. Ginzberg, *Legends of the Jews*, 7 vols. (Philadelphia, 1909–38), III, 354–382, 410–411; VI, 123–175; cf. also Philo, *De vita Moysis* 1.48; Josephus, *Antiquities* 4.6.2.

49. *Bat Rabim*, no. 68, fol. 110b. The literature on Joan of Arc is extensive. See, for example, C. W. Lighthody, *The Judgements of Joan* (London, 1962); D. Rankin and C. Quintal, *The First Biography of Joan of Arc* (Pittsburgh, 1964); W. S. Scott, *The Trial of Joan of Arc* (London, 1956); J. Quicherat, *Procès de condamnation et de réhabilitation de Jeanne d'Arc*, 5 vols. (Paris, 1841–49).

50. *Bat Rabim,* no. 68, fol. 110b. On Merlin, see E. Anwyl, *Encyclopedia of Religion and Ethics,* ed. J. Hastings, 12 vols. (Edinburgh, 1908–22), s.v. "Merlin"; K. Thomas, *Religion and the Decline of Magic* (London, 1971), pp. 394–410. On ancient Near Eastern parallels to the Merlin legend, see M. Gaster, "The Legend of Merlin," in *Studies and Texts in Folklore, Magic, Medieval Romance, Hebrew Apocrypha, and Samaritan Archeology,* 2 vols. (New York, 1971), II, 965–984.

51. *Bat Rabim,* no. 68, fol. 110b. Yagel apparently referred to Molcho's collection of sermons, originally published in Salonika in 1529. On Molcho see M. Idel, "Solomon Molcho as Magician" (in Hebrew), *Sefunot,* n.s., 3 (1985), 193–219.

52. On Nifo's view of prophecy, see Thorndike, *History of Magic,* VI, 484–487; on Pomponazzi's view, see ibid., V, 98–110, and A. H. Douglas, *The Philosophy and Psychology of Pietro Pomponazzi* (Cambridge, 1910), pp. 287–291.

53. On Cardano's view of prophecy, see Thorndike, *History of Magic,* V, 574–575; W. G. Waters, *Jerome Cardan: A Biographical Study* (London, 1893), pp. 104–117, 249; G. Saitta, *Il pensiero italiano nell'umanesimo e nel Rinascimento,* 2 vols. (Bologna, 1950), II, 202–226. For additional references, see Chapter 2, note 15, above.

54. Girolamo Cardano, *Opera Omnia,* 10 vols. (Lyons, 1662; reprint, New York and London, 1967), III, *De Rerum Varietate,* chap. 43, entitled "Hominis mirabilia," pp. 160–161, 163.

55. On Cardano's further influence on Yagel, see Chapter 6.

56. See note 6 above.

57. This is a summary of the theme of Céard's *La nature et les prodiges.* See esp. pp. vii–xiv, 485–493. Cf. the reconstruction by Park and Daston, "Unnatural Conceptions." Céard's explanation of the sixteenth-century fascination with monsters is reinforced by anthropologists Mary Douglas and Edmund Leach in their discussions of cultural anomalies and taboos. According to their view, each person attempts to perceive the world as a stable entity in which all objects have recognizable shape, location, and permanence. An anomaly constitutes an uncomfortable fact that refuses to fit into any established system of classification, seemingly defying cherished assumptions. Such anomalies attract maximum interest and often elicit intense feelings of taboo. See M. Douglas, *Purity and Danger* (London, 1966), esp. pp. 48–53; E. Leach, "Anthropological Aspects of Language: Animal Categories and Verbal Abuse," in *Mythology,* ed. P. Maranda (London, 1972), pp. 39–67. My thanks to Professor Ronald Weissman of the University of Maryland for these references.

6. Comets and the New Heavens

1. See esp. *Beit Ya'ar ha-Levanon,* Bodleian Ms. Reggio 9, pt. 1, chap. 6; pt. 2, chaps. 21, 25, 26; Bodleian Ms. Reggio 10, pt. 4, chaps. 96, 97; *Be'er Sheva,* Bodleian Ms. Reggio 11, pt. 2, chaps. 2–4, 16–19.

2. On the *Centiloquium* see M. Steinschneider, *Die hebräischen Übersetzungen des Mittelalters und die Juden als Dolmetcher,* 2 vols. (Berlin, 1893), II, 527–529. On its currency in the sixteenth century, see the numerous references in Thorndike, *A History of Magic and Natural Science,* 8 vols. (New York, 1929–41), VI, index; Ptolemy, *Centiloquium.*

3. *Peri Megaddim,* Bodleian Ms. Reggio 8, fols. 101a–b. If we are to accept this statement at face value, we can conclude that Yagel knew Arabic and Greek in addition to Latin and Italian.

4. The large literature on the Christian response includes T. S. Kuhn, *The Copernican Revolution: Planetary Astronomy in the Development of Western Thought* (Cambridge Mass., 1957); idem, *The Structure of Scientific Revolutions* (Chicago, 1962); A Koyre, *From the Closed World to the Infinite Universe* (Baltimore, 1957); K. Scholder, *Ursprünge und Probleme der Biblekritik in 17 Jahrhundert* (Munich, 1966); R. S. Westfall, *Science and Religion in Seventeenth Century England* (Ann Arbor, 1973); B. Willey, *The Seventeenth Century Background* (New York, 1935); E. A. Burtt, *The Metaphysical Foundations of Modern Physical Science,* rev. ed. (London, 1932); and A. Funkenstein, "The Dialectical Preparation for Scientific Revolutions," in *The Copernican Achievement,* ed. R. S. Westman (Berkeley and Los Angeles, 1975), pp. 165–203. See also the works cited in the Introduction above, notes 4–6. The few investigations of Jewish thought include A. Neher, "Copernicus in the Hebraic Literature from the Sixteenth to the Eighteenth Century," *Journal of the History of Ideas,* 38 (1977), 211–226; H. Levine, "Paradise Not Surrendered: Jewish Reactions to Copernicus and the Growth of Modern Science," in *Epistemology, Methodology, and the Social Sciences,* ed. R. S. Cohen and M. W. Wartofsky (Cambridge, Mass., 1983), pp. 203–225. On Neher's premature evaluation, see Levine and also D. B. Ruderman, "The Impact of Science on Jewish Culture and Society in Venice," in *Gli ebrei e Venezia,* ed. G. Cozzi (Milan, 1987), pp. 417–448.

5. On Gans's astronomical writings, see A. Neher, *Jewish Thought and the Scientific Revolution of the Sixteenth Century: David Gans (1541– 1613) and His Times,* trans. D. Maisel (Oxford, 1986); G. Alter, *Two Renaissance Astronomers: David Gans and Joseph Delmedigo,* Rozpravy Ceskoslovenske Akedemie, vol. 68 (Prague, 1958), II, 1–77.

6. On Delmedigo, see I. Barzilay, *Yoseph Shlomo Delmedigo, Yashar of Candia: His Life, Works and Times* (Leiden, 1974). On the general involvement of Jews in astronomy in the fifteenth century and later, see B. Goldstein, "The Hebrew Astronomical Tradition: New Sources," *Isis,* 72 (1981), 237–251; idem, "The Survival of Arabic Astronomy in Hebrew," *Journal for the History of Arabic Science,* 3 (1979), 31–39 (esp. 38–39).

7. See Neher, *Jewish Thought and Scientific Revolution,* pp. 251–260; and idem, "Copernicus in the Hebraic Literature."

8. *Be'er Sheva,* pt. 2, chap. 15, fols. 48b–53b.

9. Aristotle, *Meteorology* 1.7, trans. H. D. P. Lee (Cambridge, Mass., 1952), pp. 48–57. See also J. L. Jervis, "Cometary Theory in Fifteenth-Century Europe" (Ph.D. diss. Yale University, 1978), pp. 7–10; C. D. Hell-

man, *The Comet of 1577: Its Place in the History of Astronomy* (1944; reprint, New York, 1971), pp. 16–39.

10. Jervis, "Cometary Theory," pp. 9–10.

11. See Jervis, "Cometary Theory," and Hellman, *The Comet of 1577*, for a comprehensive discussion.

12. On Cardano see G. Gliozzi's articles in *Dizionario biografico degli' Italiani*, 29 vols. to date (Rome, 1960–), XIX, 758–763: and in *Dictionary of Scientific Biography*, 16 vols. (New York, 1970–80), III, 64–67. See also J. Céard, *La nature et les prodiges: l'insolite au XVIe siècle en France* (Geneva, 1977), pp. 229–251; J. C. Margolin, "Analogie et causalité chez Jérome Cardan," in *Sciences de la Renaissance*, VIIIe Congrès International de Tours (Paris, 1973); Thorndike, *History of Magic*, V, 563–579. See also Chapter 2, note 15, and Chapter 5, note 53, above.

13. Girolamo Cardano, *Opera Omnia*, 10 vols. (Lyons, 1662; reprint, New York and London, 1967), III, 420 (*De Subtilitate*, bk. 4) and 1–2, 274–276 (*De Rerum Varietate*, bks. 1, 14); Hellman, *The Comet of 1577*, pp. 91–96; Jervis, "Cometary Theory," pp. 198–199. A parallax is the apparent displacement of a celestial body as a result of being observed from the surface instead of the center of the earth or as a result of being observed from the earth instead of from the sun.

14. *Be'er Sheva*, pt. 2, chap. 15, fol. 48b.

15. Ibid., fol. 49a.

16. Hieronymus Cardanus (Girolamo Cardano), *In Cl. Ptolemaei Pelusiensis IIII de Astrorum Iudicijs, ut Vulgo Vocant Quadripartitai Constructionis* (Basel, 1554), pp. 150–156. On Yagel's familiarity with Abi l-Ridjal (Aben Ragel), see Chapter 5, note 43, above.

17. Yagel also quotes Cardano's commentary on Ptolemy in *Be'er Sheva*, pt. 2, chap. 19.

18. Cardano, *Opera Omnia*, III, 7–8 (*De Rerum Varietate*, bk. 1, chap. 2); *Be'er Sheva*, pt. 2, chap. 10, fols. 36a–38a.

19. *Be'er Sheva*, pt. 2, chap. 10, fol. 36a.

20. Ibid., fol. 37a.

21. Ibid., fols. 37a–b.

22. Ibid., fol. 37b. On Yagel's familiarity with Cordovero's work, see Chapter 9. Yagel might have considered, nevertheless, Yehudah ha-Levi's critique of the four elements in *Sefer ha-Kuzari* V, 14.

23. Cf. Funkenstein, "Dialectical Preparation," pp. 165–166.

24. *Be'er Sheva*, pt. 2, chap. 15, fols. 48b–50b.

25. Ibid., fols. 50b–53a; cf. Cardano, *Opera Omnia*, III, 150–156.

26. *Be'er Sheva*, pt. 2, chap. 15, fol. 50b.

27. On Cecco see G. Sarton, *Introduction to the History of Science*, 5 vols. in 3 (Washington, D.C., 1927–48), III, 643–645; Thorndike, *History of Magic*, II, 948–968; Hellman, *The Comet of 1577*, p. 56; Jervis, "Cometary Theory," p. 29.

28. *L'acerba, Lo illustro poèta Cecho d'Ascoli: con el momento nova-*

mente trovato, et nobilmente historiato: revisto . . . Nicolaus Massettus mutinem as lectorum (Venice, 1560), fols. 13b–15a; *Be'er Sheva,* pt. 2, chap. 15, fols. 50b–51a.

29. Cardano, *Opera Omnia,* III, 153–156; *Be'er Sheva,* pt. 2, chap. 15, fols. 51a–52a.

30. Cardano, *Opera Omnia,* III, 155; *Be'er Sheva,* pt. 2, chap. 15, fol. 52a.

31. *Be'er Sheva,* pt. 2, chap. 15, fol. 52b; *Compilatio Leupoldi Ducatus Austrie Filij de Astrorum Scientia Decum Continens Tractatuns* (Augsburg, 1489), fols. 41a–44a. On Leopold's cometary theory see Sarton, *History of Science,* II, 996; Hellman, *The Comet of 1577,* pp. 54–55; Jervis, "Cometary Theory," p. 32.

32. *Be'er Sheva,* pt. 2, chap. 15, fols. 53a–b; for Albertus Magnus' commentary on comets, see the translation by L. Thorndike in *Latin Treatises on Comets between 1238 and 1368 A.D.* (Chicago, 1950), pp. 62–76. See also idem, *History of Magic,* II, 517–592; Jervis, "Cometary Theory," pp. 34–36.

33. *Be'er Sheva,* pt. 2, chap. 15, fol. 53b.

34. Ibid., fol. 49b. Samuel's quotation is from B. T. Berakhot 58b.

35. *Be'er Sheva,* pt. 2, chap. 15, fol. 50b.

36. Ibid.

37. Ibid., fol. 53b. Isaac Cardoso, *Philosophia Libera* (Venice, 1673), p. 210, and David Gans (in Neher, *Jewish Thought and Scientific Revolution,* pp. 274–275) also mention the astronomical passage of Samuel. For a similar exegesis of a rabbinic passage (B.T. Pesaḥim 94b) reconciling the rabbinic view with the new astronomy, see Neher, *Jewish Thought and Scientific Revolution,* pp. 205–215; and idem, "L'exégèse biblique juive face à Copernic au XVIième et au XVIIième siècles," in *Travels in the World of the Old Testament: Studies . . . to Prof. M. A. Beck* (Assen, 1974), pp. 190–196. For earlier exegesis on the same passage, see I. Twersky, "Joseph ibn Kaspi, Portrait of a Medieval Jewish Intellectual," in *Studies in Medieval Jewish History and Literature* (Cambridge, Mass., 1979), p. 256, n. 52.

For other contemporary Jewish opinions on Aristotle's cometary theory, see David Gans, *Neḥmad ve-Na'im* (Jessnitz, 1743), sha'ar 12, pp. 79b–80b, who still supports it; and Joseph Delmedigo (*Sefer Elim* [Amsterdam, 1629], pp. 431–433; I. Barzilay, *Yoseph Shlomo Delmedigo, Yashar of Candia: His Life, Work and Times* [Leiden, 1974], pp. 162–163; and J. Fünn in *Ha-Carmel,* 6 [1867], 342–344), who openly criticizes it.

38. See esp. M. Nicolson, "The Telescope and Imagination," in *Science and Imagination* (Ithaca, N.Y., 1956); S. Drake, *Discoveries and Opinions of Galileo* (Garden City, N.Y., 1957), including a translation of the *Sidereus Nuncius,* which I used; E. McMullin, ed., *Galileo, Man of Science* (New York, 1967); and E. Cochrane, *Florence in the Forgotten Centuries 1529–1800* (Chicago, 1973), pp. 165–182. On the problem of the name of the instrument Galileo used, see E. Rosen, *The Naming of the Telescope* (New York, 1947).

39. "My witness . . ." is a paraphrase of Job 16:19.

40. *Beit Ya'ar ha-Levanon,* pt. 4, chap. 98, fol. 226a.

41. Ibid.

42. The chapter is not dated but was probably written close to 1613, the date of the previous chapter.

43. See Barzilay, *Yoseph Shlomo Delmedigo,* p. 150, and Delmedigo, *Sefer Elim,* pp. 300–301, 417, 432, 433.

44. *Beit Ya'ar ha-Levanon,* pt. 4, chap. 98, fol. 226b. The reference is to B.T. Eruvin 43b.

45. *Beit Ya'ar ha-Levanon,* pt. 4, chap. 98, fol. 227a. See *Il commento di Sabbatai Donnolo sul Libro della Creazione,* ed. D. Castelli (Florence, 1880), p. 5. On the *Baraita de-Shemu'el,* see *Jewish Encyclopedia,* 12 vols. (New York, 1902), II, 520.

46. *Beit Ya'ar ha-Levanon,* pt. 4, chap. 98, fol. 227a.

47. Ibid., fol. 227b. Yagel's view here of not trusting the senses is in sharp contrast to his general stance of trusting the senses over philosophy. See above, Chapter 3 and the Afterword.

48. Ibid. Cf. *Bat Rabim,* Ms. Moscow Günzburg 129, fol. 144b. See also S. Heller-Wilensky, *R. Yizhak Arama u-Mishnato ha-Pilosofit* (Jerusalem, 1956), p. 117; Steinschneider, *Die hebräischen Übersetzungen,* p. 550–552; B. Goldstein, "Astronomy in the Middle Ages according to Hebrew Sources" (in Hebrew), *Korot,* 4 (1968), 679–690; idem, *Al-Bitrūjī on the Principles of Astronomy* (New Haven, 1971).

49. Quoted from Galileo in Cochrane, *Florence in the Forgotten Centuries,* p. 166.

50. See, for example, *Be'er Sheva,* pt. 2, chaps. 2–4.

51. *Beit Ya'ar ha-Levanon,* pt. 4, chap. 35.

52. Ibid., chap. 97; *Be'er Sheva,* pt. 2, chap. 20.

53. *Beit Ya'ar ha-Levanon,* pt. 2, chap. 21, fol. 96a. See O. Gingerich, "The Role of Erasmus Reinhold and the Prutenic tables in the Dissemination of Copernican Theory," in *Colloquia Copernica,* ed. J. Dobrzycki (Breslau, 1973), II, 43–62, 123–125.

54. *Beit Ya'ar ha-Levanon,* pt. 4, chap. 98, fol. 227b.

55. Ibid., fol. 228b.

7. On Stretching the Permissible

1. *Beit Ya'ar ha-Levanon,* pt. 2, Bodleian Ms. Reggio 9, chap. 31, fols. 113a–114b (this manuscript contains parts 1–3).

2. Ibid., fol. 114b.

3. Ibid., fol. 113a.

4. Ibid., fol. 114b. On *shi'ur komah,* see G. Scholem, "Shi'ur Komah," *EJ,* XIV, 1417–19; idem, "*Shi'ur Komah*—The Mystical Image of God" (in Hebrew), in *Pirke Yesod be-Havanat ha-Kabbala* (Jerusalem, 1977), pp. 153–186; idem, *Jewish Gnosticism, Merkabah Mysticism, and Talmudic Tradi-*

tion (New York, 1965), pp. 36–42, 56–64, 129–131, and the appendix by S. Lieberman in ibid., pp. 118–126; A. Altmann, "Moses Narboni's Epistle on *Shi'ur Komah,*" in *Jewish Medieval and Renaissance Studies* (Cambridge, Mass., 1967), pp. 225–288; and M. S. Cohen, *The Shi'ur Qomah: Liturgy and Theurgy in Pre-Kabbalistic Jewish Mysticism* (Lanham, Md., 1983).

5. The phrases "things that are above us" (based on the Socratic dictum known in Latin as *quae supra nos, ea nihil ad nos*) and "to dare to know" (*sapere aude*, a Horatian motto) are both borrowed from C. Ginzburg, "High and Low: The Theme of Forbidden Knowledge in the Sixteenth and Seventeenth Centuries," *Past and Present*, 73 (1976), 28–41. For a sentiment in rabbinic literature similar to that of the first phrase, cf., for example, B.T. Ḥagigah 13a; *Bereshit Rabbah*, 8, 2.

6. *Beit Ya'ar ha-Levanon*, pt. 2, chap. 31, fol. 113a. See also Scholem, "Shi'ur Komah," pp. 173–74; Moses Cordovero, *Shi'ur Komah* (Warsaw, 1883). On the doctrine of the four worlds in kabbalistic thought, see G. Scholem, "The Four Worlds," *EJ*, XVI, 641–643.

7. On the doctrine of the four worlds, essentially the three worlds of medieval philosophy—angelic, heavenly, and sublunar—with the addition of the world of the godhead, see Scholem, "The Four Worlds." Scholem indicates that the doctrine in Spanish kabbalah originated in a different manner. Yet the first formulation (three plus one) would appear to reflect the manner in which Yagel understood the doctrines of three or four worlds, since he used them more or less interchangeably.

8. *Beit Ya'ar ha-Levanon*, pt. 2, chap. 31, fol. 113a. Yagel's shepherd, born in a natural state and endowed with the ability to understand the nature of the universe, is clearly reminiscent of Ibn Tufayl's Hayy ibn Yaqzan, the archetype of the innately gifted, self-taught man. See *Ibn Tufayl's Hayy Ibn Yaqzan*, ed. and trans. L. E. Goodman (New York, 1972).

9. *Beit Ya'ar ha-Levanon*, pt. 2, chap. 31, fol. 113b. On the significance of the big mechanical clock located in the center of medieval European towns, see C. Cipolla, *Clocks and Culture 1300–1700* (New York, 1967), pp. 37–47.

10. *Beit Ya'ar ha-Levanon*, pt. 2, chap. 31, fol. 113b. On early conceptions of clockmaking, see D. S. Landes, *Revolution in Time: Clocks and the Making of the Modern World* (Cambridge, Mass., 1983). On the origin of the ancient water clock, or clepsydra, see Cipolla, *Clocks and Culture*, pp. 37–38.

11. *Beit Ya'ar ha-Levanon*, pt. 2, chap. 31, fol. 114a. Note the parallel between the shepherd's construction of the clock as a metaphor regarding his understanding of God's creation with a similar usage among the Deists of the seventeenth and eighteenth centuries. See, for example, Fontenelle's declaration in his *Conversations on the Plurality of Worlds:* "I esteem the universe all the more since I have known that it is like a watch. It is surprising that nature, admirable as it is, is based on such simple things"; quoted in E. Cassirer, *The Philosophy of the Enlightenment* (Boston, 1955),

p. 50. Compare also Robert Boyle's comment that the world "is like a rare clock, such as may be that at Strasbourg, where all things are so skillfully contrived, that the engine being once set a moving, all things proceed, according to the artificer's first design"; quoted in E. M. Klaaren, *Religious Origins of Modern Science: Belief in Creation in Seventeenth-Century Thought* (Lanham, Md., 1985), p. 155. See also A. Funkenstein, *Theology and the Scientific Imagination from the Middle Ages to the Seventeenth Century* (Princeton, 1986), pp. 317–327.

12. *Beit Ya'ar ha-Levanon*, pt. 2, chap. 31, fol. 114a. For the phrase "the head of the citadel," see *Bereshit Rabbah*, 39, 1.

13. *Beit Ya'ar ha-Levanon*, pt. 2, chap. 31, fol. 114a.

14. Ibid., fol. 114b.

15. Ibid.

16. On the superiority of practical magic over speculative philosophy according to Yohanan Alemanno, see M. Idel, "The Study Program of R. Yohanan Alemanno" (in Hebrew), *Tarbiz*, 48 (1979), 319; idem, "Magic Temples and Cities in the Middle Ages and the Renaissance," *Jerusalem Studies in Arabic and Islam*, 3 (1981–82), 187.

17. See Chapters 2 and 3 above.

18. *Beit Ya'ar ha-Levanon*, pt. 4, Bodleian Ms. Reggio 10, chaps. 107–109, fols. 242b–248b.

19. Ibid., chap. 34, fols. 79a–81b.

20. *Be'er Sheva*, Bodleian Ms. Reggio 11, pt. 2, chap. 22, fol. 77b. This chapter was published by A. Neubauer in "Materials on the Ten Tribes and the Children of Moses" (in Hebrew), *Kovez al Yad*, 4 (1888), 138, under the incorrect title *Beit Ya'ar ha-Levanon*.

21. Azariah de' Rossi, *Me'or Einayim* (Vilna, 1866), Imre Binah, chap. 2, pp. 81–90. For a good summary of the rabbinic attitudes and uses of Ben Sira, see M. S. Segal, *Sefer Ben Sira ha-Shalem* (Jerusalem, 1953), pp. 36–46.

22. *Be'er Sheva*, pt. 2, fol. 80b.

23. De' Rossi, *Me'or Einayim*, pp. 85.

24. Ibid., p. 87; *Beit Ya'ar ha-Levanon*, pt. 4, chap. 34, fol. 79a. Maimonides uses the expression in the introduction to his commentary on Avot.

25. *Beit Ya'ar ha-Levanon*, pt. 4, chap. 34, fol. 80b.

26. Ibid.

27. Ibid., fol. 81a. For a rabbinic definition of these various types of magic, see B.T. Sanhedrin 65a–b; but cf. *EJ*, s.v. "Magic," XI, 706.

28. *Beit Ya'ar ha-Levanon*, fol. 81a.

29. See E. Cochrane, *Historians and Historiography in the Italian Renaissance* (Chicago, 1981); Y. Yerushalmi, *Zakhor: Jewish History and Jewish Memory* (Seattle, 1982), chap. 3. Cf. the early view of Maimonides in S. W. Baron, "The Historical Outlook of Maimonides," in *History and Jewish Historians* (Philadelphia, 1964), pp. 109–163.

30. *Beit Ya'ar ha-Levanon*, pt. 4, chap. 34, fol. 81a.

31. Ibid., chaps. 99–104, 105, and 106, respectively.

32. Ibid., chap. 107, fols. 242b–245a.

33. For a discussion of this text and other rabbinic writings on magic, see Y. Bazak, "The Laws of Magic and the Laws of Planting Gourds" (in Hebrew), *Bar Ilan University Annual*, 6 (1968), 156–66; L. Blau, *Das Altjüdische Zauberwesen* (Budapest, 1898); M. Smith, *Jesus the Magician* (New York, 1978), esp. pp. 77–79; J. N. Lightstone, *The Commerce of the Sacred: Mediation of the Divine among Jews in the Graeco-Roman Diaspora* (Chico, Calif. 1984), pp. 17–56; J. Trachtenberg, *Jewish Magic and Superstition: A Study in Folk Religion* (1939; reprint, New York, 1970), esp. pp. 14–22; G. Scholem, *Reshit ha-Kabbala ve-Sefer ha-Bahir* (Jerusalem, 1962), pp. 17–22, 57–61; M. Margalioth, *Sefer ha-Razim* (Jerusalem, 1966); S. Lieberman, *Tosefta Ke-Feshuta*, 8 vols. (New York, 1955–73), III, 22–29, 82, 83, 88, 94, 102–103; idem, *Greek in Jewish Palestine* (New York, 1942), pp. 92–114; B. Lewin, *Oẓar ha–Gaonim*, IV/2 (Haifa, 1930), 14, 21; L. Nemoy, "Maimonides' Opposition to Occultism," *Ha-Rofe ha–Ivri*, 2 (1954), 102–109; J. Goldin, "The Magic of Magic and Superstition," in *Aspects of Religious Propaganda in Judaism and Early Christianity*, ed. E. S. Florenza (Notre Dame, 1976), pp. 115–147; A. J. Zimmels, *Magicians, Theologians, and Doctors* (London, 1952); M. Fishbane, "Aspects of Jewish Magic in the Ancient Rabbinic Period," in *Perspectives in Jewish Learning*, ed. N. Stampfer, II (Chicago, 1979); E. Urbach, *Ḥazal: Pirke Emunot ve-De'ot* (Jerusalem, 1971), pp. 82–103; S. W. Baron, *A Social and Religious History of the Jews*, 18 vols. (New York, 1952–83) II, 15–23, 334–335; VIII, 3–16. These works refer to all the major classical sources. On magic in the *Sefer ha-Zohar*, see D. Cohen-Aloro, "From Higher Wisdom to the Wisdom of the Leaves of the Tree: Magic in the *Sefer ha-Zohar* as a Condition Engendered by Adam's Sin" (in Hebrew), *Da'at*, 18 (in press). For a discussion of the place of magic in the Jewish culture of the Renaissance, see M. Idel, "The Magical and Neoplatonic Interpretations of the Kabbalah in the Renaissance," in *Jewish Thought in the Sixteenth Century*, ed. B. Cooperman (Cambridge, Mass., 1983).

34. B.T. Sanhedrin 67b.

35. B.T. Sanhedrin 65b.

36. Cf. *Tur Yoreh De'ah*, 179, Beit Yosef.

37. *Beit Ya'ar ha-Levanon*, pt. 4, chap. 107, fol. 242b.

38. Ibid. On the ten sayings, see Avot 5, 1; Avot de-Rabbi Natan 31b, etc.

39. *Beit Ya'ar ha-Levanon*, fol. 243a.

40. For a similar threefold division of the magical arts, see Moses Isserles, *Torat ha-Olah* (Lemberg, 1858), 3, 77, discussed in Trachtenberg, *Jewish Magic and Superstition*, p. 21.

41. *Beit Ya'ar ha-Levanon*, fol. 243a.

42. Ibid., fol 243b. Cf. Bodleian Ms. Reggio 8, fol. 46a, where Yagel offers some additional definitions of both general magic and natural magic.

43. Henry Cornelius Agrippa, *Three Books of Occult Philosophy Written*

by *Henry Cornelius Agrippa of Nettesheim*, trans. J. F. London (London, 1651), p. 1. For further discussion of Agrippa's influence on Yagel regarding the concept of the triadic universe, see Idel, "Magical and Neoplatonic Interpretations," pp. 224–226. See also idem, "Differing Conceptions of the Kabbalah in the Early Seventeenth Century," in *Jewish Thought in the Seventeenth Century*, ed. I. Twersky and B. Septimus (Cambridge, Mass., 1987), p. 31, n. 154, where Idel mentions a possible medieval source for Agrippa's threefold division of magic.

44. Agrippa, *Occult Philosophy*, pp. 2–3.

45. In Bodleian Ms. Reggio 8, fol 43b, Yagel refers to Cocles' work published in Bologna in 1504, pp. 20a–21a.

46. Marsilio Ficino, *Opera Omnia*, 2 vols. (Basel, 1576; reprint, Turin, 1962), I, 573; quoted in C. Webster, *From Paracelsus to Newton: Magic and the Making of Modern Science* (Cambridge, 1982), p. 58. See also E. Rice, Jr., "The *De Magia Naturalis* of Jacques Lefèvre d'Etaples," in *Philosophy and Humanism: Renaissance Essays in Honor of P. O. Kristeller*, ed. E. P. Mahoney (Leiden, 1976), p. 21.

47. Giovanni Pico della Mirandola, *Opera omnia*, 2 vols. (Basel, 1557–73), I, 167, 169–170; quoted in Webster, *From Paracelsus to Newton*, p. 59. Cf. Idel, "Study Program of Alemanno," pp. 303–331, esp. pp. 326–327. See also idem, "Magical and Neoplatonic Interpretations."

48. Martin Del Rio, *Disquisitionum Magicarum* (Lyons, 1608), bk. 1, chap. 2; quoted in S. Clark, "The Scientific Status of Demonology," in *Occult and Scientific Mentalities in the Renaissance*, ed. B. Vickers (Cambridge, 1984), p. 357.

49. I have used the edition titled *Natural Magick* (London, 1658).

50. Francesco Giuntini, *Speculum Astrologiae* (Lyons, 1575), pp. 47b–48a.

51. B.T. Sanhedrin 65b.

52. *Beit Ya'ar ha-Levanon*, pt. 4, chap. 107, fols. 243b–244a. Cf. Bodleian Ms. Reggio 8, fol. 46a, the only place where Yagel mentions Agrippa's name, although he often uses his work.

53. See G. Scholem, *On the Kabbalah and Its Symbolism* (New York, 1960), pp. 158–204 (published in Hebrew in *Pirke Yesod be-Havanat ha-Kabbala u-Semaleha* [Jerusalem, 1977], pp. 381–421), esp. pp. 169–171, 175, regarding the commentary on Judah b. Barzilay on *Sefer Yeẓirah*.

54. Scholem, *On the Kabbalah*, pp. 170–71.

55. Ibid., pp. 171, 174, 177, 184, suggested by the verse in Gen. 12:5 on the "souls" Abraham made in Haran.

56. Meir ibn Gabbai, *Avodat ha-Kodesh* (Venice, 1566), 2, 31; Moses Cordovero, *Pardes Rimmonim* (Krakow, 1591), 24, 10; Abraham Azulai, *Ḥesed le-Avraham* (Amsterdam, 1685), 4, 30 (mentioned in Scholem, *On the Kabbalah*, p. 194). For additional references, see Scholem's book.

57. Discussed by Scholem, *On the Kabbalah*, p. 197, and see sources in his n. 2.

58. E. M. Butler, *The Myth of the Magus* (Cambridge, 1948), p. 157. On

Bacon see also S. C. Easton, *Roger Bacon and His Search for a Universal Science* (Oxford, 1952); F. Alessio, *Mito e scienza in Ruggero Bacone* (Milan, 1967); L. Thorndike, *A History of Magic and Experimental Science,* 8 vols. (New York, 1923–58), II, 617–691.

59. *De Occulta Philosophia,* bk. 2, chap. 50; quoted in F. A. Yates, *Giordano Bruno and the Hermetic Tradition* (New York, 1969), p. 136. For a similar passage in the writing of Yohanan Alemanno, see Idel, "Magical and Neoplatonic Interpretations," pp. 213–214.

60. My discussion of Camillo is based primarily on F. A. Yates, *The Idea of Memory* (Chicago, 1966), pp. 129–170. See also F. Secret, "Les cheminements de la kabbale à la Renaissance: Le théâtre du monde de Giulio Camillo Delminio et son influence," *Rivista critica di storia della filosofia,* 14 (1959), 28–59.

61. Bodleian Ms. Reggio 8, fol. 92a.

62. G. Betussi, *Il Raverta* (Venice, 1544), ed. G. Zonta (Bari, 1912), p. 133; quoted in Yates, *Idea of Memory,* p. 133.

63. Quoted in Yates, *Idea of Memory,* p. 152.

64. Ibid. For a convenient summary of the *Asclepius,* see Yates, *Giordano Bruno,* pp. 35–38.

65. Thorndike, *History of Magic,* VI, 431.

66. *Beit Ya'ar ha-Levanon,* pt. 4, chaps. 92–94, fols. 206a–214b.

67. Ibid., chap. 107, fol 244a; cf. Bodleian Ms. Reggio 8, fol. 46b, for some variations.

68. *Beit Ya'ar ha-Levanon,* pt. 4, chap. 107, fol. 244a, incorporating some additions to the earlier version in Bodleian Ms. Reggio 8, fols. 46b–47a.

69. *Beit Ya'ar ha-Levanon,* pt. 4, chap. 107, fol. 244a.

70. Ibid., fol. 245a.

71. B.T. Sanhedrin 93b.

72. *Beit Ya'ar ha-Levanon,* pt. 4, chap. 108, fols. 245a–b.

73. Ibid., fol. 245b. Cf. the spelling of his name in his earlier version of this passage, in Bodleian Ms. Reggio 8, fol. 48a. Yagel's reference is in *Gebri Regis Arabum . . . Summa Perfectionis Magisterii in Sua Natura* (Gedani, 1682), bk. 1, chap. 5 ("De his quae oportet artificem considerare"), pp. 7–10. On Jabir ibn Hayyan, see M. Plessner's article in the *Dictionary of Scientific Biography,* 16 vols. (New York, 1970–80), VII, 39–43; idem, "Geber and Jabir ibn Hayyan," *Ambix,* 16 (1969), 113–118.

74. *Beit Ya'ar ha-Levanon,* pt. 4, chap. 108, fol. 245b.

75. Agrippa, *De Occulta Philosophia,* bk. 2, chaps. 35–47.

76. *Beit Ya'ar ha-Levanon,* pt. 4, chap. 108, fols. 246a–b. On the permissibility of the third type, he offers as an authority, R. Solomon b. Adret. See his *responsa,* II, 281; IV, 245; and V, 119; and Zimmels, *Magicians, Theologians, and Doctors,* p. 136.

77. *Beit Ya'ar ha-Levanon,* pt. 4, chap. 109, fols. 248a–b.

78. See Agrippa, *De Occulta Philosophia,* bk. 3, chaps, 4–8; the trinity is discussed in chap. 8.

79. *Beit Ya'ar ha-Levanon,* pt. 4, chap. 109, fol. 247b; cf. Isa. 27:1.

80. Ibid., fol. 248b.

81. See Idel, "Study Program of Alemanno" and "Magical and Neoplatonic Interpretations." See also F. A. Yates, *The Occult Philosophy in the Elizabethan Age* (London, 1979).

82. *Beit Ya'ar ha-Levanon*, pt. 4 chap. 109, fol. 247b. On the rabbinic image of Abraham as physician and magician, see Lieberman, *Tosefta Ke-Feshuta*, VIII, 984–985.

83. *Beit Ya'ar ha-Levanon*, pt. 4, chap. 109, fol. 248a.

84. D. P. Walker, *Spiritual and Demonic Magic from Ficino to Campanella* (London, 1958), pp. 8–10.

85. *Beit Ya'ar ha-Levanon*, pt. 2, chap. 31, fol. 114b.

86. Ibid., fol. 114a.

87. For a similar discussion of magic and the laws of creation, see *Be'er Sheva*, pt. 2, chap. 26, fol. 85b.

88. See Idel, "Study Program of Alemanno," "Magical and Neoplatonic Interpretations," and "Major Currents in Italian Kabbalah (1560–1660)," in *Italia Judaica*, II, ed. S. Simonsohn and G. Sermoneta (Rome, 1987).

89. See D. B. Ruderman, "The Impact of Science on Jewish Culture and Society in Venice," in *Gli ebrei e Venezia*, ed. G. Cozzi (Milan, 1987), pp. 417–448.

8. On Divine Justice, Metempsychosis, and Purgatory

1. On Barukh Abraham da Spoleto b. R. Petaḥiah, see M. Mortara, *Mazkeret Ḥokhmei Italiyah: Indice alfabetico dei rabbini e scrittori Israelitici* (Padua, 1886), who mentions his presence in Ferrara in 1579 and in Modena in 1584. He is also mentioned in other sixteenth-century rabbinic *responsa*. Yagel's summary of Barukh Abraham's sermon is in *Bat Rabim*, Ms. Moscow Günzburg 129, no. 69, fol. 112b. Numbers 69–73 (fols. 112b–116b), all penned by Yagel, include Yagel's response, his account of his visit to Judah Sommo, the rabbi's reply, and a short letter from Mordecai Dato.

2. Yagel apparently was living in Rubeira at the time; see Chapter 1, note 48, above. Yagel first calls Spoleto "an excellent rabbi in *halakhah*"; *Bat Rabim*, no. 69, fol. 112b.

3. Ibid.

4. Ibid., fols. 112b–113a.

5. Among them were Menahem Recanati, Elijah de Vidas, and Meir ibn Gabbai. Isaac Abrabanel was the only nonkabbalist, but neither was he known primarily as a legal scholar. On their views on *gilgul* into animals, see Menahem Recanati, *Perush ha-Torah Al Derekh Ha-Emet* (Venice, 1523), *parshat* Noah and *parshat* Shemini; Meir ibn Gabbai, *Avodat ha-Kodesh* (Venice, 1566), 33, 34; Isaac Abrabanel, *Perush al ha-Torah* (Venice, 1579; Jerusalem, 1964), on Deut. 25:5; idem, *Ma'ayenei ha-Yeshu'ah* (Ferrara, 1551), p. 50a. Cf. B. Z. Netanyahu, *Don Isaac Abravanel: Statesman and Philosopher* (Philadelphia, 1953), pp. 117, 296. For the texts of Recan-

ati, ibn Gabbai, and others on metempsychosis, see R. Elior and M. Oron, eds., *Ha-Gilgul: Leket Mekorot* (Jerusalem, 1980). The rabbi also mentions Elijah de Vidas' *Reshit Ḥokhmah* (Venice, 1579) as a source, but the specific reference is unknown to me. On the general interest of Safad kabbalists in *gilgul*, see R. J. Zwi Werblowsky, *Joseph Karo: Lawyer and Mystic* (Philadelphia, 1977), pp. 234–256, esp. his discussion of Solomon Alkabetz; see also the masterly discussion by G. Scholem in *Pirkei Yesod be-Havanat ha-Kabbala u-Semaleha* (Jerusalem, 1977), p. 308–357. For an abbreviated English summary, see idem, *Kabbalah* (Jerusalem, 1974), pp. 344–348. See, more recently, M. Idel, "Explorations in the Method of the Author of *Sefer ha-Meshiv*" (in Hebrew), *Sefunot*, n.s., 2 (1983), 225.

6. The relations between Jewish law (halakhah) and kabbalah have recently engaged the attention of a number of historians. See, for example, M. Benayahu, "Kabbalah and Halakhah—A Confrontation" (in Hebrew), *Da'at* 5 (1980), 61–116; J. Katz, "Post-Zoharic Relations between Halakhah and Kabbalah" (in Hebrew), *Da'at*, 4 (1980), 57–74 (English version in B. Cooperman, ed., *Jewish Thought in the Sixteenth Century* [Cambridge, Mass., 1983], pp. 283–307; idem, *Halakha ve-Kabbala* (Jerusalem, 1984). On one halakhic context, that of the commandment of levirate marriage, related to the kabbalist notion of *gilgul*, see E. Gottlieb, "A Debate on Gilgul in Crete in the Fifteenth Century" (in Hebrew), *Sefunot*, 11 (1969), 43–66 (republished in Gottlieb's *Meḥkarim be-Sifrut ha-Kabbala*, ed. J. Hacker [Tel Aviv, 1976], pp. 370–396; E. Kupfer, "On the Cultural Image of Ashkenazic Jewry and Its Sages in the Fourteenth and Fifteenth Centuries" (in Hebrew), *Tarbiẓ*, 42 (1973), 125–30.

7. On Judah Sommo Portaleone, see S. Simonsohn, *History of the Jews in the Duchy of Mantua* (Jerusalem, 1977), esp. pp. 658–664; see also Sommo's Hebrew play. *Ẓaḥut Bediḥuta de-Kiddushin*, ed. H. Schirmann (Jerusalem, 1946). Cf. D. Kaufmann, "Leone De Sommi Portaleone (1527–92): Dramatist and Founder of a Synagogue in Mantua," *Jewish Quarterly Review*, 10 (1898), 445–455.

8. *Bat Rabim*, no. 71, fol. 114a.

9. Ibid.

10. Ibid., fol. 115b.

11. Ibid., fol. 116a.

12. I was unable to identify the source of that tradition. On Cordovero's view of *gilgul*, see his *Shi'ur Komah* (Warsaw, 1843), chaps. 3 and 4; S. A. Horodetsky, *Torat ha-Kabbala shel R. Moshe Cordovero* (Jerusalem, 1951), pp. 191–193; M. Cordovero, "A Rumor on the Matter of Gilgul" (in Hebrew), in Y. Ashkenazi, *Sefer Heikhal ha-Shem* (Venice, 1605).

13. *Bat Rabim*, no. 72, fol. 116a.

14. Ibid., fol. 116b.

15. *Gei Ḥizzayon*, pt. 1, ed. A. B. Mani (Alexandria, Egypt, 1880), pp. 18a–b.

16. Ibid., pp. 18b–19a.

17. Ibid., p. 41a. See Mani's note on the same page for the correct reading of this line.

18. Ibid., pp. 41a–b.

19. Ibid., p. 41b.

20. Diogenes Laertius, *Lives of Eminent Philosophers*, trans. R. D. Hicks (Cambridge, Mass., 1958), 8.36, pp. 352–353. Moshe Idel has recently identified Rabbi Lappidot with Rabbi Lappidot Ashkenazi, a figure with occult powers living in Safad who maintained relations with Moses Cordovero and Ḥayyim Vital. He also offers a number of parallel versions of this story current in sixteenth-century Safad, especially the version of Judah Hallewa, the kabbalist from Fez, Morocco. See M. Idel, "R. Judah Hallewa and his *Ẓafenat Pa'ane'aḥ*" (in Hebrew), *Shalem*, 4 (1984): 126–127, 146–148.

21. *Beit Ya'ar ha-Levanon*, pt. 3, Bodleian Ms. Reggio 9, chap. 12, fols. 131a–b.

22. Ibid., fol. 131b.

23. Ibid.

24. Ibid. In chap. 13 Yagel presents the view of a rabbinic scholar who believed in the kabbalah but who "was close to the sect of the Karaites, following a literal interpretation of the text according to their own reason." This anonymous scholar rejected *gilgul* altogether, offering in his defense the rational views of Saadiah Gaon and Jedaiah Bedersi (c. 1270–1340), author of the *Iggeret ha-Hitnaẓẓelut* (Warsaw, 1882). Saadiah's views are found in his *Sefer Emunot ve-De'ot* (Jerusalem, 1970), 6, 8. Leone Modena quotes the same two authorities in his own discussion of the concept of metempsychosis, *Sefer Ben David*, published by E. Ashkenazi in *Ta'am Zekenim*, ed. R. Kirchheim (Frankfurt am Main, 1854), p. 63. For an illuminating comparison of Modena's view of *gilgul* with those of Elijah Gennazano (fifteenth century) and Joseph Delmedigo (seventeenth century), see M. Idel, "Differing Conceptions of Kabbalah in the Early Seventeenth Century" in *Jewish Thought in the Seventeenth Century*, ed. I. Twersky and B. Septimus (Cambridge, Mass., 1987).

For other critics of the concept of *gilgul*, see Joseph Albo, *Sefer ha-Ikkarim*, ed. I. Husik (Philadelphia, 1946), bk. 4, chap. 29; Judah Ḥayyat, *Minḥat Yehudah*, in *Ma'arekhet ha-Elohut* (Ferrara, 1558), p. 204b; Isaac Cardoso, *Philosophia Libera* (Venice, 1679), bk. 6, quaest. lxxviii (cf. Y. Yerushalmi, *From Spanish Court to Italian Ghetto* [New York, 1971], pp. 256–259); and Uriel da Costa in C. Gebhardt, *Die Schriften des Uriel da Costa* (Amsterdam, 1922), p. 61.

25. On *gilgul* in the *Gallei Razayya*, see R. Elior, "The Doctrine of Gilgul in the Book *Gallei Razayya*" (in Hebrew), in *Meḥkarim be-Kabbala Mugashim le-Yishayahu Tishbi*, ed. Y. Dan and Y. Hacker (= *Meḥkarei Yerushalayim be-Maḥshevet Yisra'el*, 3 [1984]), pp. 207–239. On *gilgul* in Safad, see the sources listed in note 5 above and Idel, "R. Judah Hallewa."

26. G. Scholem, *Major Trends in Jewish Mysticism* (New York, 1961), pp. 280–284.

27. Ibid., p. 283.

28. See esp. M. Idel, "The Magical and Neoplatonic Interpretations of the Kabbalah in the Renaissance," in *Jewish Thought in the Sixteenth Century,* ed. B. Cooperman (Cambridge, Mass., 1983), pp. 224–227.

29. In addition to Scholem, *Pirkei Yesod;* Werblowsky, *Joseph Karo;* Elior, "Doctrine of Gilgul"; Gottleib, *Meḥkarim be–Sifrut ha–Kabbala;* and Idel, "Explorations in Method," see Manassah ben Israel, *Nishmat Ḥayyim* (Amsterdam, 1651), pt. 4, chaps. 6–23; L. Nemoy, "Biblical Quasi-Evidence for the Transmigration of Souls," *Journal of Biblical Literature,* 59 (1940), 159–166.

30. See esp. Scholem, *Pirkei Yesod,* pp. 334–337; and Elior, "Doctrine of Gilgul," pp. 228–229, who provides references to the authors of *Sefer ha-Temunah* and of *Sefer ha-Peliah* and the writings of Joseph of Hamadan and Menahem Recanati on the belief in transmigration into animals. Joseph of Hamadan's identification of *gilgul* into animal bodies with the punishment of hell parallels Yagel's identification of it with purgatory. See Scholem, *Pirkei Yesod,* p. 335, and Elior and Oren, *Ha-Gilgul,* pp. 69–107. Yagel may have known of Joseph's views through the summaries supplied in Recanati's commentary. See A. Altmann, "On the Question of the Authorship of the *Sefer Ta'amei̯ Miẓvot* Attributed to R. Isaac ibn Parḥi" (in Hebrew), *Kiryat Sefer,* 40 (1964–65), 256–276, 405–412.

31. Yagel uses Boethius' Lady Philosophy as a character in part 2 of his *Gei Ḥizzayon.* See the introduction to my forthcoming edition.

32. The passages in Plato (especially *Phaedrus* 249b, *Phaedo* 81e, *Timaeus* 42c, and *Republic* 10.618a–620d) have been cited and discussed in a number of scholarly works. See H. S. Long, *A Study of the Doctrine of Metempsychosis in Greece from Pythagoras to Plato* (Princeton, 1948); E. Ehnmark, "Transmigration in Plato," *Harvard Theological Review,* 50 (1957), 1–20; R. S. Bluck, "The *Phaedrus* and Reincarnation," *American Journal of Philology,* 79 (1958), 156–164; idem, "Plato, Pindar, and Metempsychosis," ibid., pp. 405–414.

33. Plato, *Phaedo* 81e, in *Plato's Phaedo,* trans. R. Hackforth (Cambridge, Mass., 1955), p. 89.

34. See Long, *Doctrine of Metempsychosis;* Walter Burkert, *Lore and Science in Ancient Pythagoreanism,* trans. E. L. Minar, Jr. (Cambridge, Mass., 1972), pp. 120–124; A. V. Williams Jackson, "The Doctrine of Metempsychosis in Manicheism," *Journal of the American Oriental Society,* 45 (1925), 246–268.

35. See esp. J. Dillon, *The Middle Platonists 80 B.C. to A.D. 220* (Ithaca, N.Y., 1977), p. 377; R. T. Wallis, *Neoplatonism* (New York, 1972), pp. 92, 113.

36. Augustine, *City of God,* trans. D. S. Wiesen (Cambridge, Mass., 1957), III, 394–395.

37. See esp. Wallis, *Neoplatonism,* p. 113, where specific references are given; H. Dorrie, "Kontroversen um die Seelenwanderung im Kaiserzeit-

lichen Platonismus," *Hermes*, 85 (1957), 414–435; Dillon, *Middle Platonists*, p. 377; E. R. Dodds, *Select Passages Illustrating Neoplatonism* (London, 1923), pp. 90–92.

38. See Idel, "Magical and Neoplatonic Interpretations."

39. Augustine, *City of God*, III, 394–395.

40. M. Kuntz, *Guillaume Postel, Prophet of the Restitution of All Things: His Life and Thought* (The Hague, 1981), pp. 104–105; F. A. Yates, *Giordano Bruno and the Hermetic Tradition* (Chicago, 1964), p. 249.

41. Marsilio Ficino, *Opera Omnia*, 4 vols. in 2 (Basel, 1576; reprint, Turin, 1967), I/1, 395, 420; P. O. Kristeller, *The Philosophy of Marsilio Ficino* (Gloucester, Mass., 1964), pp. 118, 361.

42. Kristeller, *Marsilio Ficino*, p. 408.

43. Henry Cornelius Agrippa, *Three Books of Occult Philosophy Written by Henry Cornelius Agrippa of Nettesheim*, trans. J. F. London (London, 1651), pp. 474, 480–481.

44. Johann Reuchlin, *De Arte Cabalistica*, trans. M. Goodman and S. Goodman (New York, 1983), bk. 2, p. 169.

45. J. D. Spense, *The Memory Palace of Matteo Ricci* (New York, 1984), pp. 251–252.

46. See *Beit Ya'ar ha-Levanon*, pt. 4, Bodleian Ms. Reggio 10, chap. 51.

47. *Sefer Tikkunei ha-Zohar*, ed. R. M. Margaliot (Jerusalem, 1948), *tikkun* 70, esp. 121b–126a.

48. Much material on earlier works on physiognomy is found in L. Thorndike, *A History of Magic and Experimental Science*, 8 vols. (New York, 1941); on the sixteenth century, see esp. V and VI. On Jewish interest in the field, see G. Scholem, "Chiromancy," *EJ*, V, 477–479 (republished in *Kabbalah*, pp. 317–319); idem, "Recognition of the Face and the Orders of the Lines" (in Hebrew), in *Sefer Assaf* (Jerusalem, 1953), pp. 459–495; idem, "Ein Fragment zur Physiognomik und Chiromantik aus der Tradition der spätantiken jüdischen Esoterik," in *Liber Amicorum: Studies in Honour of Professor Dr. C. J. Bleeker* (Leiden, 1969), pp. 175–193 (which is based on the previous Hebrew article); I. Gruenwald, "New Selections from the Literature of Recognition of the Face and the Orders of the Lines" (in Hebrew), *Tarbiz*, 40 (1970–71), 301–319; idem, *Apocalyptic and Merkavah Mysticism* (Leiden, 1980), pp. 218–224; P. Schäfer, "Eine neues Fragment zur Metoposkopie und Chiromantik," *Frankfürter Judaistische Beiträge*, 13 (1985), 61–82.

49. Thorndike, *History of Magic*, V, 50–68; VI, 160–61.

50. Giambattista della Porta, *Della fisonomia dell'huomo* (Venice, 1652), p. 101: "E dunque una scienza, che impara da segni, che sono fissi nel corpo, et accidente che transmettino i segni, investigari i costumi naturali dell'animo."

51. Ibid., p. 102: "legge, o regola di natura, che con certa regola, norma et ordine di natura si conosce, che de tal forma di corpo, si conosce tal passione dell'anima."

52. On the earlier periods see Scholem, "Chiromancy." For the sixteenth century see, for example, Ḥayyim Vital, *Be-Inyan Ḥokhmat ha-Parẓuf* (in *Sha'ar Ru'aḥ ha-Kodesh* [Jerusalem, 1912]), pp. 3a–5b; Abraham Azulai, *Ḥesed le-Avraham* (Amsterdam, 1685); Elijah Gallena, *Sefer Toledot Adam al Ḥokhmat ha-Yad ve-ha-Parẓuf* (Constantinople, 1515). See also the convenient anthology of M. Backal, *Sefer Ḥokhmat ha-Parẓuf ha-Shalem* (Jerusalem, 1967), including selections from Vital and Azulai; and L. Fine, "The Art of Metoposcopy: A Study in Isaac Luria's Charismatic Knowledge," *Association for Jewish Studies Review*, 10, (1986), 79–101.

53. See Scholem, "Chiromancy," p. 479.

54. Tobias Cohen, *Ma'aseh Tuviyyah* (Venice, 1707), pp. 74b–77a, which is based on Elijah Gallena's work. The chapter is reprinted in Backal, *Sefer Ḥokhmat ha-Parẓuf*, pp. 7–24, with illustrations that seem to be based on della Porta's book.

55. *Beit Ya'ar ha-Levanon*, pt. 4, chaps. 4–44.

56. Ibid., chap. 4, fol. 4a.

57. Nahmanides, *Perush ha-Ramban al ha-Torah*, ed. H. Chavel, 2 vols. (Jerusalem, 1959), I, 3.

58. *Beit Ya'ar ha-Levanon*, pt. 4, chap. 4, fols. 4a–b.

59. Ibid., fol. 5a.

60. Ibid., chap. 27, fol. 60a.

61. Ibid.

62. *Bat Rabim*, no. 72, fol. 116a.

63. For other contexts in which the doctrine of metempsychosis could be related to a medical-scientific theory of this period, see W. Pagel, *Paracelsus: An Introduction to Philosophical Medicine in the Era of the Renaissance* (Basel, 1958), p. 216; A. G. Debus, *The Chemical Philosophy: Paracelsian Science and Medicine in the Sixteenth and Seventeenth Centuries*, I (New York, 1977), 100–103; F. Secret, "Palingenesis, Alchemy, and Metempsychosis in Renaissance Medicine," *Ambix*, 26 (1979), 81–92.

64. See esp. J. Le Goff, *La naissance du purgatoire* (Paris, 1981) (translated as *The Birth of Purgatory* by A. Goldhammer [Chicago, 1984]); A. Michel, "Purgatoire," in *Dictionnaire de théologie catholique* XIII (Paris, 1936), cols. 1163–1326; E. Klinger, "Purgatory," in *Sacramentum Mundi*, ed. K. Rahner, 6 vols. (Basel 1968–70), V, 166–168.

65. See esp. Michel, "Purgatoire"; also the essay in the *New Catholic Encyclopedia*, II (New York, 1967) 1034–39.

66. *Oxford Dictionary of the Christian Church*, ed. F. L. Cross (London, 1974), p. 1144.

67. J. Pelikan, *The Christian Tradition: A History of the Development of Doctrine*, IV (Chicago, 1984), 137. On the Protestant critique of purgatory, see also Michel, "Purgatoire"; P. Althaus, "Luthers Gedanken über die letzten Dinge," *Luther Jahrbuch*, 23 (1941), 22–28; P. Chaunu, *Eglise, culture et société: Essais sur Reforme et Contrereforme 1517–1620* (Paris, 1981), pp. 378–380.

68. The Catholic response is fully summarized in Michel, "Purgatoire."

69. See P. Ariès, *Western Attitudes toward Death: From the Middle Ages to the Present* (Baltimore, 1974), pp. 56–66; idem, *The Hour of Our Death*, trans. H. Weaver (New York, 1981), esp. pp. 462–465; G. Vovelle and M. Vovelle, *Vision de la mort et de l'au-delà en Provence d'après les autels des âmes du purgatoire (xve–xxe siècles)* (Paris, 1970).

70. Of the immense literature on Dante's purgatory, see, for example, D. L. Sayers, *Introductory Papers on Dante* (New York, 1954), pp. 73–89.

71. See B.T. Rosh ha-Shanah 16b–17a; B.T. Shabbat 152b–153a; *Tanḥuma Vayikra*, 8; Mishnah Eduyyot 2, 10 (see Bertinora there); and Nahmanides, "Sha'ar ha-Gemul," in *Kitve Rabbenu Moshe ben Naḥman*, ed. H. Chavel, 2 vols. (Jerusalem, 1964), II, 264–311, esp. 289.

72. *Be'er Sheva*, Bodleian Ms. Reggio 11, pt. 2, chap. 7, fol. 30a.

73. I refer to Yagel's *Lekaḥ Tov*, first published in 1595. On this work and its indebtedness to Canisius, see Chapter 1, above.

74. See Le Goff, *Naissance du purgatoire*, p. 63.

75. Yet Yagel's equation of *gilgul* into animals and purgatory is imprecise in one respect. Purgatory, according to D. P. Walker, is "a morally static concept." The soul can acquire neither merit nor demerit after death. *Gilgul*, especially as it was understood by Yagel, provided the sinner with additional opportunities for moral improvement even after his earthly existence was over. See Walker's review of the translation of Le Goff's book, *The Birth of Purgatory*, in the *New York Times Book Review*, January 20, 1985.

76. See the introduction to my forthcoming edition of *Gei Ḥizzayon*.

9. Ancient Theology, the Kabbalah, and the Status of Judaism in Western Civilization

1. For an overview of this school and its legacy in subsequent centuries, see G. Scholem, *Major Trends in Jewish Mysticism* (New York, 1961), pp. 244–286.

2. On the Christian study of kabbalah in the Renaissance, see G. Scholem, "Zur Geschichte der Anfange der christlichen Kabbala," in *Essays Presented to Leo Baeck* (London, 1954), pp. 158–193; J. L. Blau, *The Christian Interpretation of the Cabala in the Renaissance* (New York, 1944); F. Secret, *Les kabbalistes chrétiens de la Renaissance* (Paris, 1964); F. A. Yates, *The Occult Philosophy in the Elizabethan Age* (London, 1979)

3. On the contemporaneous Jewish reaction to Christian kabbalah, see D. B. Ruderman, *The World of a Renaissance Jew* (Cincinnati, 1981), chap. 4 and bibliography; idem, "The Italian Renaissance and Jewish Thought," in *Renaissance Humanism: Foundations and Forms*, ed. A. Rabil, Jr., 3 vols. (Philadelphia, 1988), I, 404–412; M. Idel, "Differing Conceptions of Kabbalah in the Early Seventeenth Century," in *Jewish Thought in the Seventeenth Century*, ed. I. Twersky and B. Septimus (Cambridge, Mass, 1987).

4. See esp. *Beit Ya'ar ha-Levanon*, pt. 2, Bodleian Ms. Reggio 9, introduction and chaps. 1–3, (this manuscript contains parts 1–3).

5. On the ancient theology, see C. B. Schmitt, "Perennial Philosophy from Agostino Steucho to Leibnitz," *Journal of the History of Ideas*, 27 (1966), 505–523; idem, "Prisca theologia e philosophia perennis: Due temi del Rinascimento italiano e la loro fortuna," in *Il pensiero italiano del Rinascimento e il tempo nostro* (Florence, 1970), pp. 211–236; D. P. Walker, *The Ancient Theology: Studies in Christian Platonism from the Fifteenth to the Eighteenth Century* (Ithaca, N.Y., 1972); F. A. Yates, *Giordano Bruno and the Hermetic Tradition* (London, 1964), chaps. 1 and 2; C. Trinkaus, *In Our Image and Likeness: Humanity and Divinity in Italian Humanist Thought*, 2 vols. (London, 1970), II, 722–760.

6. See esp. Trinkaus, *In Our Image*, II, 741–742.

7. On poetic theology see Yates, *Giordano Bruno*; E. Wind, *Pagan Mysteries in the Renaissance*, 2d ed. (London, 1968), chap. 1; D. C. Allen, *Mysteriously Meant: The Rediscovery of Pagan Symbolism and Allegorical Interpretation in the Renaissance* (Baltimore, 1970).

8. Wind, *Pagan Mysteries*, p. 17.

9. Giovanni Pico della Mirandola, *De Hominis Dignitate*, ed. E. Garin (Florence, 1942), p. 162; quoted in Wind, *Pagan Mysteries*, p. 18.

10. Wind, *Pagan Mysteries*, p. 20.

11. Giovanni Pico della Mirandola, *Oratio*, trans. E. Forbes, in *The Renaissance Philosophy of Man*, ed. E. Cassirer, J. H. Randall, Jr., and P. O. Kristeller (Chicago, 1948), pp. 282–283.

12. M. Idel, "Kabbalah and Ancient Theology in R. Isaac and Judah Abrabanel" (in Hebrew), in *The Philosophy of Love of Leone Ebreo*, ed. M. Dorman and Z. Levy (Haifa, 1985), pp. 73–112. See also idem, "Kabbalah, Platonism, and Prisca Theologia: The Case of R. Menashe ben Israel," in a forthcoming volume on the thought of Manasseh ben Israel; A. Lesley, "The Recovery of the Ancients in Sixteenth-Century Italy" (Paper presented at the annual meeting of the Association for Jewish Studies, December 17, 1985).

13. Idel's contention that the Christian advocates of ancient theology assumed that there were two independent paths to universal truth is not entirely accurate. Some did acknowledge a pre-Christian revelation independent of Moses, but the more orthodox Renaissance syncretists cautiously derived the ancient theology from Moses. There also was at least one Jew (Abraham Yagel) who assumed the existence of two independent paths leading to the truth. See Walker, *Ancient Theology*, pp. 20–21.

14. Idel, "Kabbalah and Ancient Theology," pp. 98, 101, nn. 21 and 30. He quotes from *Beit Ya'ar ha-Levanon*, pt. 2, chap. 5, fol. 58b, and from pt. 1, chap. 5, fol. 10b.

15. In the other passage quoted by Idel ("Kabbalah and Ancient Theology," p. 101), Yagel cites Augustine's *City of God* rather than the *Confes-*

sions. See also Idel, p. 100, n. 29, quoting Augustine's *The Christian Doctrine* on the same idea.

16. *Gei Ḥizzayon,* pt. 2, Ms. Cincinnati Hebrew Union College 743, fol. 66b. Another passage linking Plato and Jeremiah is in *Beit Ya'ar ha-Levanon,* pt. 2, chap. 6, fol. 59a.

17. On the identity of Ham and Zoroaster, see L. Ginzberg, *Legends of the Jews,* 7 vols. (Philadelphia, 1909–38), V, 200. On the laughing, See E. M. Butler, *The Myth of the Magus* (Cambridge, 1948), p. 22

18. *Beit Ya'ar ha-Levanon,* pt. 2, chap. 14, fols. 76a–b. On Zoroaster in the Renaissance, see K. H. Dannenfelt, "The Pseudo-Zoroastrian Oracles in the Renaissance," *Studies in the Renaissance,* 4 (1957), 7–28; Ch. Wirszubski, *Sheloshah Perakim be-Toledot ha-Kabbala ha-Noẓrit* (Jerusalem, 1975), pp. 28–38. Yagel also mentions Zoraster in *Beit Ya'ar ha-Levanon,* pt. 1, chap. 4, fol. 9b.

19. *Beit Ya'ar ha-Levanon,* pt. 2, chap. 14, fol. 76b.

20. Ibid., chap. 15, fol. 77a. On Asclepius see the *New Larousse Encyclopedia of Mythology* (Singapore, 1959), p. 163.

21. On Hermes see *Be'er Sheva,* Bodleian Ms. Reggio 11, pt. 2, chap. 1, fol. 15b; *Beit Ya'ar ha-Levanon,* pt. 1, chap. 5, fol. 11a; on Homer see *Be'er Sheva,* pt. 2, chap. 18, fol. 63b; for the comparison of the homily with the myth of Prometheus, see M. Idel, "Prometheus in Hebrew Garb" (in Hebrew), *Eshkolot,* n.s., 5–6 (1980–81), 119–127.

22. On Apuleius see *Beit Ya'ar ha-Levanon,* pt. 4, Bodleian Ms. Reggio 10, chap. 101, fol. 232a. On Pythagoras see ibid., pt. 3, chap. 8, fol. 126a (the chapter is based on Agrippa's *De Occulta Philosophia,* bk. 3, chaps. 37 and 40); ibid., pt. 2, chap. 12, fols. 43a, 43b; ibid., chap. 21, fol. 95b.

23. *Gei Ḥizzayon,* pt. 2, fol. 67b.

24. *Beit Ya'ar ha-Levanon,* pt. 2, introductory chap., fols. 45a–b.

25. On Yagel's familiarity and use of Agrippa, see esp. Chapter 7 above and M. Idel, "The Magical and Neoplatonic Interpretations of the Kabbalah in the Renaissance," in *Jewish Thought in the Sixteenth Century,* ed. B. Cooperman (Cambridge, Mass., 1983), pp. 224–226.

26. *De Occulta Philosophia,* bk. 3, chap. 2. I have used the translation by J. F. London, *Three Books of Occult Philosophy Written by Henry Cornelius Agrippa of Nettesheim* (London, 1651), pp. 346–349. The theme of concealing secrets from the masses is discussed at length by Pico in the introduction to his *Heptaplus.* It is also discussed by Leone Ebreo and by Jean Bodin. For references see Walker, *Ancient Theology,* pp. 86–87.

27. *Beit Ya'ar ha-Levanon,* pt. 2, introduction, fol. 45a; Agrippa, *Occult Philosophy,* p. 348.

28. *Beit Ya'ar ha-Levanon,* pt. 2, introduction, fol. 45a; Agrippa, *Occult Philosophy,* p. 349.

29. *Beit Ya'ar ha-Levanon,* pt. 2, introduction, fol. 45b.

30. Cf. Yagel's attitude on the reading of books of magic, discussed in Chapter 7, above.

31. *Beit Ya'ar ha-Levanon*, pt. 2, chap. 1, fol. 46a.

32. He may have meant *La historia del Mondo Nuovo* (Venice, 1565) of Girolamo Benzoni, the Milanese traveler who visited Peru and described its history. Yagel also refers to Peru in *Beit Ya'ar ha-Levanon*, pt. 2, chap. 20, fols. 93b–94a; *Gei Ḥizzayon*, pt. 2, fol. 87a.

33. *Beit Ya'ar ha-Levanon*, pt. 2, chap. 2, fols. 47a–48b.

34. *Gei Ḥizzayon*, pt. 2, fol. 67b.

35. *Beit Ya'ar ha-Levanon*, pt. 2, chap. 2, fol. 47a.

36. Bodleian Ms. Reggio 8, fol. 65b.

37. Agrippa, *De Occulta Philosophia*, bk. 3, chap. 7; *Occult Philosophy*, pp. 358–362.

38. Quoted in Agrippa, *Occult Philosophy*, p. 359.

39. *Beit Ya'ar ha-Levanon*, pt. 2, chap. 2, fol. 47a. Part of this passage appeared in W. W. Hallo, D. Ruderman, and M. Stanislawski, *Heritage: Civilization and the Jews Source Reader* (New York, 1984), pp. 164–65.

40. *Beit Ya'ar ha-Levanon*, pt. 2, chap. 2, fol. 47a; cf. Agrippa, *Occult Philosophy*, pp. 359–360.

41. Cf. Agrippa, *Occult Philosophy*, p. 360; and *Beit Ya'ar ha-Levanon*, pt. 2, chap. 2, fols. 47a–b.

42. *Beit Ya'ar ha-Levanon*, pt. 2, chap. 2, fol. 47b. His source is Josephus, *Antiquities*, bk. 1, end of chap. 2.

43. Agrippa, *Occult Philosophy*, pp. 360–361; *Beit Ya'ar ha-Levanon*, pt. 2, chap. 2, fol. 47b.

44. Agrippa, *De Occulta Philosophia*, bk. 3, chap. 8; *Occult Philosophy*, p. 362.

45. Bodleian Ms. Reggio 8, fols. 66a–67a.

46. *Beit Ya'ar ha-Levanon*, pt. 2, chap. 2, fol. 47b. Hermes' prayer can be found in Marsilio Ficino, *Opera Omnia*, 2 vols. (Basil, 1576; reprint, Turin, 1962), II, 1819.

47. *Beit Ya'ar ha-Levanon*, pt. 2, chap. 2, fol. 48a.

48. On this passage in Alemanno, see Idel, "Magical and Neoplatonic Interpretations," pp. 221, 240, nn. 203, 205; p. 241, n. 222. In n. 206 Idel correctly points out that Alemanno was the source of this passage, although Yagel is not speaking here about the *ein sof*, as Idel contends. Yagel probably copied the entire passage from Alemanno's *Likkutim*, Bodleian Ms. Reggio 23, fol. 21a. (no. 2234 in A. Neubauer, *Catalogue of the Hebrew Manuscripts in the Bodleian Library*, 2 vols. [Oxford, 1886, 1906]).

49. For a brief summary, see H. E. Blumenthal, "Ḥasidei Ummot ha-Olam," *EJ*, VII, 1383.

50. *Beit Ya'ar ha-Levanon*, pt. 2, chap. 2, fol. 48a.

51. Maimonides, *Guide to the Perplexed* 2.13.

52. *Gei Ḥizzayon*, pt. 2, fols. 66a–b.

53. *Beit Ya'ar ha-Levanon*, pt. 2, chap. 2, fols. 48a–49a.

54. Agrippa, *De Occulta Philosophia*, bk. 3, chap. 10; *Occult Philosophy*, p. 366.

55. *Beit Ya'ar ha-Levanon,* pt. 2, chap. 2, fol. 49a.

56. Agrippa, *Occult Philosophy,* p. 367.

57. *Beit Ya'ar ha-Levanon,* pt. 2, chap. 3, fol. 49a.

58. Ibid. Note a similar discussion in Leone Modena, *Ari Nohem* (Jerusalem, 1971), pp. 11–13.

59. Yagel clearly alludes here to the two modes of scientific inquiry known in the sixteenth century as the compositive and resolutive methods. See the same definition by Jacob Zabarella, as summarized by N. Gilbert in *Renaissance Concepts of Method* (New York, 1960), pp. 168–173. Yagel's awareness of Renaissance discussions of method is further confirmed by his elaboration of Galen's three methods of teaching—analysis, synthesis, and diaeresis—based on a passage at the beginning of the *Ars parva,* quoted in *Be'er Sheva,* pt. 2, chap. 1. Yagel indicates there that he employs all three methods in the organization of his own composition. On the importance of this Galenic passage in the Renaissance, despite its obscurity, see Gilbert, *Renaissance Concepts,* pp. 16–22, 45–46, 99–104, 186–190.

60. *Beit Ya'ar ha-Levanon,* pt. 2, chap. 3, fols. 49a–b.

61. Ibid., fol. 49b.

62. On the sources of this tradition see Ginzberg, *Legends of the Jews,* I, 154–57; V, 117–118, 177.

63. On this tradition see M. Idel, "Iyyunim be-shitato shel ba'al 'Sefer ha-Meshiv,'" *Sefunot,* n.s., 29 (1983), 242. Yagel (*Beit Ya'ar ha-Levanon,* pt. 2, chap. 3, fol. 49b) learned of this tradition from Meir ibn Gabbai's *Avodat ha–Kodesh* (Venice, 1566).

64. *Beit Ya'ar ha-Levanon,* pt. 2, chap. 3, fol. 50a.

65. Ibid.

66. M. Idel, "Major Currents in Italian Kabbalah (1560–1660)," in *Italica Judaica,* II, ed. S. Simonsohn and G. Sermoneta (Rome, 1987), has already quoted and discussed this passage as well as the one on Cordovero.

67. *Beit Ya'ar ha-Levanon,* pt. 2, chap. 3, fol. 50a.

68. Ibid.

69. Ibid.

70. This point is made by M. Idel in "Particularism and Universalism in Kabbalah: 1480–1650" (Paper presented at the conference Jewish Societies in Transformation in the Sixteenth and Seventeenth Centuries, Van Leer Institute, Jerusalem, January 1986).

71. *Beit Ya'ar ha-Levanon,* pt. 2, chap. 3, fol. 50a.

72. Ibid.

73. Ibid., fol. 50b.

74. Ibid., fol. 51a.

75. Ibid., fols. 51a–b.

76. For an overview of the *sefirot* in Jewish mysticism, see G. Scholem, *Kabbalah* (Jerusalem, 1974), pp. 96–116.

77. For a recent survey of the controversy, see M. Idel, *Kabbalah: New Perspectives* (New Haven, 1988), chap. 6.

78. See M. Idel, "Between the Concepts of the Sefirot as Essence and Instruments" (in Hebrew), *Italia*, 3 (1982), 89–111; H. Tirosh-Rothschild, "Sefirot as the Essence of God in the Writings of David Messer Leon," *Association for Jewish Studies Review*, 7–8 (1982–83), 409–425; E. Gottlieb, *Meḥkarim be-Sifrut ha-Kabbala* (Tel Aviv, 1976), pp. 293–331; 404–422; J. Ben Shlomo, *Torat ha-Elohut shel R. Moshe Cordovero* (Jerusalem, 1965), pp. 100–169.

79. Yagel discusses the *sefirot* in *Beit Ya'ar ha-Levanon*, pt. 2, chap. 4; *Gei Ḥizzayon*, pt. 2, fols. 85a–91b; cf. Tirosh-Rothschild, "Sefirot as Essence."

80. Moshe Cordovero, *Pardes Rimmonim* (Krakow, 1591), 4, 4; *Beit Ya'ar ha-Levanon*, pt. 2, chap. 4, fol. 53a; Ben Shlomo, *Torat ha-Elohut*, pp. 124–127. On the source of Cordovero's analogies, see Gottlieb, *Meḥkarim be-Sifrut ha-Kabbala*, p. 422.

81. Cordovero, *Pardes Rimmonim*, 4, 4; Ben Shlomo, *Torat ha-Elohut*, pp. 122–123.

82. *Gei Ḥizzayon*, pt. 2, fol. 85b.

83. Idel, " Magical and Neoplatonic Interpretations," pp. 224–226.

84. *Beit Ya'ar ha-Levanon*, pt. 1, chap. 5, fol. 10b. I have followed Idel's translation, "Magical and Neoplatonic Interpretations," p. 226.

85. *Gei Ḥizzayon*, pt. 2, fols. 85a–91b.

86. Quoted in Idel, "Magical and Neoplatonic Interpretations," pp. 224–225.

87. See, for example, Pico, *Conclusiones Cabalisticae*, no. 48, quoted and discussed in Yates, *Giordano Bruno*, pp. 100–101; and Agrippa, *Occult Philosophy*, p. 367: "But the Mecubales of the Hebrew, the most learned in Divine things, have received the ten principal names of God, which by ten numerations which they call Sephiroth as it were vestiments, instruments or exemplars of the Archetype, have an influence on all things created, through the high things, even to the lowest, yet by a certain order; for first and immediately they have influence on the nine orders of angels, and quire of blessed souls, and by them into the Celestiall Spheres, Planets, and men, by which the Sephiroth everything therein receiveth power and vertue."

88. *Gei Ḥizzayon*, pt. 2, fols. 90a–b.

89. Ibid., fol. 91a.

90. Ibid., fol. 91b.

91. On this theme in the writings of Jewish thinkers of the fifteenth and sixteenth centuries, see R. Bonfil, "Expressions of the Uniqueness of the Jewish People during the Period of the Renaissance," *Sinai*, 76 (1975), 36–46.

92. *Gei Ḥizzayon*, pt. 2, fols. 75a–b. See a similar formulation quoted by M. Idel in "The Sefirot above the Sefirot" (in Hebrew), *Tarbiz*, 51 (1982), 279.

93. Idel, "Major Currents in Italian Kabbalah"; R. Bonfil, "Changes in Cultural Patterns of Jewish Society in Crisis: The Case of Italian Jewry at the Close of the 16th Century" (Paper presented at the conference Jewish

Societies in Transformation in the Sixteenth and Seventeenth Centuries, Van Leer Institute, Jerusalem, January 1986).

94. Idel, "Major Currents in Italian Kabbalah," p. 258.

95. The phrase is from Bonfil, "Changes in Cultural Patterns." It refers to Yagel's authorship of *Lekaḥ Tov*, his Jewish "catechism," based on a similar work by the Catholic theologian Canisius.

96. Cf. Idel's observations on Jewish culture in Italy and Holland by the beginning of the seventeenth century: "The Jews met this flourishing world mostly as consumers rather than contributors; they absorbed Renaissance thought, literature, mythology, and science as students learning from their masters. The self-confidence of the Jews in the supremacy of Judaism as a *modus vivendi* and as a *Weltanschauung* was waning . . . the Jewish authors' extensive use of Neoplatonic, Patristic, and scientific sources made their unconditional adherence to certain facets of Judaism problematic"; "Differing Conceptions of Kabbalah," p. 140.

Afterword

1. For a clear definition of the goals, methods, and assumptions of modern science, though anachronistically applied to the sixteenth and seventeenth centuries, see B. Vickers, "Analogy versus Identity: The Rejection of Occult Symbolism 1580–1680," in *Occult and Scientific Mentalities in the Renaissance* (Cambridge, 1984), pp. 95–163. See also D. O'Connor and F. Oakley, eds., *Creation: The Impact of an Idea* (New York, 1969), p. 16. On the medieval and Renaissance usage of the term *scientia* as distinct from *techné* or *ars*, see C. B. Schmitt, "Recent Trends in the Study of Medieval and Renaissance Science," in *Information Sources in the History of Science and Medicine*, ed. P. Corsi and O. Weindling (London, 1983), p. 223.

2. *Beit Ya'ar ha-Levanon*, pt. 4, Bodleian Ms. Reggio 10, chap. 1, fol. 2a.

3. The Maimonidean dictum (introduction to commentary on Avot; *Shemoneh Perakim*, chap. 4) quoted often in Yagel's writings.

4. Although he was reluctant to break with Aristotle's authority on the number of elements.

5. See A. Funkenstein, *Theology and the Scientific Imagination from the Middle Ages to the Seventeenth Century* (Princeton, 1986), pp. 195–198, on the ideal of knowing through doing, which characterized seventeenth-century science.

Appendix

1. See G. Bartolocci, *Bibliotheca Magna Rabbinica*, 5 vols. (Rome, 1675–94), I, 260; J. C. Wolf, *Bibliotheca Hebraea*, 4 vols. (Hamburg, 1715–33), I, no. 78; G. B. De' Rossi, *Dizionario storico degli autori ebrei e delle loro opere*, 2 vols. (Parma, 1802), I, 160.

2. See, for example, L. Della Torre, in *Archives israelites*, 24 (1863), 570–

571; M. Mortara, *Mazkeret Ḥokhmei Italiyah: Indice alfabetico dei rabbini e scrittori israelitici* (Padua, 1886), pp. 25–26; S. Fuenn, *Keneset Yisrael* (Warsaw, 1886), p. 29.

3. See Chapter 1, above.

4. On Camillo see W. Popper, *The Censorship of Hebrew Books* (New York, 1899), index.

5. See Chapter 1.

6. See M. Benayahu, "Solomon Navarro: The Author of 'The Terrible Incident regarding Joseph della Riena'?" (in Hebrew), *Tarbiz*, 51 (1982), 475: "For it seems that the famous R. Abraham Yagel Gallico, who converted and became a censor, continued during the time of his apostasy to write *responsa* [*sic*] and to exchange letters with rabbis and sages who were rooted in Judaism and scoffed at Christianity."

7. On Graziano see S. Marcus, "Graziano, Abraham," *EJ*, VII, 865; and E. Zimmer, "Biographical Details concerning Italian Jewry from Handwritten Notes" (in Hebrew), *Kiryat Sefer*, 49 (1974), 440–444.

8. On Portaleone see S. Simonsohn, *History of the Jews in the Duchy of Mantua* (Jerusalem, 1977), pp. 535, 709; I. Abrahams, "Samuel Portaleone's Proposed Restrictions on Games of Chance," *Jewish Quarterly Review*, 5 (1893), 505–515. Portaleone eulogized Hananiah Finzi at his death in 1630.

9. On Hananiah see U. Cassuto, "Jagel, Chananja aus Monselice," *EJ*, 10 vols. (Berlin, 1931), VIII, 777. On his commentary see M. Beit Arié, "*Perek Shira*: Introduction and Critical Editions," 2 vols. (Ph.D. diss., Hebrew University of Jerusalem, 1966), I, 32.

10. Beit Arié, "*Perek Shira*," I, 24.

11. See Hananiah's commentary on *Pirke Shira* (Mantua, 1661), p. 15b.

12. Ibid., p. 31a.

13. Ms. Strasbourg 4085 (Jerusalem microfilm 3960), fol. 59; also cf. fols. 97, 104.

14. Ms. Copenhagen 217/1 (Jerusalem microfilm 6925).

15. Hananiah had a son named Pelatiah who became a follower of Shabbtai Zevi and contemplated conversion to Christianity. See F. Secret, "Notes sur les hebraïsants chrétiens," *Revue des études juives*, 123 (1964), 141–142.

16. *Bat Rabim*, Ms. Moscow Günzburg 129, fol. 187b. On Trabotto see Simonsohn, *Jews in Mantua*, pp. 63, 358, 508, 510, 576, 623, 727, 737. On the different types of rabbinic ordination in Italy and the term *marbiz Torah*, see R. Bonfil, *Ha-Rabbanut be-Italyah bi-Tekufat ha-Renesance* (Jerusalem, 1979), chap. 2 and index. I could not identify Israel Foa. On the Foa family in Soragna, see R. Bonfil, "New Information on R. Menahem Azariah da Fano and His Age" (in Hebrew), in *Perakim be-Toledot ha-Ḥevra ha-Yehudit . . . le-Professor Ya'akov Katz* (Jerusalem, 1980), p. 105, n. 50.

Index

Abano, Peter, 29

Aben Ragel (Ibn Abi l-Ridjal), 78, 85, 92, 96

Abrabanel, Isaac, 123–124, 125, 142, 165

Abrabanel, Judah (Leone Ebreo), 142; on concealing secrets, 218n26

Abraham, 33, 105, 109, 112, 113, 115, 118, 119, 146, 148, 151

Abraham ben David, 151

Abulafia, Abraham, 148

Adam, 60, 62

Adret, Solomon ben, 84; on amulets, 209n76

Aelian, 60

Aglaophemus, 140

Agnon, S. Y., 83

Agrippa, Henry Cornelius, 31, 35, 102, 110–111, 112, 113, 115, 117, 118, 131, 132, 144–150, 155

Akiva, Rabbi, 118

Albertus Magnus, 47; on comets, 95

Albertus Magnus (Pseudo-), 29

Albinus, 130

Al-Biruni, 99

Albo, Joseph, 167

Aldrovandi, Ulisse, 75

Alemanno, Yohanan, 23, 118, 120, 128, 148, 155; as source for Galen, 188n40

Almagiati, Eliezer (Lazzarus), 13, 14

Almagiati, Samuel, 12

Almagiati family, 18, 21

Amsterdam, 56

Amulets, 29, 31, 35–36, 37, 40–41, 42, 117

Ancient theology, 7, 139–150

Androgyny, 52–53

Anglo, Sidney, 47

Anomaly, 200n57

Anorexia, 35

Apocrypha, 106. *See also* Ben Sira; Esdras

Apuleius, 48, 143, 146, 147

Arama, Isaac, 125

Aristotle, 124, 134, 141; on demons, 46–48, 49; on unicorns, 61, 62; on nature, 67; on comets, 90–91, 95; on the four elements, 93; and implications of telescope, 99–100

Asclepius, 113, 114, 143. *See also* Hermeticism; Magic

Ashkenazi, Eliezer, on demons, 55–56

Astrology: Jewish tradition of, 5; in medicine, 27, 30, 40–41; and cause of Siamese twins, 78; and prophecies of Nahman, 85

Astronomy: Jewish tradition of, 5; Yagel's expertise in, 21, 89–101; 16th-century Jewish knowledge of, 90

Attila, 123

Augustine, 47, 130, 143, 144, 160

Avila, child of, 84, 85, 87

Azriel ben Menahem, of Gerona, 151

Azulai, Abraham, 112

Bacci, Andrea, 64–65, 70; on secrets of nature, 66–67

Bacon, Roger, 47, 112, 113

Bagdash, 98

Balaam: as magician, 31, 47; as prophet, 86

Baraita de-Shemu'el, 98

Barcelona, 84

Bartolocci, Giulio, 166

Bar Yohai, Simon, 122, 124, 134, 135, 152. *See also* Sefer ha-Zohar

Bat Rabim, 8, 19, 25, 34, 74, 166, 167

Bedersi, Jedaiah, 212n24

Be'er Sheva, 19, 20, 71, 89